REFINER'S FIRE

THE ACADEMY OF ANCIENT MUSIC AND THE HISTORICAL PERFORMANCE REVOLUTION

RICHARD BRATBY

Elliott&Thompson

To my parents

First published 2023 by
Elliott and Thompson Limited
2 John Street
London WC1N 2ES
www.eandtbooks.com

ISBN: 978-1-78396-760-5

Images. P1: David Munrow © BBC Archive; Christopher Hogwood © A Houston; Jaap Schröder/Christopher Hogwood © John Hamilton; Peter Wadland © Decca Classics. P2: The AAM outside St Jude's © Cat Mackintosh; AAM at Kedleston Hall © BBC TV; Messiah © Cat Mackintosh. P3: *Fireworks* rehearsal © Clive Barda Photography; Christopher Hogwood/Barry Guy © Vico Chamla Venini. P4: BRIT Award, 1985 © BRITs YouTube channel; Four Seasons © Cat Mackintosh; USA tour, 1986 © Paul Hughes; Cologne © AAM archive. P5: Esterhaza, 1989 © Rosemary Rogers PR; Balloon and band Decca photo shoot, 1993 © AAM archive; Bach rehearsal at Henry Wood Hall © Malcolm Crowthers. P6: Paul Goodwin © Ron Gonsalves Management; Emma Kirkby/Andrew Manze/Christopher Hogwood © AAM archive; Triumvirate © AAM archive. P7: Libya tour, 2009 © Sir Vernon Ellis; Richard Egarr/Robert Levin © Patrick Allen operaomnia.co.uk. P8: Richard Egarr, 2021 © Mark Allen; Robert Levin, 2022 © Nick Rutter; Laurence Cummings © Mark Allen; Jubilee river pageant, 2012 © AAM archive.

All efforts have been made to acknowledge copyright for each image but if there are any omissions or errors, the publisher will be pleased to correct them for future editions.

9 8 7 6 5 4 3 2 1

A catalogue record for this book is available from the British Library.

Typesetting: Marie Doherty
Printed by CPI Group (UK) Ltd, Croydon, CR0 4YY

Contents

For sixty years a gathering has been held in this city for those most devoted to music, who at that time were committed to both its theory and its practice. Their notion was to prevent old composers, who in the previous century had happily cultivated harmony, from falling into desuetude; they founded an Academy in which the works of these artists might be performed. Nor were their efforts in vain; it grew day by day such that today it easily ranks among the most celebrated.

Letter from James Mathias, President of the Academy of Ancient Music, to David Perez in Lisbon, 1774[*]

---

[*] Quoted in Timothy Eggington, *The Advancement of Music in Enlightenment England*. Text translated from the Latin by Dr David Butterfield and the author.

Academy of Ancient Music.

THURSDAY, 31st JANUARY, 1793.

SELECTED BY

Mr. LIVIE.

ACT I.

Overture. (Esther)	*Handel.*
Air. What tho' I trace	*Ditto*
Madrigal. When all alone	*Gia. Converso.*
Duett. My faith and truth.	*Handel.*
Recit. Thrice happy Israel. ⎱	
Air. When the sun o'er. ⎰	*Ditto.*
Recit. Who quits the lilly. ⎱	
Air. Balmy sweetness. ⎰	*Dr. Boyce.*
Recit. 'Tis done. ⎱	
Air. Heart, thou seat of soft delight. ⎰	*Handel.*
Mottet. Gloria in excelsis.	*Negri.*

ACT. II.

Concerto I. Op. 2d.	*Geminiani.*
Air. Vo solcando.	*Vinci.*
Part of the Mask in the Tempest.	*Purcell.*
Air. Lord what is man.	*Handel.*
Air. Non so d'onde vieni.	*Bach.*
Air. Let the bright Seraphim.	*Handel.*
Anthem. My heart is inditing.	*Ditto.*

Introduction and Acknowledgements

The story of the Academy of Ancient Music (AAM) is the story of a revolution in the theory and practice of orchestral music. Founded in 1973 by a Cambridge harpsichordist and a record producer of genius, the Academy surfed the digital boom in recorded music during the 1970s and 1980s with unprecedented – and unrivalled – success, lifting period-instrument performance from the fringes of 1960s counterculture and putting baroque music into the pop charts. Then, as the classical-record industry faded and 1970s radicals became the 1990s establishment, the AAM faced a new challenge: reinventing itself to meet the artistic, social and economic conditions of a musical world transformed by its own revolutionary achievement.

As the Academy approaches its fiftieth anniversary, it has accrued a rich and complex history, though as an organisation it is still anything but middle-aged. In one sense, fifty is an awkward age for an orchestra. Many characters in this story are still involved and gloriously active; equally, vital personalities – particularly the Academy's co-founders, Christopher Hogwood and Peter Wadland – have already left the stage forever. That a writer as elegant and engaging as Hogwood left no memoir of his career is a source of enduring regret. Meanwhile, the existing literature on historically informed performance* deals overwhelmingly (and unsurprisingly for a field that, in its modern form, is barely half a century old) with

---

* The discussion over the correct term for the approach to music taken by the Academy of Ancient Music is ongoing, and has shifted repeatedly during the last half-century. Any attempt to summarise this debate is probably doomed but, in short, we are dealing with a conscious and serious attempt – through textual scholarship, research into performance style, and the use of historic or replica instruments – to perform music with a sound, and in a style

theoretical, aesthetic and technical questions, or takes a broad overview of the movement as a whole.

As far as I can establish, this is the first full-length narrative history of a British period-instrument orchestra; the first attempt at a comprehensive account of how one specific ensemble (arguably the most influential of them all) came into being, achieved global fame, and then remade itself, securing a future and a purpose beyond the retirement of its charismatic founder. The departure of the founding director is a challenge that many of the pioneering early-music ensembles have faced, or will face, and it forms one of the principal dramas in the Academy of Ancient Music's story. In Christopher Hogwood, the AAM was fortunate to have a founder whose generosity and open-mindedness extended to planning for his own replacement, allowing a rejuvenated Academy to build freely on his legacy under the direction of two very different but equally inspirational artistic leaders, Richard Egarr and Laurence Cummings.

This is not a biography of Christopher Hogwood but of the organisation that he created, and while it goes without saying that he plays a central role, a great orchestra is always bigger than any one individual. Fifty years on, it's almost too soon to appraise the full historical impact of the Academy of Ancient Music's trailblazing first decades. Extensive archives and a magnificent discography await future researchers. For now, as a contribution to the Academy's fiftieth-birthday celebrations, I have interviewed a broad selection of the individuals – artists, administrators, critics, collaborators and supporters – who played a role in the foundation and progress of the Academy of Ancient Music, using their first-hand testimony (I hope) to animate, clarify and enrich the tale the archives tell.

Inevitably, any such selection must be partial. Pressure of time made some interviews impossible, and mortality prevented others, although I managed to talk to all of the AAM's surviving artistic leaders and most of its general managers, as well as musicians, past and present, from all

---

and spirit, that approximates as closely as can be imagined to the style, spirit and sound with which that music would have been performed in its composer's own era.

All language is approximate, and while I am aware of the sensitivities surrounding each term, in order to avoid monotony I have used the labels 'early music', 'period performance' and 'historically informed performance' more or less interchangeably. I beg the indulgence of scholarly readers and acknowledge that terms such as *Alte Musik* and (especially) 'authentic performance' (or 'authentic instruments') are altogether more slippery, as what follows will (I hope) make clear.

sections of the orchestra. I was helped by a large number of people, first among them the AAM's former Chief Executive Alexander Van Ingen, who invited me to write this book, and his successor John McMunn, who has been a constant source of practical support and quiet confidence, finding time to answer my questions even while he steered the AAM through the deadly waters of a global pandemic. To serve as Hogwood Fellow has been one of the greatest (and most unexpected) honours of my career, and I am intensely aware of the responsibility that its name imparts.

I also wish to thank Dr Anna Pensaert of Cambridge University Library for her assistance with archive material, and my colleagues Simon Fairclough, James Jolly, Sir Nicholas Kenyon and Norman Lebrecht for support both moral and highly practical. This book would not have been possible without the co-operation – freely and unstintingly given – of more than forty interviewees, listed at the back of the book, for whose time and insights I am deeply indebted, and whose confidence I have done my best to respect. My particular thanks also (they will know why) to Anna Ambrose, Jacob Bagby, Alexandra Coghlan, Jessica Duchen, Mahan Esfahani, Simon Funnell, Charlotte Gardner, Miles Golding, Michael Guest, Michael Haas, Thomas Hewitt Jones, Stephen Maddock, Fiona Maddocks, Ben Palmer, Tommy Pearson, Stephen Preston, Bob Shingleton and Philip Siney.

And, finally, I must acknowledge my cat Rusty, whose interventions (duly and daily) on my keyboard were almost certainly well intentioned, and my wonderful wife Annette. As a writer on ancient music, I am privileged to have a partner whose profound knowledge of eighteenth-century theatre, and passion for Handel, has (I hope) taken some of the edge off the stresses, strains and spoiled weekends that accompany a project such as this. I couldn't write – I couldn't do anything, really – without her unbounded patience, encouragement and love.

Lichfield, October 2022

1

ANCIENT MUSIC

A Londoner leaving the church of St Clement Danes after Evensong on the evening of 7 January 1726 and turning into the Strand in the direction of Arundel Street might have heard music, and paused. Not the hymnody of the Georgian church, or the cries of the Thames watermen, but a different sort of music: male voices, clearly learned voices, intertwining in plangent song as they summoned the harmonies of another time to float on the night air. They might, if they were unusually well informed about the art of counterpoint and its history, have recognised the language as Italian; the sound as that of a madrigal from an earlier century. It's vanishingly unlikely that they would have recognised it as *Dolorosi Martir*, from the *Primo libro de madrigali* of 1580 by the Italian renaissance master Luca Marenzio (1553–1559).

But it wouldn't have been hard to work out that the sound was coming from the Crown and Anchor inn; and any reasonably well-connected music-lover would have been able to find out, within a few days, that they'd heard the inaugural meeting of a group of eminent music-lovers, amateur and professional, in the inn's spacious upper room. There were thirteen founder members of this new club, including representatives of two great cathedrals. They included the composer Maurice Greene (1696–1755), organist of St Paul's and future Professor of Music at Cambridge University. From Westminster Abbey came the bass Bernard Gates (1686–1773), much admired by Handel. Present, too, was the oboe virtuoso and composer Johann Ernst Galliard (1666–1749) from Saxony and the Prussian-born composer and organist Johann Christoph Pepusch (1667–1752) – not yet famous for his work on *The Beggar's Opera* (1728), but widely admired for his virtuosity and learning.[1]

And so on. Each member had subscribed two shillings and sixpence, for which they enjoyed wine and bread and the musical services of 'the Children of St Paul's Cathedral', fetched by coach to add the essential upper line to this all-male musical gathering. Informal gatherings of this sort had been taking place for over a decade, but now they were to be placed on a more regular footing. The first music heard – and from the outset the members of this select club participated as performers and scholars, as well as interested listeners – was Marenzio's madrigal. The new venture had been christened in song, and an unknown member (probably Sampson Estwick, veteran chorister of St Paul's) duly inscribed the fact in his rare manuscript copy of this 146-year-old work:

A Musick Meeting being held at ye Crown Tavern near St Clements Mr Galliard at ye head of it, & chiefly [sic] for Grave ancient Vocell Musick. Wee begann it wth ye following Song of Lucas De Marenzio Jan 7 – 1725/6.[2]

The group agreed to meet regularly to sing 'Grave ancient Vocell Musick'. By the next meeting, on 21 January, they'd been joined by the distinguished composer William Croft (1678–1727) of Westminster Abbey. On 1 March the company was swelled by three of London's pre-eminent Italian composers, Nicola Francesco Haym (1678–1729), Giovanni Bononcini (1670–1747) and Francesco Geminiani (1687–1762). Clearly, the society's principles had currency. In 1727, inspired by ideals of scholarship as well as the great musical academies of Italy (such as the Accademia de' Filarmonici in Bologna, of which Bononcini was a member), the club gave itself a name – the Academy of Vocal Music – and met regularly between the hours of 7 and 9 p.m. in the Crown and Anchor. By 1731, its activities had expanded beyond the merely vocal, and were attracting interest outside the music profession. From around 1731 until it faltered into silence in 1802, the society would be known as the Academy of Ancient Music.

Joseph Addison's and Richard Steele's magazine *The Spectator* was published from 1711 to 1712, but its character and quality had an influence out of all proportion to its short run. When the reformer Robert Rintoul set out to launch 'a perfect newspaper' in 1828 he took the title from Steele and Addison – not to pretend to any meaningful continuity, but as a salute to its enduring ethos. In the same humour, two centuries later in 1973, Christopher Hogwood would 'revive' the Academy of Ancient Music. To a mind like Hogwood's, that was never more lively than when engaged with the eighteenth century, it forged a delightful (if lightly worn) bond with the intellectual and musical life of another era. In 1998, Hogwood affirmed his own artistic descent from the singers at the Crown and Anchor when he edited and published an elegant new edition of Sir John Hawkins's *An Account of the Institution and Progress of the Academy of Ancient Music* (1770) – 'published on the 25th anniversary of the recreation of The Academy of Ancient Music, 1998'.[3] The historical kinship between the eighteenth-century group and its twentieth-century namesake is tenuous in the extreme. But to Hogwood, a man who understood like few twentieth-century musicians the significance of historical detail, it had meaning: 'This new incarnation carries on many of the aspirations of its forerunners,' he wrote, in 1996.[4]

Hogwood recognised from experience that many of the challenges (and rewards) of performing ancient music were unchanging, and equally valid in 1733 or 1973. There was, for a start, the question of a working definition of Ancientness. The waters would be muddied by the emergence, in the late 1770s, of the so-called Concerts of Ancient Music (or 'Ancient Concerts') – a rival organisation to the Academy, which would endure until 1848, and which defined as 'Ancient' any music that was a minimum of twenty years old. But the Academy was never quite so dogmatic. An early minute book, from May 1731, states: 'By ye compositions of the ancients is meant of such as lived before ye end of the ~~fifteenth~~ sixteenth century.'

Even at the outset, then, there was uncertainty – or, to put it more cheerfully, open-mindedness. The Academy's approach to musical history is probably best summed up by a letter of February 1731 from its secretary Hawley Bishop to the composer Antonio Lotti (1667–1740) in Vienna. It existed, he said, for

> The Improvement of the Science, by searching after, examining and hearing performed the Works of the Masters who flourished before or about the Age of Palestrina: However, not entirely neglecting those who in our time have grown famous.

Haym listed, as part of the Academy's repertoire, vocal music by Josquin, Lassus, Palestrina, Monteverdi, Marenzio, Gesualdo and Carissimi. But the members were never narrowly exclusive in their tastes.[5] An appetite for the songs and theatre music of Purcell opened the way to instrumental performances, and the contemporary music of Handel was a fixture from the earliest meetings. What underlay the Academy's activities from the outset was scholarship: a serious interest in documenting, appraising and rescuing (through performances of the highest standard) the music of an earlier age. Catalogues were written, scores prepared and education work undertaken to train young choristers in an appropriate performance style. Then, as now, there were sceptics. Scorn was hurled, like the contents of a chamber pot from a first-storey window, on the members' enthusiasm for obsolete musical practices. An anonymous satire dating from 1734 and addressed to Handel, ridiculed

> That indefatigable Society, the Gropers into Antique Musick, and Hummers of Madrigals, they swoon on the sight of any Piece modern, particularly of your Composition, excepting the performances of their venerable President [Dr Pepusch] whose Works bear such vast Resemblance to the regular Gravity of the Antients, that when dressed up in cobwebs, and powdered with Dust, the Philharmonick Spiders could dwell on them, and in them, to Eternity.[6]

And then, as now, the notion of authenticity in performance could lead to bitter controversy. In 1728, the Academy was shaken by an accusation that a composition by Bononcini was actually by Lotti. One of the Academy's most distinguished members stood accused of plagiarism. Evidence was provided to support the accusation, and the members (according to one member, the future Earl of Egmont, John Perceval)

> were astonished that so great a man as Bononcini should descend so low as to father another man's works, and impose them on us as his own . . . [Bononcini] stormed and maintained the gentlemen had accused him falsely, insisting the music to be still his own; whereupon it was agreed to write to Vienna to the composer to know the truth. In the meantime Bononcini withdrew from our

society and many of it, who are his professed friends, taking his part, left us also.

Lotti was consulted, sworn statements were obtained, and the accusation of plagiarism was upheld, leading to a rift in the Academy's membership. There would be more over the next half-century.

And yet, the fascination – and the quality – of the Academy's work generated success and public interest beyond anything anticipated by its founders. By the early 1730s, non-professional guests were being admitted, the membership had been opened to non-musicians (including the painter William Hogarth) and (an initiative of Pepusch's) regular additional meetings of the Academy were held at which paying members of the public could enjoy ancient music for themselves. Women, too, started to attend; decades later, Laetitia-Matilda Hawkins (daughter of Sir John) recalled how concerts at the Crown and Anchor were

> held in the then sufficiently capacious and humbly decorated best room of the tavern, and ladies tolerated as auditors, only by submitting to sit in a small passage-room, made warm and comfortable, but certainly no show-shop for their finery;– this restriction to a confined spot was not felt grievous by those who loved such music and only came to hear.[7]

A niche interest pursued in private by a handful of enthusiastic professionals began to evolve into a fashionable, even mainstream taste. Later in the century, Lord Sandwich played the kettledrums at AAM concerts. And on at least one occasion, the Academy of Ancient Music's scholarship and professionalism started to seep back into the wider musical world, with far-reaching effects. In February 1731, the Academicians revived Handel's 1718 masque *Esther* at the Crown and Anchor. According to Hawkins:

> The oratorio of *Esther*, originally composed for the Duke of Chandos, was performed in character by the members of the Academy, and the children of the Chapel Royal, and the applause with which it was received, suggested to Mr Handel, the thought of exhibiting that species of composition at Covent-Garden theatre; and to this event it may be said to be owing, that the

public have not only been delighted with the hearing, but are now in the possession of, some of the most valuable works of that great master.[8]

This was the first public performance in London of a Handel oratorio. It set in train a course of development in Handel's career (and British musical life) the consequences of which are still, two centuries later, being played out. Before the end of the century, Handel's position in British musical life was established beyond challenge – an unprecedented level of popularity for a dead composer, and a spectacular vindication of the Academy's commitment to older music. At its peak, the Academy punched far above its weight: shaping taste, recovering a lost musical past and fuelling a demand for public concert-giving (and -going) that would, in the end, be its undoing. In the final quarter of the eighteenth century, concert societies such as the Ancient Concerts proliferated, offering levels of comfort and musical thrills far beyond anything possible in the Crown and Anchor.

In response, in 1783 the Academy rewrote its constitution and the following year, in the teeth of mounting competition, it left the old tavern behind to become a full-fledged concert-promoting society. It started subcontracting its performances to professional artists (at one point in the early 1790s, its orchestra was directed by the same Johann Salomon who was simultaneously promoting concerts with the visiting Joseph Haydn at Hanover Square). With the dissolution of the original Academy its sense of purpose was weakened and the spirit of collegiality was gone. Long-term members lamented the change and engineered a return to the Crown and Anchor but the energy of the founding fathers had evaporated. The final documented concert took place in April 1802. No subscriptions could be raised for a new season. 'Such, then, was the rise and fall of the Academy of Ancient Music,' writes Christopher Hogwood.

It gave way to the public concert series, the professional symphony orchestra, the music of the pleasure gardens and the opera house. But it had achieved a small musical revolution: it had established for the first time that music of the church and music of the theatre could be performed apart from their original settings, and by selecting and performing old music on a regular basis, it laid the

foundations for a new (and English) concept of a 'canon of classics', which the wider public has embraced ever since. As a private
club, it could not itself dictate public taste, but its activities paved
the way for a concert scene containing the accepted medley of
old and new that we know today.[9]

Hogwood had better reason than most to recognise the achievements of
the first Academy of Ancient Music. The venerable society, it transpired,
was not dead but sleeping.

2

THE PIPER AND THE LYREBIRD

The original Academy of Ancient Music was born at the Crown and Anchor on the Strand. Its reincarnation was conceived one night in 1972 in another pub, and it's one of the quirks of memory that we now no longer know which one. The new group had two parents: both are now dead. But what Christopher Hogwood did say is that he'd met the Decca record producer Peter Wadland, more or less by chance, at a concert at Carlton House given by the clarinettist Alan Hacker. It rings true: Hacker (1938–2012) was leading the revival of the basset clarinet, and a programme of late-classical or early-romantic chamber music – such as Hacker promoted with his ensemble The Music Party – is exactly the sort of thing that would have piqued the interest of both men. They exchanged names and met again soon afterwards at a recording session conducted by Neville Marriner with the Academy of St Martin in the Fields (ASMF).[1]

Again, the exact date and details are uncertain. Hogwood, a man who valued precise scholarship, was self-effacingly vague about the birth of his own orchestra. Possibly it was one of the sessions for Vivaldi's *L'estro armonico*, between 26 July and 26 October 1972, on which Hogwood played both organ and harpsichord continuo. Marriner's virtuoso chamber orchestra was in high demand, recording almost monthly for EMI and Philips, as well as for Decca and its subsidiary Argo. But it's Decca that concerns us here, and the Vivaldi sessions took place in St John's Smith Square. '[Wadland] came to that, and after, we went for a drink,' Hogwood told the musicologist Nick Wilson in 2003.[2] There were various pubs in the grid of streets that makes up that particular corner of Westminster. The Marquis of Granby has been suggested. But what is certain – at least, as Hogwood recalled it – is that Wadland made the proposal.

He said, since you play with that group [the Academy of St Martin in the Fields], would it be possible to conceive of a period group of about the same size playing to anything like that standard? Rather foolishly, I said, 'Yes!' Not so much because I knew the English players could, but I could see that the Dutch and the Viennese had – I could see no reason why we couldn't.[3]

Christopher Hogwood was given to understatement. Wadland, at twenty-six, was already a shrewd judge of artists and individuals, and in taking Hogwood out for a drink it's unlikely that he expected the answer to be no. He'd perceived that Hogwood, who turned thirty-one during the course of those Vivaldi sessions, was uniquely placed to give him an informed and honest answer. Hogwood's family heritage was scientific; his father had been a physicist, and when Christopher went up to Pembroke College, Cambridge, to read Classics in Michaelmas Term 1960, his ultimate ambition was to be an archaeologist.[4] Within weeks, he was on a very different path. He'd learned the piano at home in Nottingham – the harpsichord had been a subject of curiosity but little more. But as early as Cambridge University Music Club's freshers' concert, on 29 October 1960, he'd appeared in public as a harpsichordist, playing with fellow students in a Telemann trio sonata. Three weeks later, in another CUMC concert, he was providing harpsichord continuo again – this time in what he described as the 'first modern performance' of a Handel sonata for two flutes.[5]

Already, his love of discovery – and his flair for translating that excitement into performance – was taking a recognisable shape. Christopher's first two years at Cambridge saw him playing Stravinsky's Sonata for Two Pianos, singing madrigals on the River Cam, directing a student wind band in Richard Strauss and Gabrieli, and conducting a production of Sullivan's *Cox and Box*. And, of course, taking every possible opportunity to perform on the harpsichord, whether solo or as a continuo player. 'Surely the Music Faculty's harpsichord had never been so busy,' comments the musicologist Elizabeth Roche, whose husband Jerome was a Cambridge contemporary (and, as a fellow student, a frequent musical collaborator). That Christopher was not a Music undergraduate was immaterial: at Cambridge, as at Oxford, a vigorous undergraduate musical life has always thrived entirely independently of academic supervision. That autonomy can even be an advantage. As Roche puts it, the undergraduate Hogwood was

> an immensely stimulating presence, both musically and intellectually – a fine practical musician who, not being preoccupied with preparing for stiff exams in harmony and counterpoint, or producing a comprehensive folio of compositions, was able to take a broader, and often thought-provoking, approach to all sorts of musical matters. In particular his enquiring and adventurous – and where earlier music was concerned, notably forward-looking – spirit often enabled him to widen horizons by introducing his friends and acquaintants to then unusual repertory both old and new, and developing ideas spanning a wide range of interests not by any means limited to music.[6]

'Anyone who did not know him to be officially a Classicist could easily have taken it for granted that he was one of the Music Faculty's most talented – and versatile – students,' she observes.

It was also his fortune to be an undergraduate at a time when the tone of the Music Faculty was set by Robert ('Bob') Thurston Dart (1921–1971), the virtuoso harpsichordist and musicologist who would become Professor of Music at the University in 1962. Hogwood took lessons with Dart, and came to see him as a mentor – James Bowman thought that Dart was a decisive influence in his decision to become a professional musician.[7] The outwardly gruff Dart could be intensely supportive and inspiring to those who shared his enthusiasms, and his personal collection of historic instruments was itself a source of inspiration to those of a similar mindset. Hogwood's friend and fellow Pembroke undergraduate David Munrow was already a superb recorder player (although, like Hogwood, he wasn't a Music undergraduate – he was reading English). The sight of a crumhorn hanging on the wall of Dart's study prompted him to take his next step into what was then called early music.[8]

But that was (and is) one of the special qualities of a collegiate university: its ability to connect the lay enthusiast and the academic expert; to jolt the curious out of their academic ruts and to provide a constant, fertilising milieu of unexpected personal relationships. Another important presence at Cambridge at that time was Raymond Leppard, the conductor, composer and harpsichordist. He lectured at Trinity College from 1958 to 1968, and was in the process of leading the post-war rediscovery of Monteverdi with a lavish and controversial new edition of *L'incoronazione di Poppea*, presented at Glyndebourne in 1962.

And then there was the harpsichordist Mary Potts (1905–1982), in whose capacious, welcoming home Hogwood lodged for several years. He was not alone. Munrow had digs there, the harpsichord-builder Trevor Beckerleg started out in Potts's basement, and contemporaries recall a constant traffic of musical young people through her house at 54 Bateman Street – eager to play her historic instruments, and to absorb the experience and expertise of a woman who had learned her art in the 1920s from Arnold Dolmetsch, one of the founding figures of the early-music revival.[9]

Hogwood, too, was forming musical relationships that would shape his future career, and his future orchestra. Konrad Schiemann sang in the choir at Pembroke College. He recollects,

> after some rather bibulous choir supper, retiring to the Dean's room with Christopher. He wasn't in the choir, but he was there because he came to musical events; and so he'd been invited to the supper, and afterwards we made music. I remember singing the part of the Commendatore in *Don Giovanni*; it was all rather jolly. But years later, Christopher said, 'Well, the person who introduced me to Mozart opera was Konrad, who sang this part.' And so I feel this is part of my limited contribution to the musical life of the country.

(It's something of an understatement; Schiemann would become a long-serving director and supporter of the Academy of Ancient Music.)

In June 1963, meanwhile, Hogwood conducted a CUMC performance of Walton's *Façade*. The ensemble included the future conductors Christopher Seaman and David Atherton, and the concert was presided over by a choral scholar from King's College, Simon Standage, who was already making a name as a violinist.[10] That relationship, too, would have long-term consequences. 'I played with him a lot – well, with his orchestra at Pembroke College, anyway,' recalls Standage. 'And then I went abroad for about six years, and when I came back he was playing with David Munrow in the Early Music Consort.' Another King's chorister, the bass David Thomas, recalls singing in a performance at Pembroke of Handel's *Acis and Galatea*, with Hogwood on harpsichord and Munrow on sopranino recorder, 'which was very funny'.

Pembroke contacts would prove useful in 1964 when, after finishing his undergraduate degree, Hogwood won a British Council scholarship to study for a year at Charles University, Prague. 'We met first in Pembroke College,' recalls Jasper Parrott, who went on to found the HarrisonParrott artist agency in 1969.

> But my father was at that stage the British Ambassador in Prague – very much a music-lover, and a good amateur pianist. And I was also becoming infatuated with music, playing the oboe not very well, but with a lot of enthusiasm. Chris was living in austere circumstances in Prague: this was still in quite tough Communist times. So my parents invited him, whenever they could, to parties – to meet people that they thought would be useful and interesting to him.

Even for a self-taught player such as Parrott, Hogwood's determination was hard to resist. 'While Chris was in Prague, David Munrow went out to visit him at Easter [1965]. I remember ending up playing the recorder in an impromptu musical interlude in a church service at the American Embassy: Chris, David, and myself – we played a baroque trio, or something like that.'

By now, it was clear to Hogwood that his future lay with music, and his purpose in Prague was to study with Zuzana Růžičková (1927–2017), the Czech harpsichordist who had survived imprisonment and slave labour at the hands of the Nazis in Theresienstadt, Auschwitz and Bergen-Belsen, and who was pursuing her post-war career under constant surveillance from the Communist authorities – who viewed the Jewish, independently minded Růžičková as doubly suspect. 'One day in 1964 I was called to the Ministry of Culture and told I was going to teach some English students,' she recalled, in her memoir *One Hundred Miracles*:

> My first impression of Christopher was that he was a rather strange fellow. He immediately told me that he was only in Prague because of me and said he didn't want to see or hear anything of

a communist city. 'I am just coming to the musicology department to have lessons, and that's it', he declared. Of course it didn't
take him long to fall in love with Prague . . . Dear Christopher
could have been a great soloist, but he already knew that he was
a Renaissance man, wanting to focus on his conducting, editing
and scholarship.[11]

Růžičková was a peerless judge of character and artistry. Hogwood
would remain a lifelong friend, and in later years she placed him at the top
of her long list of harpsichord pupils. But Cambridge had opened so many
avenues for exploration that any one, alone, would probably never have
satisfied him. That Easter in Prague (recalls Jasper Parrott) Hogwood and
Munrow were already talking about starting an early-music ensemble of
their own. The impetus seems to have come from a concert that Munrow
had organised at Cambridge on 19 January 1963 – as Roche recalls it,
'CUMC's first concert to consist entirely of "early" music'.[12]

The group, assembled by Munrow, was called Cambridge Pro Musica
Antiqua and the programme consisted of music by Telemann, Scarlatti,
Biber, Handel and Orlando Gibbons. Hogwood was only one of two
continuo players (he was due to conduct a new production of Gilbert and
Sullivan's *Patience* later that week, and had his hands full). But, on paper,
it looks like a blueprint for what was to come: for more than a decade
after his return from Prague, Hogwood's emerging musical career would
be inextricably linked with that of his younger friend, David Munrow.

The Pied Piper

David Munrow (1942–1976) was never a part of the Academy of Ancient
Music, but he is an unignorable part of its story. Nearly five decades after
his death, his personality is still a catalysing force. 'He burst upon an
unsuspecting world,' remembered Nicholas Kenyon.[13] 'David Munrow
did not just emerge into the field of medieval and renaissance music – he
exploded into it,' wrote his former tutor Anthony Lewis.[14] His recordings still pulse with an irrepressible fantasy and verve. In his lifetime, his
enthusiasm, his energy and his impact on the world of early music were
so potent, and so life-affirming, that half a century after his death by his
own hand at the age of thirty-three, many of those who knew or were
close to him still find the subject almost too painful to discuss.

Born in Birmingham, Munrow had studied bassoon with Vaughan Allin of the City of Birmingham Symphony Orchestra – a larger-than-life musician who carried a shotgun in his bassoon case and once composed a back-to-front version of Vaughan Williams's *Fantasia on Greensleeves*, passing it off as the work of a fictional Turkish composer, Enërg Essëlv.[15] Munrow played in the Midland Youth Orchestra, branched out onto the recorder and, in 1960, spent a year teaching in Peru before going up to Cambridge. He was fascinated by the folk music and instruments of South America. 'I remember him coming back from South America with a clutch of pipes which he'd gathered there,' says Konrad Schiemann, a schoolmate of Munrow's at King Edward VI School, Birmingham. 'He demonstrated them with great competence.'

That same curiosity and open-mindedness – a practical, 'have-a-go' enthusiasm coupled to an almost theatrical urge to communicate – made Munrow a force of nature in the lively musical environment of early 1960s Cambridge. You get the impression that other, less extrovert talents were simply and happily caught up in his wake. When Hogwood went to Prague, Munrow enlisted as a postgraduate at the University of Birmingham, studying bawdy Restoration songs. In May 1965, at the Barber Institute, he assembled the largest possible band of cornetts, shawms, crumhorns, recorders and percussion, as well as modern oboes and trombones, to perform seventeenth-century Italian *canzoni* and a selection from Susato's *Danserye*. 'Elderly professors were practically dancing in their seats,' remembers Lewis.[16] From there, Munrow found an enthusiastic reception in the wind band of the Royal Shakespeare Company at Stratford-upon-Avon, whose Music Director, Guy Woolfenden, was eager to utilise Munrow's expertise with crumhorns and shawms.

In 1967, Munrow launched the Early Music Consort of London. The ideas that he'd discussed with Hogwood in Prague had developed a momentum of their own, and true to Munrow's wide enthusiasms and free-ranging interests, the Consort was a flexible ensemble, expanding or contracting to suit the music in hand. At its core, it comprised five musicians: Munrow himself, the countertenor James Bowman, viol player Oliver Brookes, lutenist James Tyler and on keyboards, harp, percussion – and, by all accounts, whatever was required – Christopher Hogwood, now twenty-six years old and styling himself 'Xris' (it was the Summer of Love, after all). 'He was quite showy,' recalled Bowman. 'He was very beautiful, with lots of long hair.'[17]

But there was nothing hippyish about the professionalism, and the determination, with which Munrow organised his new ensemble. As Bowman remembered,

> I was sceptical because I wasn't terribly keen on early music. It was usually chaotic. 'Oh, sorry. I've started the wrong piece', or 'I've got the wrong instrument. Can we start that one again?' There were early-music concerts in the sixties which sounded like something by Florence Foster Jenkins or Joyce Grenfell. But when I saw what he had on offer, I thought he was wonderful. He would start a performance with a properly planned programme, no faffing about – it was all very professional. David said, 'It's not like a school concert, with applause after every piece – the whole thing is properly presented. There is no messing around with music: it will all be in folders in front of you, and you'll just turn the page.' It was all thoroughly drilled, and Chris appreciated that.

Impressions matter. Jasper Parrott, then a junior artist agent at the firm of Ibbs and Tillett, persuaded his employers to take a chance on the new group. Two years later, when they transferred to Parrott's own fledgling agency, the Early Music Consort's reputation was already snowballing. Nothing quite like this had ever been seen in the English early-music movement.

Which is not to say that Munrow and Hogwood were operating in isolation. The idea of rediscovering and performing the forgotten music of a past era dates back (in the British Isles, anyway) at least as far as that original Academy in 1726. The history – or rather the many intertwining, overlapping and frequently contradictory histories – of the early-music movement has been extensively chronicled, embracing such landmarks as the Handel Commemorations of the 1780s and 1790s in London, Felix Mendelssohn's celebrated performance of Bach's *St Matthew Passion* in Berlin in March 1829, and the renewed interest in so-called *Alte Musik* in Germany in the first half of the twentieth century.

The European *Alte Musik* impulse was, in a large part, anti-romantic: at least partly, a reaction against the philosophical and aesthetic extremes of the late-romantic era and (it was implied) the disastrous consequences in which they were implicated from 1914 onwards. It's no coincidence that a leading German modernist composer such as Paul Hindemith, in exile from the Nazis, became a significant influence on early music in the USA. Meanwhile, in Thomas Mann's novel *Doktor Faustus* (1943–7) the narrator Serenus Zeitblom is a mild-mannered, viola d'amore-playing devotee of *Alte Musik* who is able to stand apart and observe in horrified detachment as post-romantic German music (personified by the possessed, Schoenberg-inspired composer Adrian Leverkühn) spirals into insanity and cataclysm.

For English readers in the post-war era, early-music revivalists had a rather less flattering fictional image: the prim middle-class *bien-pensants* of Kingsley Amis's *Lucky Jim* (1957), all floral-print frocks, amateur recorder recitals and enforced jollity through the medium of compulsory madrigal-singing. To readers at the time, the characters of Amis's satire were recognisable as disciples (at a generation's remove) of the French-born Arnold Dolmetsch (1858–1940), who had settled in Haslemere in Surrey after the First World War, and established himself as a scholar, a performer and a maker of historic instruments. Dolmetsch made lutes and, later, at the encouragement of William Morris, harpsichords. He's sometimes credited with the construction of the first recorder of modern times. As with Continental devotees of *Alte Musik*, Dolmetsch's interest in the past was a reaction against industrial modernity, but rooted in the Fabian tradition and the very English loam of Morris's Arts and Crafts Movement.

Dolmetsch was bearded and knickerbockered, and his circle of pupils was occasionally compared with a cult. Perhaps unfairly, early music acquired a reputation as the leftish preserve of what George Orwell described as 'every fruit-juice drinker, nudist, sandal-wearer, sex-maniac, Quaker, "Nature Cure" quack, pacifist, and feminist in England'. Yet Dolmetsch's legacy was fertilising, and largely benign. Nor was it as doctrinaire as some detractors liked to imply. Mary Potts, Hogwood's teacher and sometime landlord, had studied with Dolmetsch and bought her Burkat Shudi harpsichord from him in 1929 (he suggested to her that it would serve as a stopgap until she could acquire a modern iron-framed instrument).[18] Howard Mayer Brown, writing in 1988, maintained, 'It is no exaggeration to say that even today almost everyone involved in early music in England has been touched in some way by Dolmetsch, by his students, or by his students' students.'[19]

In the period after the Second World War approaches to early music were diverging along different paths in different places. The Dutch harpsichordist, conductor and musicologist Gustav Leonhardt (1928–2012) had founded his Leonhardt Ensemble while studying in Vienna. An interpreter of striking personality and rigour, he had already embraced the use of reproduction historic harpsichords and built on the scholarship and the growing pool of *Alte Musik* performers that he had encountered in Vienna. 'It's no problem getting hold of a facsimile edition of early music,' he remarked. 'What else is there to add?'[20] Leonhardt frequently collaborated with Nikolaus and Alice Harnoncourt, string players in the Vienna Symphony Orchestra who had founded their own pioneering period-instrument orchestra, Concentus Musicus Wien, in 1953, and spent four years researching and rehearsing playing techniques before giving their first official public performance in Vienna's Schwarzenberg Palace in May 1957. By 1962 they were making commercial recordings. (Leonhardt's group had made its LP debut in 1954.)

In the UK, the future pioneers of period performance took a slightly less rigid approach. Roger Norrington was in the generation ahead of Hogwood and Munrow at Cambridge, and founded his first early-music group, the Schütz Choir, in 1962. 'We knew nothing,' he says.

It wasn't really very historically informed. But singing music which no one had ever heard before in this country led us to using old instruments, because Schütz requires the zink and the cornetto and so on. So having done some things with modern instruments, we thought we'd really better try to use the old ones. I also met Thurston Dart at Cambridge, when I was reading English, and I was instinctively interested in his lectures about old music. Dart told me quite a lot about the influence of the Italian style on English music via the Netherlands – I remember having a long talk with him about that. But for the Schütz Choir in 1962 and for quite a while after that, I didn't know anything about it. I used instinct. There was no scholarship in that at all.

There's an innate British tendency to downplay the amount of effort that lies behind creative achievement, particularly when it's of a scholarly nature. Still, it's possible to sense that same, pragmatic spirit of open-minded exploration – of learning through doing, of trusting to instinct and of doing whatever it takes to get the show on the road – in Munrow's approach, and also in that of the Irish scholar and conductor Michael Morrow (1929–1994). Morrow launched his ensemble Musica Reservata in 1960 with the avowed intention of breaking away from a 'mish-mash of University Choral Society sounds', with the strict qualification that any historically informed performance could only ever be 'a more or less successful counterfeit'.[21]

The style was raucous, improvisatory and sometimes ramshackle. Both Munrow and Hogwood played with Morrow during the 1960s, and the soprano Emma Kirkby attended Musica Reservata's concerts as a student. 'They were immense fun, with lots of eccentric renaissance instruments and a lot of inspiration – but mainly chaotic,' she recalls. 'That was really the milieu in which a lot of future directors worked. I think they got the inspiration from Michael Morrow, but they also discovered how not to put on concerts.'

The traditional orchestral scene in Britain, meanwhile, was approaching the baroque revival – and the question of historical-performance practice – via its own process of evolutionary compromise. The mid-twentieth century saw a fashion for chamber orchestras: using modern instruments, but in smaller ensembles, and with a leaner, livelier approach. The London Chamber Orchestra was founded in 1921, the Goldsbrough Orchestra (1947) evolved into the English Chamber Orchestra in 1960, and the Boyd Neel Orchestra (named after its founder, but referred to by players as the 'Boiled Veal Orchestra') lit up the concert landscape of the 1930s and 1940s with the athleticism and bravura of its playing, making pioneering recordings of Handel and Vivaldi, and commissioning Benjamin Britten, Gordon Jacob and John Ireland.

But none of them achieved anything like the international impact of the Academy of St Martin in the Fields – launched in November 1959 by the LSO and Boyd Neel violinist Neville Marriner (1924–2016) – which selected its players from the front desks of London's freelance symphony orchestras. Critics enthused over the freshness and crispness of the ASMF's playing; within a decade Marriner's ensemble was being described as Britain's best orchestra, and its recorded catalogue increased almost by the month. For audiences who were used to Mozart and Handel on full symphonic string sections, the energy and clarity of this world-beating chamber orchestra was thrilling, though its sound still had the reassuring polish and precision of a top symphony orchestra.

In fact, the main 'period' colour that early ASMF listeners would have heard was the jangle of the harpsichord, often played by Thurston Dart or – increasingly, from the late 1960s – Christopher Hogwood. As Munrow's reputation skyrocketed, Hogwood kept a foot in both worlds. It was undeniable that the energy and freewheeling spirit of the Early Music Consort – fronted by Munrow, with his youthful enthusiasm and puckish humour – had caught the spirit of the time. Medieval music was funky: Steeleye Span took plainchant into the pop charts, and in 1970 Munrow and the Consort provided the score for the BAFTA- (and later Emmy-) winning BBC TV drama series *The Six Wives of Henry VIII*. Members of the Consort played with folk-rock bands, and collaborated with Peter Maxwell Davies and his Fires of London on Ken Russell's 1971 cinematic shocker *The Devils* (the Vatican called for it to be banned). Munrow composed the score for John Boorman's 1974 psychedelic science-fiction blockbuster *Zardoz*: supplying gemshorns and notch flutes as Sean Connery roamed an apocalyptic future clad in red Y-fronts.

As the 1970s progressed, the Early Music Consort would tour Europe, the Middle East, Australia and the USA. In August 1971, the Consort made its first appearance at the Proms. 'Filling the Albert Hall, of all vast spaces, with totally unamplified and glorious sound: David and Goliath was the general impression,' recalled the American musicologist Robert Donnington.[22] The counterculture was going mainstream. By now, Munrow was such a celebrity that he'd been offered his own radio series. *Pied Piper* started barely a fortnight after that Prom and ran for 655 episodes on BBC Radio 3 – twenty minutes of 'tales and music' aimed at younger listeners, and covering everything from prog rock to crumhorns. Space travel, string quartets, Bach and the life of Sir Thomas Beecham might all form the subject of one of Munrow's playful, enthusiastic mini-masterclasses. Although designed for children, Munrow's style was so accessible – and so engaging – that *Pied Piper*'s listeners were later found to have an average age of twenty-nine.

The Young Idea

The spirit of communication was infectious. Munrow was not alone: since 1969, Christopher Hogwood had been the voice of BBC Radio 3's

The Young Idea – a weekly Tuesday afternoon show comprising 'music chosen by the under-twenties'. Surviving schedules suggest that much of the music involved was being chosen *for* the under-twenties, and from Hogwood's earliest appearances on *The Young Idea* (the series had already been running for some years) his own interests and enthusiasms are obvious. Praetorius, Byrd and recordings of Frans Brüggen and Gustav Leonhardt playing Corelli jostled with Penderecki, Messiaen and William Grant Still. 'I listened to it and so did my music-loving friends,' recalls the soprano Catherine Bott. 'It was compulsory listening.'[23] Nicholas Kenyon recalls, 'He had such a deft way of illuminating what he talked about, what he played – really informative without being patronising. He set a whole new style for informed broadcasting that wasn't pompous and condescending.'

Evidently, there was more than one strong musical personality within the Early Music Consort, although for now it was Munrow's outgoing style that shaped the artistic direction of the ensemble. For all the mainstream success that greeted the EMC, and Munrow's remarkable media-savviness and professionalism, there was still an improvisatory quality – a certain on-the-hoofness – about the group's activities. Munrow, recalls the violinist Catherine Mackintosh, 'was really good fun. He was really quite driven. And just a tremendous fountain of energy.'

Mackintosh would be called in to join the core five members of the EMC whenever a programme required an additional viol or rebec, and she recalls one occasion where the spontaneous EMC spirit nearly led to a fiasco:

We were going up to do a concert with David, in quite a large group. And we went by train to Glasgow, and we had a very convivial time on the train – we had a British Railways dining-car lunch. And when we finished, we went back to our compartment and discovered to our horror that our compartment was no longer in the train. It had divided while we were having lunch, and the half which had all our instruments in it had gone off to Edinburgh. So as soon as we arrived in Glasgow, somebody had to rush off to Edinburgh and collect all these instruments – which fortunately were found. They arrived at the concert hall just in time for the concert. But there was no rehearsal that day.

What happens on tour stays on tour: there are few touring ensembles of any kind that don't have a similar tale to tell. By the standards of the time, the EMC was a paragon of organisational discipline. But Christopher Hogwood was quietly starting to hanker for a style of historic performance that was more in keeping with his own meticulous philosophy of musical scholarship. Like Norrington and Dart, Munrow took a pragmatic approach to what would later be called 'authenticity'. For Munrow, the needs of the live performance were paramount, and where individual musical instinct came into conflict with scholarship (or the lack of it), instinct took precedence. As Neville Marriner of the Academy of St Martin in the Fields got to know his brilliant, intellectual young harpsichordist, he became aware that he was dealing with an artist with a deep concern for scholarly rigour:

> For me, he was always the fresher side of musicology. With Bob [Thurston] Dart, we always felt that he was the father of our musicological ambitions. But when Christopher came along he was different. In many ways he was more specific than Bob Dart was. Bob would always say that an ornament is played the way you feel, it's put there for you to express yourself. Whereas Christopher, I think, was much more intent on accuracy.[24]

Stylistic and textual fidelity was less of an issue in medieval and other pre-baroque music, where the lack of source material more or less obliged interpreters to use their imaginations. An artist such as Munrow thrived on that sort of freedom, and Hogwood's recorded performances with the EMC demonstrate that he, too, was more than capable of rising to its creative challenges. Indisputably, however, something in his make-up – both as an individual and as an artist – craved the precision and intellectual underpinning of historical scholarship. 'He had certain principles that he wanted to apply. He wanted to have the most up-to-date scholarship in terms of what he was doing. And he always made sure there was a musicologist – if not himself – preparing editions,' says the film director Anthony Fabian, Hogwood's partner of twenty-six years. 'But what was his absolute through-line was that he did not want to put himself in front of the music. He wanted always to let the music speak for itself, to do what he would call archaeology. His artistic imprint was to be transparent.'

It was a philosophy that had less in common with the English pioneers of early music than with Nikolaus Harnoncourt – who as early as 1954 had argued that 'the attempt must be made today . . . with [baroque works] to hear and perform them as if they had never been interpreted before, as though they had never been formed nor distorted.'[25] Munrow was far from alone in taking a radically different approach. 'Christopher described it as an invention upon invention. He objected to what was going on because, although it was quite fun at first, it really became a bit of a shot in the dark. David was in some ways more of a showman than a scholar,' recalled James Bowman. As Hogwood himself put it, in 1984:

> It was an entirely new 'old' sound, but not a soul knew if it was authentic or not . . . There was a lot of showbiz attached to it. Finally my interest in this kind of music became exhausted, because we did not know whether or not what we were doing was authentic. Although the whole world thought that this type of music-making had a musicological foundation, the very opposite was the case: we had to do a lot on 'feeling', because there was insufficient basis and definite proof of the way in which music was made in the Middle Ages. In looking for an 'original sound', we were very much dependent upon hypotheses.[26]

Instead, as he explained,

> I turned to an area, to a period, which offered me reliable sources. That was the music of the seventeenth and eighteenth centuries . . . The repertoire that I played with the Academy of St Martin in the Fields aroused my attention more and more, together with the desire for an 'authentic sound', which I had preserved from my involvement with medieval music. I tried increasingly to give my solo recitals on historical instruments, too, because the harpsichords built in modern times had a sound that one could only place in the realm of the imagination or, better, of toys.[27]

Hogwood's own leaning towards a greater scholarly basis for performance – and towards the seventeenth- and eighteenth-century repertoire in which it was a more practical proposition – aligned with a particular moment in the recording industry. Munrow and the EMC had shown that early music and historically informed performance could enthuse a wide audience. Now major record labels looked to build on that discovery and to make it into a paying proposition.

The Class of '73

Already, traditional recording orchestras such as the ASMF were starting to sense the new climate. Neville Marriner joked that period instruments were 'very popular with the open-toed-sandals-and-brown-bread set'[28] but meanwhile he leaned more and more on Hogwood to produce scholarly editions of works on the ASMF's recording schedule. James Bowman remembered that Hogwood 'did a lot to make the Academy play in a more authentic way. He made them do their trills on the upper note, for a start. He put in much more tasteful ornamentation: as Neville himself used to say, "We've been Hogwood–ised."'[29]

Marriner swam with the tide – up to a point: '[Hogwood] did many editions for us, and I don't think we ever really followed them to the letter.' Hogwood recalled, 'I'd been telling them to try playing without vibrato in Vivaldi's Op. 3, and they almost did.'[30] Expression and instinct still trumped fidelity to scholarship; just a bit less so. Marriner, in later years, was 'sure the appearance of the Academy of Ancient Music was entirely due to his [Hogwood's] frustration with the other Academy'. 'Chris was quite rightly straining at the leash to move off in another direction with his own orchestra,' recalled Bowman.[31]

It was a propitious moment to do just that, in the UK at any rate. Nick Wilson has coined the phrase 'The Class of '73' to describe the cohort of British early-music ensembles that were founded around this time and subsequently went on to enjoy lasting success on disc and in the concert hall. Chronologically speaking, it's a bit of a catch-all, but it describes a definite step change in the quality and scale of early-music activity in the UK. The English Concert, formed by Trevor Pinnock in 1972, gave its first concert in 1973, made its first recording in 1974 and was signed to Deutsche Grammophon's *Alte Musik* label Archiv Produktion in 1978. Peter Phillips's chamber choir, the Tallis Scholars, gave its first concert in Oxford in November 1973.

At the instigation of Michael Tippett, Andrew Parrott – who had played with Michael Morrow in Musica Reservata – assembled the

Taverner Choir, Consort and Players for the May 1973 Bath Festival. Meanwhile, John Eliot Gardiner's Monteverdi Choir – founded in Cambridge in 1964 – had made its first appearance at the BBC Proms in 1968 (its period-instrument orchestra, the English Baroque Soloists, performed for the first time in May 1977), and Roger Norrington's Schütz Choir had been active for a decade and was recording regularly for Argo. In 1974, at Kent Opera, Norrington would take the unprecedented decision to perform Monteverdi's *L'incoronazione di Poppea* on period instruments. (The performance was in Lisbon. 'They said, well, let's take our modern instruments as well in case it doesn't work,' remembers Norrington. 'I said, "No, just the old instruments – that's it."')

The Academy of Ancient Music was born with one overwhelming advantage over its fellows: it had a record contract from the outset. In fact, as we've seen, it was Peter Wadland of Decca who conceived the idea of a sort of period-instrument ASMF – a recording orchestra *par excellence* – and correctly intuited that Hogwood, by now, would not need much persuasion. Wadland was aware that in Germany, the Telefunken label's sub-brand *Das alte Werk* had built a relationship (and a catalogue) with Gustav Leonhardt, and with Harnoncourt's Concentus Musicus Wien. HMV had reaped the fruits of its confidence in Munrow and the Early Music Consort, and major labels were now looking to sign the emerging historically informed ensembles. Andreas Holschneider, the head of Deutsche Grammophon's Archiv label, attended the debut performance of The English Concert on 4 May 1973 and expressed an interest, but waited another five years before offering the ensemble a contract.[32] Decca, meanwhile, had acquired the long-established French early-music publishing house Éditions de l'Oiseau-Lyre, and put Wadland in charge.

Early L'Oiseau-Lyre releases under Wadland's direction had concentrated on eighteenth-century repertoire, but they also included contemporary music by Hans Werner Henze, Tōru Takemitsu and Peter Maxwell Davies. They were eclectic, pursuing no particular stylistic angle: Thurston Dart, the English Chamber Orchestra and the Fires of London were equally likely to appear. After his drink with Hogwood, Wadland saw a new and more focused way forward: a specialist early-music label and a bespoke ensemble with which Decca could surf the rising tide of interest in historically informed performance. He spoke to a sceptical Ray Minshull (the long-serving Head of A&R at Decca Classics) and persuaded him to back a recording of Thomas Arne's Eight Overtures in Eight Parts with a new ensemble to be assembled, directed and managed as a wholly independent body by Christopher Hogwood. 'We came up with the idea that if we combined enough of these small groups – and we knew one or two oboists, horn players, and so on – we might just manage to make an orchestra,' said Hogwood. 'So we did it.'[33]

It will have been around this time that Hogwood made the news known to Neville Marriner. 'He wrote a very polite letter saying that he hoped we wouldn't mind if he was starting his own orchestra,' recalled Marriner. 'For him, it was a great joy to have an orchestra where he could actually reproduce the sound that he really wanted.' In fact, Hogwood continued to work on projects with the ASMF for several years after setting up his new orchestra, and it was almost certainly the ASMF – combined with his own deep knowledge of eighteenth-century musical history – that inspired the name Academy of Ancient Music.

He doesn't, at that point, seem to have over-thought it. 'It was a title from the very early eighteenth century, of a group of people who met in London to both sing and play music that they saw as being ancient if it was at least twenty years old. It seemed to me a rather appropriate title to go off with,' he told Lucie Skeaping on BBC Radio 3 in 2013.[34] Three days of recordings were scheduled at All Saints' Church in Petersham, West London. For the first time in nearly two centuries, the Academy of Ancient Music was to meet, on Monday, 17 September 1973.

3

CREATING A SOUND

The Academy of Ancient Music had a name, and it had a recording contract. As yet, it didn't have any musicians. Part of the appeal of recording
Arne's overtures was that they did not require a large orchestra. John
Dunkerley (Decca's senior balance engineer from 1968 to 1997) recalls,
'It required a very small string section, fairly cheap to put together. There
weren't very many original-instrument players at that time. It seemed to
be a very good way of putting one's toe in the original-instrument waters,
which were then, basically, very small beer.'[1] According to Emma Kirkby,
Wadland might have had another, more pragmatic motive: 'Radio 3, back
then, thought it was nice to start with overtures in the morning, so they
were always playing them.' Twenty-three players (including Hogwood,
directing from the harpsichord) were required for the September 1973
Arne sessions, but those players still had to be found and booked before
the process of creating a recording – let alone an orchestra – could begin.

'It was almost like an audition record,' says Dunkerley. 'It was very
much a testing of the waters by Peter and Christopher, to see whether it
would be a success.' No problem: looking back at those early days at the
time of the AAM's fortieth anniversary, Christopher Hogwood made it
sound easy. There wasn't a large pool of players who owned the necessary
instruments, or understood the techniques necessary for playing therm.
But as Hogwood recalled,

> they all knew each other. When you knew one, you knew the
> lot. There was, and had been, of course, a big school of English
> consort-playing. So many of these English players, interestingly,
> were as adept on the viol as they were on the violin and I think

that made a special cast to the style that was developed here
– in contrast to what we already knew well from Amsterdam
and from Vienna, from Eduard Melkus, from Leonhardt, from
Harnoncourt . . .

And so we knew our people. Yes, we knew Jenny Ward Clarke
and Cat Mackintosh and Duncan Druce, and Trevor Jones, who
were already string-playing friends, usually in a consort setting.
We put them together: Tess [Miller] played the oboe and we
found Alan Civil was quite prepared to risk his life on the natural horn, and a few people on the natural trumpet, and out of
that very small group of players we met in a church in Petersham
and that was the beginning of the Academy of Ancient Music.
And after introducing people to each other, we then recorded
Arne overtures.[2]

The list of players on that first recording is a potted survey of the
state of the UK early-music scene in the early 1970s – and a harbin-
ger of things to come. Players such as the violinists Duncan Druce (the
orchestra's leader on that first session), Simon Standage and Catherine
Mackintosh, and the oboist Tess Miller, would go on to play significant
roles in the life of the Academy of Ancient Music. There were early-music
veterans such as the bass player (and pioneering viol player) Francis Baines
(1917–1999) – a regular at Benjamin Britten's Aldeburgh Festivals, where
he was the resident expert on the hurdy-gurdy and shawm – and future
stars. Nicholas McGegan, later director of San Francisco's Philharmonia
Baroque Orchestra and the Göttingen Handel Festival, was in the orchestra that Monday morning, aged twenty-three and playing the flute.

And then there were artists such as Simon Rowland-Jones (viola
player of the recently formed Chilingirian String Quartet), the timpanist, composer and future TV producer Robert Howes and Alan Civil
(1929–1989), the virtuoso principal horn of the Philharmonia and BBC
Symphony Orchestra and a legendary figure on the London session scene
(he played on *Revolver* and *Sgt. Pepper's Lonely Hearts Club Band* and was
one of only five session musicians ever credited by The Beatles). Civil was
a supremely versatile player, and was willing, when pressed by Hogwood,
to turn his hand to a valveless instrument (for the recording, he used a
French-made horn dating from 1815) even if, at heart, he was one of the

many seasoned industry pros who (in the words of Catherine Mackintosh) 'thought we all ate brown rice and wore sandals'. (John Dunkerley admits that he and his colleagues at Decca referred to Hogwood and his kind as 'the nut-cutlet brigade'.) In an interview with Nick Wilson in 2003, Hogwood recalled:

> If we couldn't fill the gaps, we persuaded good professionals like Alan Civil to drop the modern horn and pick up an ancient horn. They didn't always do it on the same basis as we did. They were doing it more as a joke – to show that the old instruments didn't work – whereas we were doing it to show that the old instrument did it better. So there was a little bit of 'Ho ho, listen to this funny noise on the horn.' And I might say, 'Alan, couldn't you use your lip to make it slightly more in tune, or put your hand in,' and we got some very interesting results, because they were total professionals in another field, whereas we were total amateurs in this field.[3]

'We had some fabulous musicians, actually,' says Catherine Mackintosh.

> There were quite a few people in the mainstream orchestras who were intrigued by playing on old instruments. I remember that first recording in Petersham – there was a moment where we were taking a rather long time doing a take of a section which the horns weren't in. And there was suddenly a very strange noise, and it was Alan who had fallen asleep just in front of the altar and was snoring loudly.

The fact remained, though, that even in a period-instrument orchestra of twenty-three, in 1973 there were still gaps that needed to be filled. The world of historically informed performance was close knit precisely because it was small. In the long term, that was a problem that would start to remedy itself – as the musicians of 'The Class of '73' demonstrated that it was possible to sustain a career as a period-performance specialist. In the medium term, though, it was a problem. Speaking to the first ever industry-wide conference on 'The Future of Early Music in Britain', held at the Royal Festival Hall in May 1977, Christopher Hogwood described the dilemma: 'There are far too few players doing far too much work.'

It was brought out recently, I think, at a Continental music festival that featured English early-music groups in its programme. It had booked a large number of named groups and then was rather horrified to discover that in fact all the different names amounted to the same group of players, who in some cases were expected to divide themselves into thirds every evening of the week and perform in different places.[4]

Undoubtedly, with demand for historically informed players rapidly outstripping supply, there was a great deal of overlap between the personnel of, say, the AAM, The English Concert and the Early Music Consort. There had to be, if orchestral recordings (even on the modest scale of the Arne disc) were to be made. In 1977 Hogwood summarised the problem by thinking the unthinkable: could a period-instrument orchestra ever assemble enough players to record a late Mozart symphony?

If five players drop out of any of the established London string orchestras, you can replace them. If five baroque violinists go ill, you can't produce another five. Yet we manage somehow to perform in the correct orchestral proportions a lot of orchestral music that on the face of it we shouldn't be able to perform, and it's done by a much maligned promiscuity; everybody has to play for everybody else simply in order to muster a string section of the size that existed even in the most modest of eighteenth-century establishments. If you were to try and perform music from a little later in the eighteenth century – some of Mozart's larger-scale symphonies for instance – you would find yourself some twenty players short in the violin section alone.[5]

History is peppered with ironies that are visible only with hindsight. Yet in setting up an orchestra drawing on a wide pool of freelance musicians, with the proficiency to produce commercial recordings to a high standard on a strict deadline and budget, Hogwood and Wadland were emulating the very pattern of work that had made London's conventional orchestras so highly regarded and commercially successful. The parallel with the Academy of St Martin in the Fields is significant: consciously or not (and it was far from a straightforward or immediate process), they were injecting the homespun, experimental world of early music with the efficiency, professionalism and rigour of the freelance London orchestral model. They weren't entirely alone in this but with its Decca deal the Academy of Ancient Music moved instantly to the front of the field, learning and adapting at speed and on the job. The AAM was in the vanguard of the process – call it professionalisation, commercialisation or simply a collective artistic coming of age – that would make it possible for historically informed musicians to make an entire career out of what had (until now) been a fringe or a sideline.

Human Resources

It's worth stepping back for a moment to look at the different paths that individual musicians had taken to reach this point – and the motivation behind their decision to master techniques and instruments with which there was (at that time, anyway) no realistic prospect of earning a living. For Catherine Mackintosh, the seed was sown at school, and by a committed modernist.

> I went to Cranbourne Chase, where we did a lot of renaissance singing and playing. My teacher for O-level music was Harrison Birtwistle. He was very interested in medieval and renaissance music: we sat down with him at the beginning of the year and made a list of all the composers that we ought to be talking about. By the end of the year, when the exam came up, we'd only got as far as Bach.
>
> He introduced me to wonderful English viol music and lute songs – Julian Bream, Peter Pears, Monteverdi operas. And so I was quite in love with this pre-classical music before I'd even got to the Royal College of Music. Then, while I was at the College, a notice went up saying that if anybody would like to learn to play the viol, Marco Pallis, who was the director of the English Consort of Viols had very kindly donated a chest of viols to the college. [Pallis – a Liverpudlian mountaineer and Buddhist of Greek descent – was one of Arnold Dolmetsch's most committed pupils, and had formed his first viol consort in 1935.]
>
> I learned to play the treble viol quite quickly. I played in the English Consort of Viols for quite a few years. Pallis was a sort

of a tutor to me really; he gave me my first baroque fiddle bow, and my first treble viol. And so I began playing in the early-music groups that were around then – particularly Musica Reservata – and because I was a violinist I picked up a lot of the medieval fiddles and rebecs and things quite quickly. I gave up my plans to become a virtuoso modern violinist when I was still at college. I was one of the few people who was playing pretty much full-time on early instruments.

Even so, at this point – the late 1960s – there wasn't sufficient work to pay the bills.

No, there certainly wasn't enough. I was teaching kids at the same time. I suppose the first baroque gig that I did might have been with Roger Norrington's Schütz Choir, which was not professional at the time. I used to sing with them. And occasionally he did a concert with a small chamber group – the London Baroque Players, which later morphed into the London Classical Players. I played the fiddle, and Francis Baines was on the double bass. I got paid three quid for it.

I felt very lucky, in some ways. Looking back on my trajectory as a musician, I spent two years being chiefly a viol player, which I don't think anyone could do now. I played masses of renaissance music, and I played with Anthony Rooley in the Consort of Musicke; I was a founding member of that group also. And then along came the Academy of Ancient Music in 1973, so I started playing baroque music. And then after a few years of doing that, we started playing classical music. Actually, I had been playing with Chris quite a lot before that. We'd done some BBC programmes; I'd played sonatas and trio sonatas with him. So I guess he knew about me, and we were a fairly small pool of baroque players at that time. And of course there were other groups such as The English Concert, which started around the same time. We all played in everything in those days.

Although Simon Standage sat next to Duncan Druce on the front desk of that first Arne recording, he would spend much of his early career as the leader of The English Concert. But his musical roots were so entwined with Hogwood's that it was a simple and most natural thing to move across for projects with the AAM:

> The English Concert was at the other end of the spectrum to the Academy, as regards regular personnel. It seemed almost by design that Chris was happy with a changing personnel, whereas The English Concert was the most constant of any of those groups. I know that we were accused of being the same players with different conductors, but The English Concert was very consistent, personnel wise.
>
> I'd been at Cambridge with Chris and I played with him a lot at Pembroke College, so I played with the Early Music Consort as well. We were on modern instruments at the time, and it was Chris who said to me, 'Why don't you get yourself a proper baroque instrument?' So I did.

In the late 1960s and early 1970s, the acquisition of a good baroque violin was more easily said than done. Standage turned first of all to J & A Beare, the long-established London dealers, who were unable to help, though one of their experts, Peter Biddulph, had a lead:

> He said, 'In Paris, Étienne Vatelot has a fiddle in original condition.' I was freelancing as an associate member of the London Symphony Orchestra at the time, but I had some time off. We had two small boys then; so we piled into our Renault 4 and drove to Paris. I went into Vatelot's shop and he showed me an instrument by Roze, a well-known French eighteenth-century maker. I said yes and had to go back to my hotel to get my American Express. And in the meantime, while I was doing that, somebody arrived from the Paris Conservatoire, which at that time was just around the corner on the Rue de Madrid. They wanted to buy it because they had three others and they wanted to make up a quartet of Roze instruments. But Vatelot told them, 'I'm afraid it's been sold.' So I was lucky to get it. It was a strange instrument, made in Orléans. It cost all of £200.

Significantly, though – and even after that trip to Paris and the invest-ment of £200 – Standage continued to maintain a career in the orchestral mainstream:

> I joined the LSO in the first place in order to be able to get a mortgage, but I thoroughly enjoyed it. The LSO under André Previn had played a lot of Vaughan Williams and Walton and Ravel; I can't remember playing a Beethoven symphony, and obviously there was no Bach. It was when I went to the English Chamber Orchestra that I found myself playing baroque reper-toire, and that was what I found unsatisfactory. I realised that there was something not quite right about playing Bach the same way that you play the Tchaikovsky Serenade. We had Raymond Leppard a lot, and Barenboim was a regular visitor, and I thor-oughly enjoyed that. But it did strike me that there was something not quite right about the instrument I was playing, which is why I got interested in the baroque violin. The business of playing in a symphony orchestra is famously bad for your health. The attrac-tion of baroque music for me is that it was chamber music. The English Concert started off as a group of three or four people.

Orchestral projects, even on the relatively modest scale of the AAM's Arne overtures, were the exception rather than the rule in the salad days of 'The Class of '73' – achievable, with much careful diary management, primarily for recording sessions. When the embryonic AAM ventured away from Decca recordings and into the concert hall (or the BBC studio) it was predominantly as a chamber ensemble. Although he wasn't present at the Arne sessions, a regular AAM member in the 1970s was the cellist Anthony Pleeth. As the son of the distinguished cello soloist William Pleeth (best remembered today as the teacher of Jacqueline du Pré), he could easily have made a career on a modern instrument. Instead, he found himself drawn into a fascinating and very different world:

> I had a trio with Trevor Pinnock and the flautist Stephen Preston. We played modern instruments, because that's all there was. But we used to listen to Frans Brüggen and Gustav Leonhardt and Anner Bylsma – the first Dutch recordings on authentic instruments.

Then the others started going onto baroque instruments and I joined them about a year later – I can't remember why that was. Maybe it was because David Rubio was making my first baroque cello for me – I was about twenty-one or twenty-two, so that would have been around 1970. Trevor being a harpsichordist, I can remember being at his first wife's family home in Cobham in Surrey, and listening to Brüggen and Bylsma, and getting the taste for it. For the next three or four years I spent a lot of time at the British Museum, researching cello repertoire. Then in 1974 or 1975, Chris Hogwood had the idea of recording the Geminiani cello sonatas.

Hogwood was a tireless archive researcher, so their interests naturally brought them into each other's orbit.

I can't remember how I met Christopher Hogwood – whether Catherine Mackintosh or Duncan Druce introduced us. But he must have been aware of what I was doing with Stephen and Trevor. The circle of people playing so-called authentic instruments was pretty small at the time, so anybody that was doing that sort of thing in England was known to everybody else.

The small size of that circle meant frequent compromises with players whose motivation was more financial than scholarly. James Bowman's impression was that 'they couldn't give a stuff about all that. If Chris told them what to do, they'd do it. There was none of this delving around in the Bodleian Library. No, thanks! If you're a musician, you want to earn the money and do the work. You don't want to be discussing sesquialtera on page 76, and all that sort of thing. You just want to get on with it, don't you?'

Emma Kirkby draws the distinction more subtly:

I mean, everybody had a good go, and some people were very accomplished and some people were perfectly efficient. But the remarkable ones were the ones who said, 'Yes, OK, I'm doing this, but I'm also going to go to the Netherlands and have some lessons with Jaap Schröder, or go to Harnoncourt in Salzburg,' or whatever. They went and found out about the slightly more established schools of playing. But, being British, they picked up ideas and information from quite a number of sources, and were much less likely to become too influenced by any one of them. There's a slightly anarchic streak in English players, which is quite good, actually. I don't think we do gurus in quite the same way as they did on the Continent at that time.

She adds, 'I say "we", but I'm talking particularly about the players – the proper musicians, as opposed to the singers, who were feeling their own way.'

Bowman was in the vanguard of the vocalists who were 'finding their own way'. His own career had taken him from an organ scholarship at New College, Oxford, to an encounter with Munrow (they were both booked to play 'an awful concert' with the Dunstable Consort), and on to membership of the Early Music Consort. Meanwhile he had built an active concert and operatic career that extended from Britten's English Opera Group to the Royal Opera House.

Bowman, like Kirkby, would become intimately associated with the Academy of Ancient Music in its first decade. He'd been offered a choral scholarship at King's College, Cambridge, but had been rejected by the college on non-musical grounds. The bass David Thomas did sing at King's, and – almost inevitably – was drawn into the orbit of David Munrow:

The David I knew at Cambridge was a rather small, very active-looking little bloke who had a terrific sense of humour. I used to play the cello and I remember doing the *St Matthew Passion* with one of the littler colleges; the conductor was hopeless, poor chap. David was leading it and we were in fits the whole way through. He was really naughty, and terrific fun. We used to meet them at parties and in people's rooms – he was always larking about and having a roistering time.

Kirkby, on the other hand, had never expected to make a career as a singer. While studying Classics at Somerville College, Oxford, she'd sung with the amateur Schola Cantorum of Oxford under the direction of her future husband, Andrew Parrott. Then she became a school teacher, but found herself increasingly in demand on the semi-professional fringes of the emerging early-music scene, singing particularly with Parrott's Taverner Choir. 'I started singing with the Taverner Choir before I threw my life into singing as a profession,' she recalls. 'My first recordings were not with Taverner, but in fact with Anthony Rooley and the Consort of Musicke. That would have been something like 1974 or 1975: it was called *Musicke of Sundrie Kinds*.' Parrott was chorusmaster, and that same recording also featured David Thomas and Catherine Mackintosh. 'But the point is that was done for L'Oiseau-Lyre and Peter Wadland, who was backing both the Academy and the Consort of Musicke. So it was really through Peter.'

And so, in turn, Kirkby came to record with the AAM. Already, the partnership between Wadland and Hogwood was having a catalytic effect on the wider early-music scene. Artists from the fringe were being brought together in new and ever more fruitful combinations. A cottage industry was becoming a commercial force, and careers were blossoming on soil that had formerly proved barren. 'From 1975, I stopped school teaching and had a go at singing, thinking, "Oh, you can always go back to teaching if it doesn't work,"' says Kirkby. She never did – and for that, like many other artists, she thanks Peter Wadland.

The Silent Partner

The name of Peter Wadland (1946–1992) is no longer as well known as it deserves to be – and certainly not as familiar as that of Christopher Hogwood. To some extent, that's as he would have expected: for a record producer, the artists and the recorded performance are paramount. But it's also because Wadland died of AIDS on 30 June 1992, at the age of forty-six.

Too early, by any standards, and certainly too early for his memory to be caught and preserved in the amber of the internet, though at least one national newspaper carried an obituary. But Wadland is remembered with intense fondness and admiration by all who were involved in the early days of the Academy of Ancient Music. No recording is possible without someone behind the control desk. In the case of the AAM, Wadland was behind the whole orchestra: the impetus behind Hogwood's decision to take the plunge, and the man whose personal rapport with Hogwood and unflagging behind-the-scenes advocacy at Decca would supply rocket fuel for the new orchestra's first two decades.

'He was an imp-like chap – very slim and slender and bouncy and cheerful, who just had this mission,' recalls Sir Nicholas Kenyon. As Wadland's vision for L'Oiseau-Lyre and the AAM took shape, he created Florilegium, a new historically informed sub-label within a label, with the Arne disc as one of its inaugural releases: 'He and Chris just saw eye to eye about what could be done.' Wadland, like Hogwood, was intensely aware of the economics and practicalities of the recording industry, and they were on the same page from the outset. For Emma Kirkby, Wadland was 'absolutely crucial'. Catherine Mackintosh remembers 'an extraordinary guy, very focused, very willing, with an excellent pair of ears'. Those ears were the first to hear any AAM recording, and it's no exaggeration to say that the group's sound, at least in that first decade, was in part Wadland's creation.

And yet Wadland was anything but dogmatic – as far removed as could be imagined from the ascetic 'nut cutlet' image of the early-music movement. Brought up by a German mother in Antwerp and Brussels (he was trilingual – always an asset in a milieu as cosmopolitan as the music business), he discovered classical music as a schoolboy in the record library at King's College, Taunton. By the time he joined Decca, aged twenty-two, he'd acquired a deep knowledge of recorded music, and a broad and eclectic personal taste.[6] 'I don't think you would ever hear him playing baroque or early music if you went round to his house,' says James Jolly, editor in chief of *Gramophone* and a close friend of Wadland's. 'He liked the great virtuoso pianists – the Jorge Bolets and Shura Cherkasskys of this world, both of whom he produced. He was also quite an opera buff, and I think he had great flair for it.

'He was one of those people who never appeared to take anything particularly seriously, but underneath it, he was incredibly serious. He was very funny, and he was a great *bon viveur*. He was very European in his outlook, and he was incredibly gregarious; his house was always full of musicians who were coming over to perform in London.' Wadland's enthusiasms embraced contemporary composers as well as performers:

He had a lovely modern house in Camden Mews, in Camden. It had this amazing open-plan top floor with a balcony. I remember one Christmas going round there, and there was Peter with Hans Werner Henze and his other half, and various other people. Henze was smoking dope throughout the entire meal and everyone was virtually catatonic at the end of it. I don't know if he and Henze had a thing, but they were very close, and Henze wrote little pieces in manuscript for Peter – little musical in-jokes.

That gift for conviviality and good conversation provided another point of connection with the more reserved Hogwood. Anthony Fabian remembers dinners with Wadland:

He was very camp, a very charming and pleasant and naughty sort of person. He was very jovial. As I say, 'naughty' is the main quality that I would attribute to him: he was gossipy and enjoyed fun. He loved wine – his favourite was a white burgundy. And he and Chris really did enjoy a great personal and professional friendship, with a tremendous mutual respect. He was very persuasive and well liked within Decca. I have to say that Peter was responsible for Chris's career taking off. If it hadn't been for Peter's agreement to that first record – well, Chris would've taken off eventually, but Peter was absolutely the spark that enabled that to happen. It was a great friendship and Peter was utterly supportive of all Chris's projects up until he died. It was one of Chris's very few close friendships, I would say. He had very few close friends.

At Decca, too, Wadland was a force of nature – the diametric opposite of the stereotypical record-company 'stiff in a suit'. He treated L'Oiseau-Lyre – and Florilegium within it – as his private realm. 'He was the most musically tolerant producer on staff,' says the producer and scholar Michael Haas, a long-term colleague at Decca.

He never, and I really mean never, left a performance halfway through. Decca paid for us to go to as many performances as we liked and we were always offered the very best seats: front row, Grand Tier at the Royal Opera. It was easy to get fed up if someone was off, and just 'call it a night' and leave. Peter never did. His other principle, which was perhaps a weakness, was that he would only work with people he could get along with. If someone was confrontational or difficult or likely to storm out of the studio, they simply weren't allowed to appear on a Peter Wadland production. Fortunately, he got on very well with a huge number of extremely gifted artists.

But Peter would never say anything negative – at least, I can't recall him dishing the dirt on anyone. For someone who dropped out of education, having attended some very fine schools in both Belgium and England, he was the most informed person I can recall, on almost any subject. His work was his main personal interest, but he loved ballet and he loved the piano and was an expert on both. His autograph collection gave you a real picture of who he was – he wasn't interested in just collecting the signature; he approached composers with manuscript paper and asked them to write something for him. He even kept his letter to William Walton asking for something, over which Walton replied – scrawled across the top of Peter's letter – 'I don't have anything to write!'

Peter's other interest was sex. Lots and lots of it. Promiscuous, confrontational and unapologetic – he already had regular visits to the local 'clap clinic' and used his spare opera ticket to invite his 'clap doctor' to join him from time to time. He even introduced him as 'This is X, my clap doctor.' Peter was not going to be intimidated by rules and regulations regarding sexual decorum. He was in the first generation of gay liberation and saw any attempt to stymie sexual freedom, whether it was undercover policemen or AIDS or the *Sun*, as just new hurdles to leap across. For him, sexual liberation was also a liberation from long-term commitment, but he did have an enormous circle of absolutely devoted friends. Some he slept with, but many were simply friends in a more traditional sense. He found sex highly amusing – he found promiscuous sex even funnier. I could go on about some of the things he would regale us with – arriving at the office, dishevelled with leaves and sticks still in his hair from an all-nighter on the Heath or Common.

Bundled with Wadland's free-spirited approach came a meticulous care for the detail of his recordings. For the new Florilegium series, Wadland penned the mission statement:

The Florilegium series presents performances of music from the renaissance to the romantic periods on original instruments or authentic copies, based on the most recent research into the original texts, instrumentation and performing styles of each period.

Wadland even specified the cover designs – a crucial part of a recording's identity and sales appeal in the era of big 12-inch LP sleeves. The basic colour was white, serving (in the words of the design journalist Jeremy Hall) 'to underline the purity and stripped-down nature of the interpretation'.[7] Around it was an ornate decorative border, derived from the decoration of a Ruckers harpsichord, to add a touch of rococo flair. And in the middle, chosen to complement the music, either by the performers or (equally often) by Wadland himself, an old-master painting. For Vivaldi, a Canaletto; for Dowland, a miniature by Nicholas Hilliard. And for Arne's overtures, Hogarth's *An Election Entertainment*: bustling, colourful imagery for this very English music.

'He had very good taste,' remembers James Jolly. 'He had some very nice bits of art. In fact he left me a painting by Rudolf Sauter, who was John Galsworthy's nephew. The consistency of L'Oiseau-Lyre as a label is completely due to Peter. He would make sure that they got exactly the right cover photograph; he would pore over the notes; he was obsessive about the typography – every last detail.'

That obsession with detail would prove crucial for the fledgling Academy of Ancient Music. The basic idea had been to create a period-instrument equivalent of Marriner's Academy of St Martin in the Fields, a group so consistently proficient that it could produce a saleable recording with a minimum of takes. Nicholas Kenyon witnessed the process at first hand:

I remember going to a Marriner recording of Schubert's Ninth Symphony. At the end of it, they had some time left over and had decided to do a Mozart *Adagio and Fugue*. The way they did it was extraordinary: they just put the orchestral parts out, Neville beat his way through it, then went into the recording control room to listen to it – and decided on that basis what needed to be changed in order to mould it into a performance. It was not the usual way of making records, but it was very successful.

It became evident that the AAM would not be able to operate that way. An orchestra assembled from the most disparate extremes of a deeply heterogenous early-music movement and supplemented by have-a-go session players, was not likely to produce a cohesive (or even very accurate) sound from the first note – quite apart from the technical difficulties of playing period instruments in what was (for the time) an unusually large ensemble. From the outset, multiple takes were the norm – a situation to stretch the patience even of seasoned artists and engineers.

'Let's say – putting it kindly – that tuning took longer,' says Dunkerley, who would become a regular part of the Florilegium team. 'I have very unfond memories of woodwind tuning, and horns with crooks. Lots of plumbing noises.' Catherine Mackintosh remembers, 'We had a terrible time recording in that Petersham church – why they chose it I can't imagine, because it was right underneath the flight path to Heathrow Airport. Luckily, with this music, no take really needed to last for very long! Christopher and I would listen to the first edits, and then we went through and tried to get rid of all the imperfections that we could. The recording engineers were extremely good.'

Wadland kept the show on the road. 'He was quite different in the studio,' says Jolly.

Well, actually he still had that slightly flippant side, but underneath he was absolutely razor sharp. There are some producers who are very control-freakish in their sessions, and everything is under control. Peter never gave that impression, although the sessions always were incredibly organised. He was very meticulous; he used to annotate everything, and he was very good with people. There's a whole spectrum of the way producers work, but he really brought out the best in artists. And he'd be very quick about spotting when people were getting unhappy or angry or frustrated, immediately homing in and defusing any situation like that.

It was interesting. I think he was a very good complement to Chris, and some of the other more intellectual academic artists he recorded on L'Oiseau-Lyre – people like [the American pianist and musicologist] Joshua Rifkin. Because Peter wasn't really an intellectual. He was very much an instinctive musician; gut feeling was very much how he worked. And he relied on the Hogwoods and the Rifkins to bring their academic credentials. But he attended to the musical side very well indeed. They were both great sticklers for detail. Peter knew exactly what was going on under the bonnet of his recordings.

And so, over three days at Petersham – with Hogwood directing from the harpsichord, Wadland encouraging and troubleshooting from the control desk, and the players sawing bits off their instruments if necessary to make things work – the eight Arne overtures were recorded for release the following year. The ensemble sound is unpolished by the comparison with the standards that would be achieved in future years. 'Raw vigour, with the emphasis on the raw,' remembers Catherine Mackintosh. 'Gradually Peter managed to edit things so that the rawness was slightly edited out.' But the overwhelming impact is the precision (despite everything), the clarity and the energetic, upfront verve that no one yet knew would become defining elements of the Hogwood–Academy of Ancient Music sound. This is inventive, ebullient music and there's an excitement and immediacy about the music-making that's exactly what you'd expect from a group of players who were creating something unprecedented – to all intents and purposes, the first true orchestral recording ever made by British performers on period instruments.

Hogwood wrote the sleeve notes, and helped Wadland pick out an eighteenth-century cartoon of Arne at the organ to decorate the back of the LP sleeve. It was the first orchestral release on Florilegium, and it made a genuine impact. The musicologist Stanley Sadie reviewed it for *The Times* on 23 November 1974, noting, as a preliminary, that the group used 'authentic instruments' (the quotation marks were Sadie's own – an early reminder that the authenticity, or otherwise, of Hogwood's project would never be entirely uncontentious). But he was entirely persuaded that he was hearing a sound from out of history:

I cannot remember hearing before an orchestra with so natural and convincing an eighteenth-century sound. The ensemble does not have the kind of surface polish that one expects from, say, the ECO or the St Martin's Academy, but the effect is delightfully fresh and vigorous.[8]

The idea of historically informed performance as a stripper of 'surface polish' – a kind of sonic Nitromors – was one that Hogwood would embrace, and which would come to haunt him. For now, though, critics took the AAM's first recording in good faith, and with real enthusiasm. Lionel Slater, in *Gramophone*, announced the AAM as 'the latest of several practical musicological groups', and concluded, 'Hogwood's talented team emanates a feeling of freshness in its playing, and there is a pleasing spontaneity in the added graces; that the occasional one doesn't quite come off is of very little importance in the overall impression . . . I look forward', he added, 'to more recordings from this group.' He wouldn't have long to wait.

4

Making a Name

A successful first recording is an excellent calling card for a new group. But, even in the 1970s, it wasn't in itself sufficient to sustain a full-time ensemble. Certainly, if the Arne disc had been conceived (as John Dunkerley remembered it) almost as an 'audition record', it was a success. BBC Radio 3 took it up, with vigour, from the instant that it was released in November 1974. The eight sprightly pieces did indeed become fixtures on its morning *Overture* slot (Arne had clearly displayed considerable foresight in deciding not to publish them as symphonies). Before long they were popping up (by listener request) on *Your Concert Choice*.

The name of the Academy of Ancient Music was starting to become known, and further recording projects were booked, as Wadland and Hogwood backed their hunch in the face of disbelief from the Decca top brass. There was a disc of Johann Stamitz symphonies and a concerto with Alan Hacker (with Hogwood directing a 26-piece orchestra from the harpsichord), followed by Vivaldi's *Stabat Mater* and *Nisi Dominus* with James Bowman as soloist – the group's first vocal recording. 'Nobody else had done the piece before I did it, and now everybody does it,' recalled Bowman. 'It was Chris who encouraged me to sing it, very much so. Decca said, "Oh, this won't sell." They paid me £100 and said, "Bugger off." It sold 300,000 copies in France.'

Outside the recording sessions, however, the Academy of Ancient Music was emerging more gradually, and with rather less of a splash. Prior to the end of 1974, when that debut recording was released, the name carried no cachet. Hogwood started by using it to describe any of the chamber ensembles he assembled to give recitals at concert clubs or universities across the UK, and those that were not given with Munrow as part of the

EMC – though of course they did tend to be drawn from the same pool of performers. The year 1974 saw Hogwood performing in chamber concerts in Devon and Birmingham; a recital in the University of Kent's Gulbenkian Theatre in Canterbury on Sunday, 26 May 1974 was announced simply as 'James Bowman (Counter Tenor), Christopher Hogwood and Ensemble', playing a programme of 'Handel, Vivaldi, Corelli and Scarlatti'.[1]

A year later, the same performers would almost certainly have been described as the Academy of Ancient Music – as they were at St Margaret's Church, King's Lynn, on Friday, 1 August 1975. 'It was a delightful mixture of Italian and English and baroquial [sic] music,' wrote the reporter of the Lynn Advertiser, over a large picture of Hogwood seated at the harpsichord: 'With Mr Hogwood and Mr Bowman were Simon Standage (baroque violin), Eleanor Sloan (baroque viola) and Oliver Brookes (viola da gamba).'[2]

The typical live AAM line-up in these first few years seems to have been a variation on this theme – essentially, a trio-sonata ensemble plus a vocalist or occasional additional instrumentalists. If it was a challenge to assemble a 26-piece orchestra for a recording session, the prospect of rehearsing and touring such an ensemble still felt like a leap too far. Besides, the network of small promoters – concert clubs, chamber-music societies, churches, schools and colleges – who still make up the grassroots of UK concert life were perfectly willing to dip a toe into what the King's Lynn reporter termed 'a delightful reconstruction of ancient music', but were more likely to do so if it could be managed on a chamber-music budget. Hogwood, in particular, was in his element as *primus inter pares* in a baroque chamber group.

'We've had so many wonderful harpsichord players, but he was the best continuo player I've ever known,' remembers violinist Maya Homburger, who started playing with the AAM in the 1980s.

> As a violinist, you could just float on what he did with the harmonies, and the way he filled in and improvised the figured bass. His timing was exquisite. But never too much: I mean, much as I adore Ton Koopman or Trevor Pinnock, they can occasionally go over the top with ornaments and become showy. Chris had this subtlety, but at the same time a passion, which made a harpsichord sing.

By mid-1976, when Hogwood began to record a 15-part series on the history of the trio sonata for BBC Radio 3 (it was broadcast the following year), it was as Director of the Academy of Ancient Music. His argument was that the trio sonata was as significant a form, historically, as the string quartet: typically, he published a book based on his research for the BBC Music Guide series. And the players involved were all, by now, AAM regulars – surviving call sheets list cellist Anthony Pleeth, bassoonist Hansjürg Lange, flautist Stephen Preston and violinist Eleanor Sloan, all playing for fees (generous for the era) of £30 per session (Hogwood got £50). A recording released by the National Trust in 1979 is a sort of late coda to those early chamber-ensemble days: salon music and songs by Haydn, Hummel, Weber and Stephen Storace, played by Hogwood, Preston, Pleeth and the violinist Monica Huggett with the tenor Paul Elliott. It was the AAM's first recording produced for a label other than L'Oiseau-Lyre, and still some of the most modern music, chronologically speaking, that the AAM has ever approached.

From 1976 onwards, things started to snowball. Nothing succeeds like success, and as Decca balance sheets began to sing, Wadland was empowered to think bigger. LP sales and radio airplay spread the name of the new group, so concert promoters began to think bigger too. And although the pool of available players was still too small, a regular stream of work from Hogwood (whether in the recording studio, on the airwaves or in the concert hall) made planning easier, and allowed ever more ambitious live projects. Having charmed the King's Lynn audience in 1975, Hogwood was appointed Artistic Director of the King's Lynn Festival from 1976 (he would hold the post until 1980). A year on from the AAM's Festival debut, the audience at St Nicholas's Chapel, King's Lynn, on Saturday, 24 July, saw an expanded ensemble, plus the Schola Cantorum of Oxford, playing on a new scale. The critic of the *Lynn Advertiser* didn't bother to conceal their surprise:

They presented a stirring programme of Handel. And perhaps the first thing to note about them is that they are not a collection of white-haired musical dodderers: the only ancient thing about them is their title. Under the direction of the youthful and zestful Christopher Hogwood – the Festival director himself – they are as young-looking a collection of players as it has been Lynn's pleasure to welcome outside school orchestras.[3]

The programme opened with *Zadok the Priest* and closed with *The King Shall Rejoice*. In between came *Acis and Galatea*, with a spirited team of soloists: soprano Judith Nelson, tenors Ian Partridge and Martyn Hill, and the bass David Thomas (who believes to this day that Hogwood booked him on the strength of that over-enthusiastic Cambridge college performance a decade or more previously). These pieces were, noted the reporter, 'performed for the first time using instruments and groupings genuinely of the period'. Handel might have disagreed, and the *Advertiser's* correspondent also felt that the massed forces made 'an uncertain start'. But they came together after the interval, and no one present, by the sound of it, can have failed to sense that they were at a true Festival occasion:

> One can scarcely switch on Radio 3 these Sunday mornings without hearing the Academy of Ancient Music and Christopher Hogwood in one's living room. Here they were in person, fresh-faced and innovative – and so industrious, with all that busy Handelian bowing and blowing. They were a hit and no mistake.[4]

From nought to ubiquity, in barely eighteen months: the pace – in an age before the internet, when even fax machines were in their infancy – feels breathless. A chain reaction had started whose spiralling, self-renewing energy would carry the AAM forward for the next decade and a half. The AAM gave its first concert outside the UK – in Bruges – in 1975. In September 1976 the group toured the Netherlands and, starting in November 1976, began a full-scale international tour on a scale that would seem ambitious even today, including concerts in Egypt, India, Sri Lanka, Thailand, Singapore, Malaysia, Hong Kong, Indonesia, Japan and South Korea.

The British Council was the sponsor, and its intention was to showcase the world-beating state of the art in British classical music, which at this point in the 1970s meant ancient music: a whole Academy full of it. What was now a fast-growing but still novel trend in Europe, North America and the UK was largely unheard of (and certainly unheard, beyond recordings and broadcasts) in Asia. Understandably, the Council opted to send the Academy in its chamber form. It's unlikely at this point that the AAM would have had the logistical capacity to muster its full forces for global travel, though Hogwood did lament to a Calcutta journalist that he was unable ('for economic and other policy reasons') to bring what he already described as the full 35-player orchestra along with him.[5] In addition to Hogwood, the touring personnel were Bowman, violinists Christopher Hirons and Eleanor Sloan and viola da gamba player Oliver Brookes.

This was virgin territory for historically informed performers, and the arrival of this new breed of musician provoked genuine curiosity. The *Hindustan Standard* dispatched a reporter to the Grand Hotel, Calcutta, for an interview. His opening gambit gives an interesting insight into the international reputation that the AAM had already achieved, barely two years after the release of its first recording. 'As is the case of the Academy of St Martin in the Fields, the reputation of the equally well-known Academy of Ancient Music preceded the actual arrival in Calcutta by members of the group.'

> I met them on the morning of their concert, at the Grand Hotel, where the members of the orchestra . . . were desperately trying to acquire a typical Indian tan between sips of ice-cold (Indian) beer at the hotel's swimming pool. For a group as reputable as this one they were completely relaxed, and talked animatedly about their deep commitment to performing early music as it was written, on the actual historical instruments for which it was conceived.
>
> Tall, blue-eyed Christopher Hogwood, who first formed the group some three years ago, agreed that there has recently been a widespread resurgence of interest all over Europe in attempting to capture as faithfully as possible the spirit and mood of the baroque . . .[6]

It was the first of a thousand such interviews that Hogwood would give over the course of his career. Wherever the AAM made its debut in a town or venue – Jakarta, Staffordshire or the American Midwest – that had yet to receive the Historically Informed gospel, Hogwood would step forward, cheerfully, enthusiastically and accessibly explaining, from first principles, why he and his colleagues had chosen to play this music on these odd-sounding instruments. The Calcutta programme comprised music by Purcell; the National Centre for the Performing

Arts in Bombay heard a similar programme, but at St Bridget's Convent School in Colombo, Sri Lanka, the following week, the Colombo-based *Sunday Times* reported that Hogwood 'played on a piano for the lack of a harpsichord in our country'.*

'Eager young faces' were reported to have filled the audience in Singapore. By early December the AAM was in Hong Kong. A concert at the Island School went well, but a performance at La Salle College in Kowloon, on 2 December 1976, proved less satisfactory. 'All was well until just before the entrance of the musicians, when the audience was plunged in Stygian gloom, while the players were bathed in a hellish light,' wrote the local critic David Gwilt.

> Matters were temporarily adjusted, at least to the extent where the players had enough light to play by. The audience, still in pitch darkness, were lucky enough to have memorised the names of the first few items on the programme . . . There followed *Ego flos campi* and *Salve o regina* of Monteverdi, with James Bowman, countertenor, in magnificent voice, rounding and shaping the phrases in movingly expressive manner but hampered by another annoyance – that of nearby pile-driving – putting in its tuneless notes. This made the performance like one heard on a cracked record . . .[7]

'The players and singer reacted splendidly, though, giving of their all,' he added – and after a few adjustments it seemed as if the concert was getting back on course. Windows overlooking the pile-driver were closed and the lighting was brought up, 'which only served to bring on all the overhead fans at full strength'. The band played on – a Cavalli canzona, a Purcell trio sonata and Purcell's *The Queen's Epicedium*, sung by Bowman. After the interval they continued with the second of Couperin's *Leçons de ténèbres*, a pair of Scarlatti sonatas from Hogwood, and a Handel trio sonata – all to the accompaniment (reported Gwilt) of a slightly unorthodox continuo: 'In the second half it was the turn of the local dogs to have their say, and

---

* The author can attest from personal experience to the difficulty of playing even modern string instruments in Colombo's tropical climate. In a venue without climate control, gut strings can lose pitch by as much as a whole tone during the course of a Mozart first movement.

say it they did, with full throat. In spite of this, Couperin's sonata "La Steinquerque" made a fine effect.'[8]

Other Hong Kong critics were less restrained – in fact, the conditions under which the AAM had performed became a minor local scandal. 'The diffusion of culture throughout Hong Kong is an admirable ideal,' wrote Keith Anderson (later the prolific sleeve-note writer for the emerging Hong Kong classical label Naxos), in the *Tiger Standard*:

> but to send a distinguished group of musicians to play, unadvertised, in a school hall, to the accompaniment of dogs, mass-transit, pile-drivers and incoming aeroplanes – let alone the fidgeting of restless children, the rustling of toffee papers and general air of inattention – argues, to say the least, extreme ineptitude on the part of the organisers . . .
>
> The players in question, the Academy of Ancient Music, include not only players of distinction, but arguably the best countertenor in the world at the moment, James Bowman. It says much for their good humour that neither the smallness of the audience nor the lack of preparedness of the willing boy scouts on the lights – let alone the noises off – dissuaded them from performing.[9]

The AAM, if not the hapless scouts, had Been Prepared. 'Hong Kong owes Mr Hogwood and his colleagues an apology,' Anderson concluded. Apology or no, for a group of musicians who'd learned their trade on the often eccentric fringes of the 1960s early-music scene, it was probably just another memorable concert saved by flexibility, patience and bulletproof concentration. While specialists such as Anderson and Gwilt appreciated the significance of what they were hearing – and local curiosity was high, if not particularly expert – you do get the impression that the British Council and its far-flung organisers weren't entirely sure what they were supposed do with the Academy of Ancient Music. That would change on future tours; by September the following year the AAM was travelling again, this time to Australia and New Zealand.

Back in the UK, meanwhile, and outside the recording studio, the AAM was quickly reaching a point where it had little left to prove. On 4 July 1976, it had made its first appearance on BBC Radio 3 as a 'live' ensemble rather than on disc – a programme of music by Couperin,

Rameau, Handel and Marais, recorded at the Fitzwilliam Museum in Cambridge in May the previous year. Just four performers participated – Bowman, Brookes and McGegan, with Hogwood doing double duty as presenter. The diary was filling up with (mostly small-scale) dates – the Victoria & Albert Museum, Birmingham Art Gallery, the BBC's Pebble Mill studios in Birmingham, the Wigmore Hall and the Queen Elizabeth Hall on London's Southbank – the venue for the AAM's first ever London appearance, on Sunday, 6 March 1977.

One festival, however, has a special significance for any UK-based classical ensemble: the irrefutable indicator that an orchestra is on the map. On the evening of Tuesday, 1 August 1978, at the Royal Albert Hall, the Academy of Ancient Music made its first appearance in the BBC Proms. Simon Preston directed the first half from a chamber organ; together with his superbly trained Choir of Christ Church Cathedral Oxford he was by now a regular collaborator with the AAM on disc. Judith Nelson, Emma Kirkby and Carolyn Watkinson were the soloists in Vivaldi's *Gloria* (RV589) – the work now universally known as *the* Vivaldi *Gloria*, but here receiving its first ever Proms performance. Bach's Cantata No. 50, 'Nun ist das Heil und die Kraft' followed – 'wonderfully clean and resilient', noted Edward Greenfield in the *Guardian*.[10] After the interval Hogwood stepped up to perform all three suites from Handel's *Water Music*, with an orchestra of a scale almost unprecedented in British early music, and certainly in the annals of the AAM: some 50 players.

It's easy today to underestimate the achievement that this represented: simply to assemble such a quantity of performers was extraordinary in itself, quite aside from the musical challenge of generating an artistically satisfying performance. A recording was one thing, and the AAM's recording of the *Water Music* was already scheduled for release that autumn. But to reproduce such a performance in a live concert with a national profile (it was broadcast live on both Radio 3 and Radio 4 simultaneously) and a large audience was another matter. Hogwood had almost certainly been thinking ahead to exactly this challenge when he had addressed 'The Future of Early Music in Britain' conference at the Southbank in May the previous year:

It's the same with multiple woodwind in Handel. It's all very well for scholars to tell us the proportions of a baroque orchestra with

two or three oboes playing a single line, but you cannot prac-
tise doing that on your own – you have got to get together six
oboists. And maybe not all six of those players will happily give
up several days' paid employment in order to experiment. The
sheer size of the undertaking means that there has to be some
financial inducement.[11]

The combination of a L'Oiseau-Lyre recording coupled to a prestigious broadcast Prom date provided just such an inducement – evidence
of how the Hogwood–Wadland partnership, and the early-music movement more widely, was starting to generate its own momentum. An hour
and a half before the AAM took the stage, a telegram arrived at the stage
door from Wadland, 'Wishing you all a great success tonight.' That they
made an impact is beyond question, with few reviewers failing to note
the contrast between these exotic new-old sounds and the more familiar
(and richly coloured) Hamilton Harty selection for full orchestra that had
been a Proms staple since the 1920s. 'What would Sir Henry Wood have
said, I kept wondering,' wrote Greenfield of the *Guardian*,

> to see a packed Albert Hall for music played in an archaic fash-
> ion on gut strings with no vibrato, with valveless horns, with
> baroque oboes, sopranino recorders and even a theorbo among
> the continuo instruments? What is more the main subject of all
> this archaism was one of the longest-standing Proms favourites,
> and not in half a dozen movements like the Harty but in nearly
> a score.[12]

The new conventions of historically performed practice – or at any rate,
Hogwood's notions of fidelity to the score – also came as something of a
jolt. Greenfield continued:

> I did actually suspect that some among the thousands there were
> indeed taken aback by the oddity of the timbre and by having
> the famous *Air* played like a brisk march with snapping double-
> dots . . . I was only sad that the *Allegro* that ends the F major Suite
> had to be omitted when we heard three of the shorter movements
> (authentically) six times over, with full repeats.[13]

For the most part, critics were willing to take the scholarly authenticity of the AAM's Handel at face value, and they relished the piquant sonorities of this musical apparition from another century. Hogwood's concerns about ensemble had been right: the massed oboes made an unmissable impact. Frank Dobbins, in *The Times*, noted 'all the concomitant problems of six cackling baroque oboes and insecure natural horns' – but added that 'all the parts were remarkably well executed and co-ordinated'.[14] Robert Henderson, in the *Daily Telegraph*, attempted to evoke some sense of the colours involved:

> With the First Suite dominated by natural horns and the tangy sound of six baroque oboes, the second making mellifluous play with the softer tones of flute and recorders, and the third introducing the ceremonial accents of trumpets and drums, their sharply differentiated characters were drawn with an impeccable and exhilarating blend of scholarly insight, polish, and imaginative musicianship . . . it was a performance which in its clarity of texture, its lively pace and finely sprung rhythms, cleansed this familiar music of the dust of ages.[15]

Office Space

Less than five years had passed since that first recording session in Petersham. The Academy of Ancient Music had evolved from a half-experimental session group assembled on an ad hoc basis from the contents of Christopher Hogwood's address book to an expanding orchestra with a national profile, an international touring schedule and an extensive discography. The economics of its rise are not wholly clear; but evidently – with regular income from Decca, from concert promoters and from the BBC, supplemented by discreet cross-subsidy from Hogwood's own solo, broadcasting and writing income – it was washing its face, and generating regular work for a sizeable pool of specialist players. The early-music ratchet, it appeared, turned only one way. What had seemed artistically impossible in 1972 had by 1977 become merely a question of finance and logistics.

With the AAM's Proms debut in August 1978, it became a concrete reality. Assembling a full-sized eighteenth-century orchestra on period instruments for a live performance was, demonstrably, something that could be done. Now it had been done, and from now on it would be done again – with increasing frequency and confidence. But it would need more than Christopher Hogwood's address book – to say nothing of Hogwood's own energy and increasingly scarce free time – if the AAM was to capitalise on the opportunities that were opening before it. Once again, Hogwood's Cambridge networks provided a solution, in the person of a young American archaeology graduate called Heather Jarman.

Hogwood was lodging at the time with Nicholas Shackleton, a pioneering palaeoclimatologist and great-nephew of the famous explorer Ernest Shackleton, who was also an enthusiastic collector of early woodwind instruments – and his wife Judith. After graduating from Berkeley, Jarman had 'bummed around Europe' with her future (now ex-) husband, a Cambridge archaeologist, and had met the Shackletons in Crete, shortly after working on an archaeological dig in Epirus. 'And because I was madly in love with my husband-to-be, I went back to Cambridge and I lived in Cambridge from then on,' she recalls.

I went to live in England at the end of 1967. I loved cooking, and so did my ex-husband, so we'd invite the Shackletons to dinner and Christopher would trail along. But I didn't actually work with him until 1976. I decided I'd had enough of Cambridge academic life – it was very male chauvinist. But I loved organising things, and so I decided to set up my own business, organising other people and providing back-up services for small businesses. Judith Shackleton came to me and said, 'Christopher needs someone to deal with his life.' He was always away performing, and since he was a lodger at her house, she was already doing his laundry, his ironing and cooking his meals. She said, 'I can't cope with the phone calls on top of that.' So I talked to Christopher and we said, 'Well, let's try it. Let's see what happens.'

So I started, and the first thing he wanted me to do was to reorganise his library. He was already a compulsive collector of books and music, and it was a total mess. So I started doing that part-time. Next, I was trying to sort out his desk, and answering the phone. And after three months he asked me, would I like to manage the orchestra?

My musical background wasn't great. I had piano lessons when I was a child, and I'd played the flute in my high-school

marching band. And when I was at Berkeley they had an absolutely phenomenal course for people who didn't want to major
in music, but were very interested in it: a year-long course on
history and theory, starting with Palestrina and going right up to
Shostakovich. I'd done that, and because I'd done archaeology and
felt a connection to the past, I was interested in what Christopher
was doing – trying to get into the heads of those historic composers and players by reading the literature, reading about the period,
trying to set them in context.

Hogwood, at the time, was running the Academy – and the rest of
his career – from a rented room in the Shackletons' house in Claremont,
Cambridge: a Victorian cul-de-sac off Hills Road. He had a bedroom,
and a second room that doubled as office and library, but as the Academy
expanded, he gradually started to colonise the house. Eventually the property next door became available and he shifted his base of operations there.
But the pace of his creative activities, by the late 1970s, was such that
administration was almost an afterthought. From 2 Claremont, Jarman's
challenge was to establish some sort of order in a professional schedule
that barely allowed a pause for breath:

Chris was still doing his BBC programme, *The Young Idea*. It was
crazy: he would dictate the script just off the top of his head – this
was in the days of typewriters. He'd record three programmes at a
time, every three weeks, but the BBC producer needed a written
script. So I would transcribe his dictation, and then we'd send the
scripts down to the BBC. Often he would go Cambridge station,
find someone who was going to London on a train, and ask them
if they could take the script to King's Cross with them and put it
in a taxi to the BBC. Later there were bike couriers, but it was
always last minute.

The Academy's work, meanwhile, was predominantly focused on
the recording studio, with live concerts happening almost as an adjunct.
Jarman remembers the typical schedule in the late 1970s:

We were doing almost solely chamber music. Small groups:
trio-sonata groups, mainly, travelling around doing gigs for the

music-club circuit. We did a couple of orchestral concerts a year, typically one at King's Lynn and one in Bruges, often with the same programme. Those were the only public orchestral concerts. All the rest was chamber music, probably three or four tours per year. I didn't go with them: Christopher kept the small groups organised, and they figured out their own travel. But I had been brought up on orchestral music, and I wanted to emphasise that, so I started trying to sell the orchestral music. Not against Christopher's wishes, of course – but it was probably because of me that we started increasing the percentage of orchestral music.

More orchestral work, of course, required more players – which in turn required more administration:

I was doing all the selling, all the contracting, all the fixing, all the booking of travel. I started selling on the Continent as well. Early music was becoming very popular then, so we weren't the only people in the field: there was The English Concert and John Eliot Gardiner and the rest. We'd all got going at about the same time and we were all fighting over the same players. The limitation on work wasn't what we could sell to promoters; it was whether we could get the performers.

When I started, of course, I hadn't a clue about fixing an orchestra. Christopher was still playing for the ASMF and he suggested that I talk to their fixer. I adopted her method of everything – you'd have a grid and pencil in the musicians you wanted, ticking them off as they were confirmed. This was all done by phone, of course. And I started a group calendar, around 1979–80, so all of us could tell each other what we were planning – so that we could book recording weeks when, say, The English Concert wasn't working. We collaborated on that because it was in all our interests to make sure we could get the players.

Cycles

By 1979, however, one crucial figure was missing from the early-music scene. David Munrow had continued to run the Early Music Consort, and Hogwood had continued to play as a member of the group even as the AAM gathered momentum. Munrow was aware that Hogwood was pursuing a different artistic path; and it seems likely, in the light of Hogwood's snowballing career, that both men will have felt their collaboration was reaching a natural end. 'David was very charitable about it,' recalled James Bowman – who sensed a certain friction between the two, particularly during the recording of one of the EMC's later projects, a disc of Purcell odes. The fact that Hogwood and Wadland were about to begin a long-term Purcell project of their own would have had little effect on Munrow's own plans, but it can't have helped defuse tensions.

> Most of the players were ones that Chris had earmarked for the AAM. They didn't fall out, exactly, but Chris wasn't very pleased that David had rather poached them for his recording. Chris being so discreet, he never had an all-out row with him. It was all rather understated, but we knew what was going on. It wasn't a happy time, I'm afraid, and David's recording wasn't terribly successful. David loved Purcell, but it just didn't have the spark, which Chris was very good at getting. It didn't work: his tempi were a bit on the slow side. Chris was very good at imparting electricity to Purcell. Chris appreciated David's talents, but felt that he was exceeding them by encroaching on other territory.

There were some tensions at times. Chris was not the easiest person,' recalls Jasper Parrott. And Purcell felt like Hogwood's, rather than Munrow's, natural domain: positively avant-garde by comparison with the renaissance and medieval programmes with which the EMC had made its name. Munrow was still hugely popular and energetic but the early-music scene was expanding in all sorts of directions, and by 1976, no one ensemble had a monopoly on the public's imagination, or the record industry's interest. Still, it wouldn't have been in Hogwood's nature to have quarrelled with Munrow, and he was booked to play on an EMC tour in the late spring of 1976, arranged by Jasper Parrott's agency. It never happened. On 15 May 1976 David Munrow was found dead by his own hand at his home in Chesham Bois, Buckinghamshire. He was thirty-three years old, and had been suffering – unknown to his public – from depression.

A life-force had been extinguished, and the shock and sense of loss that greeted Munrow's death extended far beyond the early-music world. 'As far as I am concerned, there will never be anyone else like him, nor would I wish there to be,' wrote Bowman, in a published tribute.[16] For Bowman, and for many other early-music pioneers of the 1960s generation, it drew a line. 'I didn't sing any more of that early stuff after David's death. I gave it up. I didn't want to do it any more. If David wasn't there to direct it, I wasn't interested. I went on to doing Vivaldi and Handel after that.' Hogwood's outward reaction, typically, was reticent. 'He didn't ever want to talk to me about it,' recalls Tony Fabian. 'There was a sense of betrayal, I think, when Chris moved away from the Early Music Consort, and so there was a lot of guilt around that. There was a slightly messy, uncomfortable feeling around all of that, and therefore he didn't want to talk about it.'

'Christopher hid his feelings,' says Jarman. 'It's not something he would have discussed. He was very English, very Cambridge. He just didn't talk about emotions.' The Early Music Consort died with Munrow, and the AAM, in its chamber form, took over the cancelled tour. In the studio, however, Wadland's ambitions for Hogwood's ensemble were escalating in scale and range. He paired the Academy with the Choir of Christ Church Cathedral, Oxford, for a series of recordings, released between 1978 and 1979 directed by the Christ Church's own organist, Simon Preston – choral works by Handel, Vivaldi and (a sign of things to come) Haydn.

This was the first time that the Academy had been directed by anyone other than Hogwood, but Preston (1938–2022) was an artist of considerable prestige in his own right and operating on his own territory. Since Hogwood was relatively inexperienced with choral music, it made sense to hand over to Preston. The crystalline, chamber-sized sound of an Oxford collegiate choir in high-classical repertoire was refreshing to some, and startling to others. 'It's not the easiest thing to keep the Haydn pot a-boiling with an all-male choir of about 30 voices pitted against an orchestra of roughly the same size,' commented *Gramophone*, of Haydn's *Missa Sancta Ceciliae*.[17] Preston's interpretative philosophy was strikingly akin to Hogwood's own. 'Handel has to sound natural,' he told the American critic Bruce Duffie, a decade later in 1990. 'So many people these days sort of fiddle around with Handel, and they try and interpret Handel.'

. . . the more naturally it's performed, the better the music sounds. For a long time, I subscribed to the view – especially with the organ concertos – that they needed fleshing out a bit. There was a lot missing, and that literally meant to double-dot everything, and that you had to put trills in whenever you possibly could, and all that sort of rubbish. But if we go back just to the way that the music is, the way it's on the printed page, it's amazing. Then, when you play it as it is, and you realise how extremely Handelian it sounds, or how natural it sounds, there's very little need for performers to get in the way of it.[18]

None of this implied any reduction in Hogwood's recording work with the Academy. Between the Arne release in November 1974 and the end of the decade, the AAM was making a recording, on average, every three months. There's an irresistible sense of enthusiasm – and momentum – about the sheer quantity and variety of their recorded work: Stamitz, Geminiani, Vivaldi, Locke, Rébel and Bach; and not just J. S. Bach either. Hogwood's lifelong affinity for the classical era produced spirited LPs of symphonies by Johann Christian and Carl Philipp Emanuel. Wadland, meanwhile, was already thinking long-term. A 1976 disc of Purcell's incidental music from *Abdelazer*, *The Gordian Knot Untied* and *The Married Beau*, with the soprano Joy Roberts, carried the unassuming title *Purcell Theatre Music*. As under-recorded but valuable English music, it was a natural progression from the Arne and, with an orchestra of fewer than twenty players, it was a low-cost, low-risk proposition for Wadland's sceptical label bosses. But flip to the reverse of the LP sleeve and the mask slips: *Purcell Theatre Music* is now *Purcell Theatre Music Vol. 1*. Wadland and Hogwood were already thinking ahead.

The Academy of Ancient Music's cycle of recordings of Purcell theatre music would eventually encompass eight volumes of LPs (the CD re-release runs to six well-packed discs), released over nearly a decade between 1976 and 1985. Its steady progress was evidence that the early-music world now had the capacity for large-scale, long-term recording projects, and that the record-buying public was eager to hear the result. It presented huge quantities of historically significant music, for the first time, in a historically informed style, and brought Hogwood and the AAM into collaboration with a generation of sympathetic and highly skilled singers: Bowman, naturally, but also Judith Nelson, Emma Kirkby, Julian Pike, Rogers Covey-Crump, David Thomas and Michael George, as well as Andrew Parrott's Taverner Choir. 'Chris phoned me up and said, "Hello, David,"' recalls Thomas.

> I hadn't seen him for a long time. And he said, 'Would you like to come and see me in Cambridge, because I'm looking for a bass singer?' He'd already started recording the Purcell and he'd been using a different bass, a very fine singer, but didn't like his approach – he probably thought he wasn't as good at words or something. So I came up, and we had a chat and went for an Indian meal, and got on very well. He invited me to do Locke's *Tempest* music, and from then on I did practically everything with him for years and years.

For Emma Kirkby, too, Purcell marked the start of an enduring musical relationship, not just with Hogwood and the AAM but with her colleague Judith Nelson. It helped that she was already recording for Florilegium, and known to Peter Wadland.

> I was already recording Dowland with Anthony Rooley's Consort of Musicke. The first things I did for Chris were part of his Purcell project. I was brought in as another soprano alongside Judith Nelson, which was lovely. And then from then on, I did quite a few things with Judy – she was ten years older than me, a lovely singer and incredibly kind. I was very lucky, actually, to work with her because she was the perfect duet partner. She was already working with William Christie and René Jacobs in France. They discovered her for the Academy just in time – it always takes a few years to be in a country before you are noticed. They used her quite a lot, but Purcell was the first thing. I did a couple of duets with her, and a trio with David Thomas. Peter Wadland had very clear ideas about what he wanted – he liked voices that were very definite.

The Purcell project also accelerated the AAM's own evolution as an ensemble, and refined its recording technique. With a major long-term project on the books, Catherine Mackintosh took Duncan Druce's place as leader of the orchestra (though Druce continued to play viola). 'I've always absolutely adored Purcell, so I was in seventh heaven,' she says. The Decca engineer John Dunkerley became part of the regular Florilegium technical team, as the sessions moved from All Saints, Petersham, to the Church of St George the Martyr in Holborn, and finally to Kingsway Hall, also in Holborn. (Even with the relatively short takes required by Purcell, the aircraft noise above Petersham was becoming unmanageable.)

But the process of learning from experience – not picking it up as they went along, exactly, but meeting each fresh challenge with renewed curiosity, followed by research and thorough preparation – was already part of the AAM's modus operandi. Within half a decade of its foundation, the Academy of Ancient Music had already acquired a musical personality and a creative philosophy, grounded in Hogwood's own approach to musical scholarship and performance. It had begun its evolution from a chamber ensemble and occasional recording orchestra to a full-scale period-instrument orchestra, with a growing schedule of live concerts. It had started to acquire the characteristics of an established ensemble: an international profile, a tour diary, a discography, a stable roster of regular players and collaborators and – crucially – the beginnings of a back office. And it had established an artistic bridgehead in classical repertoire (Stamitz, and J. C. and C. P. E. Bach) that had, until now, been considered beyond the scope or capacity of the early-music movement.

The Academy was no longer just a side project by David Munrow's harpsichordist, though Hogwood continued to subsidise the group from his own BBC and solo earnings. 'We expect to be £3,000 in the red this year,' he told an interviewer from *Gramophone* in December 1979.[19] But the Purcell project demonstrated that L'Oiseau-Lyre was committed to the AAM for the long haul, with every expectation of commercial success. Glossy, shelf-filling orchestral and operatic box sets were the luxury products of the late LP era. The Purcell series showed that the derided 'nut-cutlet brigade' could deliver a big prestige project, and things were about to get a great deal bigger. Paul Griffiths, looking back over the 1970s in *The Times* in the last week of 1979, described it as 'the decade when we learned to love early music':

When I first went to hear David Munrow's Early Music Consort in 1968 their programme whipped snappily through the history of music at the royal courts, from twelfth-century France to seventeenth-century England. And one was not too much per-turbed by this for, since all the music was pretty odd, it scarcely mattered that some of it was odder, and differently odd.

The seventies have made those potpourri programmes unthink-able, and my earlier ignorance would now be barely excusable in anyone with any pretensions to musical sophistication. Early music has become big business for the record industry . . . It also seems likely on the basis of what has happened during the last ten years, that the experience of early music will have more and more influence on the ways we play and hear the music of later times. Again, the signs are already there. The final month of the decade has seen the release of a recorded set of Mozart symphonies played in as near as possible the original manner with authentic instru-ments used and every detail of eighteenth-century style faithfully copied. Works only two centuries old are now early music.[20]

The Academy of Ancient Music would see to that.

5

MOZART AND MESSIAH

It's 18 October 1978, and a BBC Two film crew has taken over the Marble Hall of Kedleston Hall, in Derbyshire. Cables snake across the ornate floor; runners and producers clutch clipboards beneath Corinthian columns. In the centre of the room, Christopher Hogwood sits at a harpsichord. He turns towards the cameras and begins to speak.

Over the next five years, we shall be recording afresh all Mozart's symphonies. It will be a voyage of rediscovery. Rediscovering the real Mozart is a little like restoring a painting – accumulated dust and layers of varnish are removed and a new painting is revealed – new, that is, to us. In music, too, when the intentions of the composer can be discovered, and when these intentions are realised on the instruments of the period, then the music is revitalised in just the same way as that painting. We are more or less used to hearing revitalised masterpieces of the middle ages, the renaissance, even of such great baroque composers as Bach. The anachronism of playing Bach on the piano is dying out – it is more common to find him played on the instruments he knew – organ, clavichord and harpsichord.

Now, if such a process is valid for Bach and his predecessors, why not later composers? Would we restore a Rembrandt and not a Van Gogh? So just as Bach can be revitalised by studying his original scores, and reading about his performances from eyewitnesses, so we can extend the process to Mozart, Beethoven, Brahms, even Debussy. By studying their manuscripts and instruments, by returning to the colours, the style and the clarity of their individual periods we can rediscover their works with the eyes and ears of a contemporary listener.[1]

It isn't so much a justification as a manifesto. The early-music movement is no longer speaking simply to scholars and *Gramophone* subscribers. The BBC documentary *Come Back Mozart*, when it appears, will be broadcast nationally at 8.05 p.m. on 15 February 1980 – a prime-time Friday night slot, in an era when British viewers only had three TV channels to choose from. By then, the first volumes of the Academy of Ancient Music's Mozart symphony cycle would already be in the shops, but Hogwood and Wadland, with the support of the BBC producer Roy Tipping, were planning ahead. They were preparing to make the case for the project to the wider musical public; to BBC Two's entire viewership, in fact. And, of course, they were staking their claim to wholly new territory for the early-music movement. Mozart was the domain of Herbert von Karajan, Carl Böhm and Leonard Bernstein; boxed symphony cycles were the preserve of major symphony orchestras. Period-instrument groups stuck to the baroque. Anything later than Handel was neither necessary nor practical.

Hogwood, Wadland and the Academy were crossing a frontier, and planting a flag. The tone – this being Hogwood – was genial and articulate, but his argument was uncompromising. Bach on the piano is an 'anachronism'. The 'real Mozart' was about to be restored, with all that 'accumulated dust and layers of varnish' removed by expert hands. 'By recording all his symphonies in roughly the order in which he composed them,' he continued,

> we are hoping to learn for ourselves the nuances of the styles which Mozart developed. By the time we reach the works written at the end of his life we will be immersed in the music of Mozart in a way unique since his death. Where then do we start removing the dust from his music?
>
> It's rather like the build-up to an assault on Everest, and over the next five years we'll be putting the results of this research and our experiments into practice and on to record. The result will be analogous to what happens to fine old oil paintings when, dark and faded with a patina of dirt and oxidation, they eventually get

cleaned and restored. Inevitably, critics, historians and the public are forced to re-evaluate these newly emerged works of art. I'm quite prepared to believe that Mozart done in this style will be startling for some people, inspiring for others, but that no one who is interested in these beautiful pieces will in future be able to ignore the historical and musical implications of these first authentic performances in modern times.[2]

Seventeen months earlier, Hogwood had suggested in public that a period-instrument performance of a later Mozart symphony in the UK was practically impossible.[3] That such a project was conceivable, let alone viable, is proof of just how quickly the early-music scene was developing, and how swiftly the bandwagon was starting to roll – even while Hogwood argued that the musical logic of a move from Rembrandts into Van Goghs was inescapable. 'A turning point came, I think, when we recorded and played in concert Philipp Emanuel Bach,' he told an interviewer, some years later:

And this suddenly sorted out those people who wanted to go on, and were professionally equipped to go on to later playing styles and those who were really baroque and earlier. It opened the way, I think, for people to begin to say, well, what about the school after the galant, the beginnings of classical music. We had already accompanied some of the early Haydn Masses. We were looking at classical idiom and my feeling was that it would be nice to try a couple of Mozart symphonies and see what happened. And I put this idea forward and again, to my surprise, the then very adventurous record chiefs thought about it for a bit and somebody came along and said, 'Well, we really need a new set of Mozart symphonies.'[4]

He makes it sound as simple as that; and perhaps, in that golden age of global classical LP sales, it really was that simple – certainly with Peter Wadland there to make the case. Hogwood's initial idea – to record Schubert – might have been a step too far but, by now, Decca knew that the Academy of Ancient Music could deliver a viable product, and Mozart was a saleable name. It was down to Hogwood and Jarman to supply the musical side of things; Wadland, Dunkerley and the L'Oiseau-Lyre team would do the rest. Hogwood began the Mozart cycle the way he began all his major projects: by doing his scholarly homework and consulting the relevant authorities. 'The only problem was, none of us had great experience, particularly in string-playing styles, orchestrally, for classical music,' he recalled.

> So because Jaap Schröder, the Dutch violinist, had been run-
> ning the Esterhazy Quartet and recording and playing Haydn and
> Mozart for a long time, I thought he would make an excellent
> partner. And purely by chance, while we had started looking into
> the musicological edge of this, we discovered that over quite a
> few years, Neal Zaslaw in Cornell University had been running
> seminars amongst his students for establishing historical principles
> and texts and performing evidence for the Mozart symphonies.[5]

Zaslaw advised on style and on editions, and helped establish appropriate orchestral configurations for each work. The first jolt to convention came with the decision (typical of Hogwood) to make this the most comprehensive Mozart symphony cycle on disc – including works, such as the single-movement C major Sinfonia K.35, or the five-movement work K.250/K.248b that Mozart extracted from his *Haffner Serenade* – that had not traditionally been part of the numbered canon of 41 Mozart symphonies. Invitation cards went out from Decca House for 'a reception to announce the recording of THE FIFTY SYMPHONIES OF MOZART' (the capitals were deliberate) at Ely House, Dover Street, on 29 September 1978. The AAM had acquired a logo, too: the elegant, calligraphic rendering of the group's initials that it uses to this day.

But the most striking innovation, in a musical world that expected its Mozart to come from the baton of a single all-powerful maestro, was Hogwood's decision to share the artistic direction of the project with the Dutch violinist and classical-period specialist Jaap Schröder. Schröder (1925–2020) cited his musical heroes as Jacques Thibaud and Stéphane Grappelli, but he was a formidably knowledgeable early-music specialist, who'd worked with Gustav Leonhardt and Frans Brüggen and whose Quartetto Esterházy, founded in 1972, was (in his own words) 'the first quartet to focus on sound and style-related questions of musical interpretation, using appropriate instruments and bows'.[6] Hogwood sat at the harpsichord and Schröder, as concertmaster, took the leader's seat on violin, and together they co-directed each symphony. 'That was how many eighteenth-century orchestras ran,' explained Hogwood.

> The first violin was literally the leader and waved a bow which ensured a good unanimity from the upper strings and the winds whereas the bass end – the cello, the continuo, the double bass and so on – would be controlled often by the composer sitting at the keyboard.[7]

'The idea came from Neal [Zaslaw], who was our guru musicologist,' says Heather Jarman. 'There would have been the joint directorship between Mozart at the keyboard and the leader of the orchestra.' It presupposed a lively and sympathetic collaboration between Hogwood and Schröder and that, in the main, seems to have been the case. 'They were very polite to each other. It seemed to work,' says Catherine Mackintosh. 'I'm not sure how inspiring it was for the rest of us.' At times, the collaborative spirit could get out of hand. 'Jaap was standing up and leading for the early sessions,' says Simon Standage. 'I remember one session in particular where we were in quite an interesting seating arrangement, and the session was stopped. And at that point about five people stood up because, well, Jaap was already standing, of course; Chris stood up, Catherine no doubt stood up – the responsibility for direction of the group had that many people involved.'

As the cycle progressed, Hogwood relinquished the harpsichord for the later symphonies and conducted instead. But the collaboration with Schröder and Zaslaw did inject fresh ideas into an Academy that now found itself on a vertiginous stylistic learning curve. Mackintosh was grateful for the opportunity to sit back from the leader's role. 'I quite enjoyed the sessions because I wasn't actually in the hot seat and Jaap was doing a marvellous job teaching us about articulation, and about Mozart. He did have a slightly different way of doing things, but it wasn't as exaggerated as some of the Dutch specialists.'

Wadland's recording team, too, had to adapt quickly to a new area of historically informed style. Recording this much music with this many period woodwind and brass players was still terra incognita, and tales persist of repeated struggles with intonation, and movements patched together by the engineers from countless three-bar takes. 'Jaap did an awful lot on those symphonies – basically giving us his own ideas of practice, and in which direction they should go. So there was a lot of discussion going on,' says John Dunkerley.

> How you bow things, how you approached some of the entries, and things like that. He was leader, but also almost co-conductor, because Chris was a harpsichord player, and he didn't know all that much, at that point, about string playing. Of course we had Neal Zaslaw, who attended a lot of the sessions. He did all the research on the different set-ups for the orchestra, and he gave me a lot of problems because I had to try and convert his ideas into something one could practically record.

Zaslaw researched appropriate orchestral layouts for specific symphonies. A sinfonia that began life as an operatic overture for a theatre's orchestra pit would have a different seating plan from a work composed for a public hall in Vienna or an open-air celebration in Salzburg. It was all factored into the evolving cycle. 'He would give me some diagrams of how they would have sat. There were some that were almost like a very narrow pit, with the players stretched out either side. I had to convert that into something that would be sensible,' says Dunkerley. 'As we got to the larger orchestra set-ups, it became a little less challenging. We started in a church in New Southgate. Then we moved to St Jude's, Hampstead, and that proved problematic in the winter months because, being on the top of the hill, it caught all the wind and rain. Then we were allowed into the Kingsway Hall, and it's almost as though that was a coming of age.' Until its demolition in 1998, this former Methodist Church in Holborn was famed in the record business as one of the world's finest acoustics for recorded orchestral music.

The first volume, released in late 1979, comprised three LPs containing eleven symphonies from the years 1772–3. Seven box sets would be released in total, with the last appearing in the spring of 1983: twenty-three LPs in total. By any standards, that was a lot of Mozart to get through. For the first time, the members of the Academy started to experience a sensation that was all too familiar to the hard-bitten freelance players of London's symphony orchestra circuit: routine.

'It was a bit of a production line really, just getting through them,' says Catherine Mackintosh. 'It became a bit humdrum, and I do remember thinking when we finished each recording that I wouldn't listen to it for another ten years.' Bass player Barry Guy was a bit more energised by the project. He was one of the first of the AAM's second generation of players: he hadn't been present in 1973 but had been recruited by Hogwood after the group's founding bass player, the veteran Francis Baines, had been discreetly 'retired' (Baines's term) by Hogwood in the late 1970s.

It was a revelation in a way. First of all, there are so many Mozart symphonies that are never heard. With each session and every new symphony, it was like a first performance for me. Chris was very aware of the internal balance of the orchestra. For many years I'd found Mozart problematic in so-called modern orchestras, because the whole balance always seemed to be a little bit awry. There was always something too loud or something too soft or the clarinets were too assertive. But with the correct instruments, suddenly all of the balance and all of the internal sounds somehow resonated.

Guy, along with several members of the orchestra, had developed a very particular coping strategy:

These blocks of symphonies came along every couple of months. There were so many sessions, and there was so much music to get through, that you became a little bit of an automaton. After you've done some takes, then the engineers would say, 'Oh yeah, can't we redo such and such? We need this, we need that.' I said, 'Well, there are so many symphonies and there are so many whiskies out there. Why don't we write a tasting book of whiskies, to be completed at the end of the symphonies?' So we had a whisky club throughout the Mozart symphony sessions.

Catherine Mackintosh observed rather than indulged. 'Unlike some of my colleagues, I think I probably wouldn't have been a very effective player if I had! It was Barry plus four or five of them anyway. They always wore suits when they were doing their whisky tasting.' Guy recalls that it was all highly professional.

It wasn't about getting pickled in the afternoon session; it really was just a tasting. We were all encouraged on our travels to pick up unusual whiskies. Sometimes if you were in Scotland, you'd end with an unmarked bottle, which you'd picked up at this distillery or other. Then you'd bring it along and we would all taste it and write it up. It was very methodical: we'd write up the year, the distillery and so on. Chris Hogwood knew all about it because in the afternoon breaks, we'd be lined up on the stage in Walthamstow Town Hall with all these tiny little bottles. As ever, he was very tolerant.

Meanwhile, throughout the Mozart years the Academy maintained a full schedule of concerts, touring and other recordings – Handel, Monteverdi, Muffat, Vivaldi and of course the ongoing Purcell series. Emma Kirkby observed the players from the outside:

I remember an absolutely glorious session in St Jude's in Hampstead. It was an afternoon session and the string players had been recording Mozart in the morning. Or perhaps not exactly the same day, but it was in the middle of a patch of Mozart recordings, and it did have that slightly more pressured – not quite mechanised, but very exacting and slightly difficult feeling – of having to get it right. They were very exhausted by all that.

And it was a balmy September afternoon in St Jude's, and the sun was pouring through the windows and we started recording 'Gentle Morpheus' from Handel's *Alceste* – that gorgeous song in E major, where the strings just make this purring sound, because it's a lullaby. And the beam on all their faces! I can't tell you. They said, 'Oh, this is so much more fun!' It was just such a joy. It had an incredibly radiant feeling because of the contrast with how hard they'd been working with the Mozart.

There was still a broad and vocal constituency of critics who had yet to be persuaded of the musical merit of historically performed performance – quite apart from its claims to 'authenticity'. The critic of *Classical Music* attended an AAM trio-sonata concert at the Wigmore Hall in February 1979, apparently expecting to be disappointed, and wholly immune to

Hogwood's skills as a presenter. 'Somehow the craving for authenticity has opened the floodgates to anyone who can play the fiddle without vibrato, or pluck a few chords on a lute, with little or no concern for either the interpretation or aesthetic effect of the works being performed,' he wrote.

> In most respects this was a trying affair, and matters were not improved by Christopher Hogwood's lengthy and surly introductions to the music. Clearly sensing the presence of a fanatical and grim-faced early-music crowd, he took the opportunity to pillory much music written after about 1800. This would not have been so bad if the playing had been interesting. As it was, rhythms were slack and intonation was often abysmal.[8]

Possibly the sheer pace and quantity of the Academy's work was starting to show. But if the Mozart symphonies became a routine for the players, the impact of the recordings themselves was electrifying. Alan Rich, of *New York* magazine, spoke for the consensus when, in the autumn of 1980, the first volume hit record shops in the USA:

> All right, you may say, the scholarship is in order; what does this possibly have to do with the results? Well might you ask, and often have I asked the same; the tendency of inadequate or sleep-inducing musicians to hide behind the concept of 'authenticity' is a painful reality on today's musical landscape. I need only cite such matters as the Telefunken series of Bach cantatas, in the bloodless if elegant performances under Gustav Leonhardt and Nikolaus Harnoncourt, to demonstrate the vast chasm that can yawn between correctitude and communication.
>
> *Can* yawn, but needn't: these new Mozart performances are just wonderful from any standpoint . . . the exuberance and vitality of the performances add to the authenticity of performance the authentic depiction of Mozart's own surging, torrid creative drives . . . All this is marvellously attended to in these performances of sublime, seraphic love and energy.[9]

'How sublime it all is, how vivid,' he went on, before concluding that 'no recording project in years has so revitalised my joy in record listening.'

Successive volumes were greeted with undimmed enthusiasm; sales were buoyant as record collectors built their way to a Mozart cycle of unprecedented completeness and originality. 'Those records really took off with the record-buying public,' says Nicholas Kenyon. 'They were perceived as really fresh, and really innovative, because they started with Volume Two or Three, with works that were comparatively unfamiliar at that point. So it made a huge impact.'

Gramophone journalists were invited to the penultimate recording session at Kingsway Hall. A couple of days earlier, on 4 March 1982, the entire team had celebrated with a post-session party, complete with a specially baked cake featuring (a typical Hogwood touch) an acrostic made up of the letters WAM and AAM. By the time the last volume was released in the spring of 1983, the cycle had already made history. Summing up the final volume for *Gramophone*, Stanley Sadie – himself a Mozart scholar of international standing – concluded:

> I shall not attempt to summarise these recordings – either this box or the whole – in a glib final sentence or two. As I have indicated, not all the playing or ensemble is perfect and there may well be reservations about the expressiveness of the slow movements. But the set as a whole represents a remarkable achievement, making us listen afresh time and again, to perceive things in the music that have previously been obscure. Certainly it will have to be regarded as a landmark, not only for the early-music movement, but also in the history of recording.[10]

That judgement has stood. At the end of the 1980s, in December 1989, Sadie, writing again for *Gramophone*, nominated the AAM Mozart cycle as the most significant recording of the decade – a verdict unaffected by the vast sales and revolutionary changes that had defined recorded in music in the ten years since the start of the cycle (the first commercial compact discs had gone on sale in the spring of 1982). With the launch of their Mozart cycle Christopher Hogwood and the Academy of Ancient Music were now a significant presence at the top table of the international recording industry, with a growing market in the USA. The whole field of period performance was buoyed up – and pushed into the spotlight – by their success.

'By the early 1980s, the academic question of how late early music should go had been overtaken by practice,' writes Nick Wilson. 'The success of recordings like the Academy of Ancient Music's complete Mozart symphonies demonstrated that the tide was not to be turned.'[11] But another AAM recording was to have an even wider international impact. Alan Rich, in September 1980, already had an inkling of what to expect, and he ended his Mozart review with one almighty teaser:

> I have also, by the way, heard an even later Hogwood album, his version of Handel's *Messiah*, which will be issued here this fall. Not being one to break release dates, I will merely breathe the news that however many performances of the music you already own, you'd better husband your shekels for this one.[12]

The Refiner's Fire

The idea of a historically informed recording of Handel's *Messiah* was not new, exactly. The great Westminster Abbey Handel Commemoration festivals of the late eighteenth century had been among the first major occasions in British musical life at which ancient music had taken a central place. Since that time, *Messiah* had become part of the fabric of musical life in the English-speaking world – the cherished common property of every amateur choral society, and an annual fixture at Easter and Christmas. If any one work of the baroque era can be said to have enjoyed an unbroken performance tradition in the British Isles, it's *Messiah*. Handel's score assumed almost infinite forms as communities reinvented and adapted it to the tastes of their time and the circumstances of specific performances.

The widely used edition by Ebenezer Prout (1902) represented, for its time, the state of the scholarly art (and restored Handel's high, virtuosic baroque trumpet parts), but by the late nineteenth century *Messiah* could be heard performed by brass bands, Welsh male-voice choirs, in arrangements for salon orchestra and solo piano, and in increasingly colourful versions for full symphony orchestra. Prout devised parts for flutes, clarinets and trombones; in 1959, Sir Thomas Beecham recorded an edition by Eugene Goossens that added piccolo, contrabassoon, four horns, trombones, tuba, two harps, triangle, cymbals and bass drum – though his choir of 80 singers was positively chamber-sized compared to some Victorian performances. At their peak, the great Handel Festivals held at the Crystal Palace in Sydenham at intervals from 1857 onwards mustered a chorus of 2,700 and an orchestra of 460.

In the aftermath of the First World War, a cautious reaction set in, and there were various attempts to present *Messiah* in something like its eighteenth-century scale and scoring. Overwhelmingly, however, performers and listeners conceded that some updating or expanding was necessary and, indeed, very much in the spirit (if not the letter) of Handel's intentions, though most attempted some sort of compromise. Sir Malcolm Sargent's 1959 Liverpool recording is perhaps the most typical document of *Messiah* as it was widely performed at the start of the stereo era: a large (but not enlarged) orchestra playing with rich, romantic expression, the amateur voices of the sizeable (but not vast) Huddersfield Choral Society and a line-up of soloists whose CVs embraced Wagner and Puccini as well as years of experience on the oratorio circuit.

When Neville Marriner and the Academy of St Martin in the Fields planned a recording of *Messiah* for Argo in the first half of 1976 with the ASMF's own chamber chorus, Marriner turned to Hogwood, who duly prepared a new performing edition modelled on a very particular historical moment. 'Based on the first London performance of March 23rd 1743' declared the cover, and you can sense Hogwood the scholar throwing down a gauntlet to two centuries of generalised, augmented and cut performances – as well as the very notion that there exists a single, fixed and definitive object called 'Handel's *Messiah*'. Hogwood supplied sleeve notes and played chamber organ on Marriner's recording, and the result was warmly received, with the critic Joseph Green finding 'a freshness, lustre and emotion hidden previously beneath the layers of varnish accumulated through the years'. The reference to 'varnish' is suspiciously Hogwoodish, and Green concluded that 'Hogwood has done a great service to music in raising the music from the dead.'[13] Performed on modern instruments, Marriner's was, in 1976, the most historically informed *Messiah* yet committed to disc.

Christopher Hogwood was never likely to let that stand, though he was not the first to perform *Messiah* on period instruments. Roger Norrington had conducted a period-instrument version in the early 1970s at Handel's parish church of St George's, Hanover Square. 'I'd done quite a lot of Handel with modern instruments, but this was the first time with period instruments, so I was really genned up on how I thought it really should be played – the tempi, the phrasing, the original instruments and the small professional choir,' says Norrington. 'It was very exciting indeed – in fact, unhistorically, the soloists came from the choir. Chris Hogwood was in the audience, and he dashed off and ended up recording it himself. He saw that it could be done.'

It didn't happen quite as quickly as that but, by 1979, the idea had acquired a momentum of its own. The orchestra required for *Messiah* in any 'authentic' version was smaller than the ensembles that the AAM was regularly fielding for the Mozart sessions, and the ongoing relationship with Simon Preston's Christ Church choir was producing excellent results. Still, it represented something of a gamble: the early-music movement's boldest sally yet into the heartlands of the canon. This wasn't a question of refreshing unheard Mozart symphonies for an audience of record-collectors and connoisseurs. *Messiah* is a work that even the most casual music-lover feels they own. If there was an (as yet undiscovered) ceiling to the growing public appetite for historically informed performance, this project, in all likelihood, would be the one that crashed headfirst into the joists.

'*Messiah* had been over-recorded even in those days, so there was a pressure from our recording company not to do the same version,' said Hogwood.[14] Circumstance, as well as scholarship, provided a solution. Emma Kirkby had not expected to be involved at all: 'Christopher had intended, I think, for James Bowman to do it, but then James got pharyngitis and that wiped him out for several months. He recovered, and came back singing even better, but that was one of the reasons Chris turned to this slightly different version of *Messiah*, because it was one for which Guadagni, the castrato, was not available to Handel. So the arias that James would have sung were not needed to be sung by a man.' The non-availability of Bowman, and Hogwood's detailed knowledge of the original source material 'naturally led to the account books and surviving performing parts for the performances at the Foundling Hospital in 1754'.[15]

That decision led to some distinctly fresh – and, at the time, startling – textual decisions. 'In those days the vast majority of listeners were used to hearing cut *Messiah*s, so just to hear every piece was a surprise for a lot of people,' remembered Hogwood.[16] There were unfamiliar arias, and familiar arias in dramatically rewritten forms, as well as some distinctive quirks of instrumentation. The AAM fielded 26 strings for *Messiah*, and oboes and bassoons were doubled. 'The oddity is two horns – what did they play?' observed Hogwood. 'We know they were there, but there is no independent part for them. We tried using them to double the trumpets an octave below. Whether that is right or wrong, nobody is quite sure, but I don't think anybody has ever complained since!' Catherine Mackintosh collaborated with Hogwood to prepare the string parts: 'We worked a lot together, just the two of us, on the score. It's one of the things I feel most proud of.'

The recording sessions took place between 1 and 12 September 1979 at St Jude's Church in Hampstead. Wadland and Dunkerley worked hard to accommodate Hogwood's ideas about layout. 'Chris particularly wanted the soloists very close to him, so we parted the woodwind and put them just there,' says Dunkerley, who placed the choir to the front and right of the orchestra on temporary wooden staging. Hogwood conducted, with Preston playing organ continuo. Kirkby remembers the musical aspects of the sessions as intensely rewarding. The recording would later be credited with bringing her name to an international audience, although Judith Nelson sang the majority of the soprano arias. 'That's perfectly true,' says Kirkby.

> It was immense luck for me that Judy was there. She sang all the arias that people expect the soprano to do, all those arias that have that enormous baggage of everybody else's performances. She was older than me, and more experienced, and she knew just how to relax and do it her way. I was very glad that Judy was doing 'I Know that My Redeemer Liveth' because I'd heard it sung a few times, wonderfully enough for me to think, 'Gosh, that must be hard.' I'm glad I didn't have to attack it then. These days, I love to sing 'Redeemer' but I think you do need a certain courage to do it and realise that it is a beautiful bit of joyful argument. It's rhetorical. It's an earnest exposition of faith, and it doesn't have to be flashy. But that's the sort of thing that frightens you when you're young, and as I say, I think I was just very lucky. I had very little to compare my 'But Who May Abide' or my 'Thou Art Gone Up On High' with. So I just got on with it, really.

Hogwood paced *Messiah* as a fast-moving music drama: 'We made sure there weren't great gaps between movements. I do like continuity, without too much space for you to open your handbag and find a cough sweet!'[17] Midway through the sessions, on Sunday, 9 September, the entire team decamped to the Royal Albert Hall to perform in a BBC Prom – the first time that *Messiah* had been broadcast nationally with a period-instrument orchestra and historically sized forces. The sound of the AAM's Handel was already familiar from the previous year's Prom, but the sound of those famous choruses sung by the 31 boys and men of the Christ Church choir came as a delightful shock even to Kirkby:

> Because I didn't have anything with chorus, when I finally heard the chorus, it was wonderful because it was such a special sound, with the boys' voices. That's one of the strengths of that recording. It's slightly dangerous, if you like, but it's that hugely enthusiastic sound. You just have to smile when you hear it. There were lots of selling points in our *Messiah* and that was definitely one of them.

The recording was released in October 1980, and it is hard to overstate its impact. 'If I were to tell you that a new *Messiah* had appeared that eclipses all other *Messiahs*, would you believe me?' asked Eric Salzman in the US magazine *Stereo Review*.

> Hogwood has an orchestra of ancient instruments, real ones or copies thereof. He has a chorus of boys and men – small, crackerjack. He has a cast of singers with beautiful, pure (but not cold) voices. And he has the parts for and accounts of the Foundling Hospital version of 1754, together with the most up-to-date how-to information on mid-eighteenth-century performance practice. The resulting sound is simply wonderful: luminous, transparent, gratifying. But there's even more to it than that, for this performance is not so much a triumph of more scholarship as it is a triumph of musicality and intelligence. Everything is phrased, everything sings and not flat-out in-out but a rising and a falling like the very breath of life.[18]

'Shall I stick my neck out?' he concluded. 'Okay. I think this is the most absorbing and moving performance of *Messiah* I've ever heard.' Peter Davis, in *The New York Times*, was scarcely less effusive:

The revelatory results are like no *Messiah* ever heard before in this century. The biting edge of the gut strings, the airy buoyancy of the total instrumental ensemble, the utter transparency of the choral singing, the sharply-etched musical profile of every familiar number freed from any suggestion of Romantic silky-rich vibrato – this is a *Messiah* that will no doubt elate baroque purists and unsettle traditionalists.[19]

That these endorsements came from the USA is significant. Combined with the Mozart cycle, the AAM *Messiah* put rocket boosters on the orchestra's international profile and made Hogwood, almost overnight, the face of early music in the USA. But of these two major projects *Messiah* had the more wide-reaching impact, redefining one of the pillars of the classical canon and doing so with such virtuosity and joy that it was no longer credible to dismiss these performers as cranks or hobbyists. Suddenly the nut-cutlet brigade was winning Michelin stars, and everyone wanted a taste. On 20 March 1982, barely a fortnight after the conclusion of the Mozart recordings, BBC Two television broadcast a complete AAM performance of *Messiah,* specially filmed in Westminster Abbey, with the same soloists as on the recording, but with the choir of Westminster Abbey (where Simon Preston had taken over in 1981) replacing the Oxford chorus.

'It was freezing cold in the Abbey. That's the main thing I remember,' says Emma Kirkby.

And we had these dresses designed by someone at the BBC, and we had a different colour for each section of the *Messiah*. I remember my 'But Who May Abide' dress because it was a slightly shiny electric blue: I wondered whether, with the 'Refiner's Fire', I was supposed to be some kind of a gas flame. But then in the Passion section, we were all in black and I had this amazing dress with lots of jet all over it, so that was quite fun. In the third section, I was in some kind of gold thing: whether it was something to do with going to heaven, I don't know. It seemed funny at the time, but to be honest, we just all got on with it. It was recorded as live – we were not miming to playback, and that sometimes meant you had to have a certain degree of ESP because of the distance between us and the band. We knew this stuff by then, we'd done it enough, but at the same time it had a real sense of occasion because I don't think there was much in the way of editing.

Once again, this was prime-time Saturday night viewing: historically informed performance was going head to head against *Dallas* and *Ken Dodd's Showbiz*. That, in itself, gives some idea of the impact of the AAM's first recorded *Messiah*. And from the dance-like opening flourish of the overture to the final, shining 'Amen', no AAM recording has won more universal and enduring acclaim. Thirty-five years later, *Gramophone* magazine could still declare, 'Nobody in their right mind doubts the seminal importance of Christopher Hogwood's groundbreaking *Messiah*.' The critic and early-music specialist Lindsay Kemp recalled his first listening as 'an awakening': 'This recording is not only one of the shining lights of "historically informed performance", forcing us to rethink what we thought we knew and strewing new ideas in our path; it is also remains one of the most deeply convincing *Messiah*s we have.'[20] For Nicholas Kenyon, it was quite simply a decisive moment in the history of the Academy of Ancient Music, and of the early-music movement more widely: 'Everybody said, "Yes, this is it."'[21]

Autumn of Discontent

The outcome of the *Messiah* project could hardly have been happier. But orchestras are social organisations, and as the Academy of Ancient Music began to act and operate more like a traditional orchestra, it started to encounter traditional problems. No two witnesses give the same account of the dispute that broke out at Maida Vale studios on 2 September 1979 during preliminary rehearsals for the *Messiah* project, but it seems to have started with a cigarette. In 1979, smoking in the workplace was a largely unchallenged norm even in orchestras, where rehearsals would take place in a fug of tobacco smoke and one of the orchestra manager's duties before each rehearsal was to place ashtrays among the music stands. 'I can still see those ashtrays, bronze-coloured things,' remembers the cellist Anthony Pleeth.

'And I was smoking when I was playing, which is what I always did. The cigarette went between the first and second fingers on the right hand when you're holding the bow.' Accounts differ as to what happened next, but it seems that Pleeth's smoke drifted towards William Christie, the virtuoso American harpsichordist whom Hogwood had brought in to play continuo. Heather Jarman recalls that Christie asked Pleeth – 'politely, for Bill' – to stop smoking. Pleeth remembers no such request. 'I just remember that he got up and rushed over to where I was playing and extinguished the cigarette on my music stand.' 'Bill turned around, grabbed the cigarette from Tony's mouth and stubbed it out on the music,' recalls Jarman.

Tempers flamed like magnesium; there was a heated verbal altercation. Pleeth demanded to see Christie's Musicians' Union card and it swiftly became clear that this was about more than just passive smoking. Pleeth was a member of the Musicians' Union – near universal for orchestral players of the era, but less common on the early-music scene. Hogwood was not a member (in Pleeth's eyes, he was 'quite to the right of me and quite anti-union'). Nor was Christie. The MU enforced its rules strictly; the late 1970s were the last hurrah of the closed shop and the union had a history of trying to bar non-British musicians from working in the UK. The post-war years – when the MU had picketed touring orchestras, and had leaned on the Labour government to prevent the Holocaust survivor Rudolf Schwarz from taking a conducting post with a British orchestra – were within the memory of many active professional musicians.[22]

'I did take umbrage to somebody coming over from America, and – because he happened to be a mate of Chris's – behaving in that way,' says Pleeth. 'He was imported, and there were lots of very good harpsichordists around by then whose noses were slightly put out of joint.' John Dunkerley felt the atmosphere turn sour. 'Poor Judith Nelson was so upset, because she was a very good friend of Bill Christie's, and she just had to carry on almost through tears.' '[Pleeth] then discussed the matter with the Musicians' Union and came back saying that another harpsichordist would have to be found to take part in our recording of *Messiah* as the American was not a Musicians' Union member,' Hogwood told the *Guardian*.[23]

The MU had flexed its muscles. Christie vanished from the sessions, and the union turned its sights on the rest of the Academy. 'The next day, Bill Christie did not turn up,' says Catherine Mackintosh, who had witnessed the explosion. 'So that's the way it was resolved temporarily.

But the spin-off was that those of us who were in the union – which was basically everybody in the group – were told by the union that we were forbidden to play with Chris Hogwood. Because Chris refused to join, the MU said, "Well, therefore, you're not allowed to play with him."'

This threw up immediate practical difficulties. Pleeth was due to play with Mackintosh and Hogwood in a forthcoming chamber tour. Hogwood's status was a grey area: the MU did not require conductors to be members but its assumptions about what constituted a conductor were fixed doggedly in a less flexible era. MU regulations made no provision for the concept of a player-director: you either played an instrument or you waved a baton. Rules were rules. The entire basis on which Hogwood directed the Academy of Ancient Music – and, by extension, the working practice of much of the early-music movement – was now under direct attack from one of the music industry's most powerful and uncompromising lobbies.

'It spread out into the whole of the music profession,' says Catherine Mackintosh. Jaap Schröder's position in the Mozart project came under question, and Simon Standage also felt the repercussions:

My group, the Salomon Quartet, was doing an educational TV programme with Chris. At that time the Musicians' Union was imposing itself to the extent that, since the rule book says that a member may not play with a non-member, a union man could come in and catch me playing with my wife on Christmas Eve in church, and I could be struck off. On this occasion I took some music for The English Concert round to Tony Pleeth's and he said, 'Oh, are you going to do that session tomorrow?' So I told him, yes, I was, because we were supporting Chris – and, sure enough, he got the union to send somebody around, and we were called before a tribunal. It let us off with a warning but, at that time, the union's strength was such that we could all have been put out of work.

As far as the union was concerned, Chris was a keyboard player, and therefore he should belong to the union. The fact that at that time he was providing heaven knows how much work for union members with the Mozart symphony series, apart from everything else, was something they couldn't understand, because they could only see him as a keyboard player. The idea of a group being conducted by somebody playing a harpsichord was totally foreign to the union. It was very alarming at the time.

The union issued a ruling that Hogwood could not direct the AAM from the harpsichord in concerts. Hogwood booked a different harpsichordist and conducted instead. Meanwhile, members of the Academy confronted the union's objections head on. Mackintosh was among several union members in the group to be summoned before a tribunal. 'We actually managed to get a very nice guy called John Turner – an extremely good recorder player who used to play with David Munrow and a great friend of Chris's – to come with us, because he was now in his second year as a solicitor,' she recalls.

We were all waiting rather nervously outside the door. Eventually the door opened and they said, 'Who is this?' We said, this is our solicitor, John Turner, and they said, 'You can't. We can only allow union members in this meeting.' Of course, they hadn't realised that he was also a union member. So he came in. And the situation was solved by Tony Pleeth not playing on this tour.

The notion that blanket enforcement of outdated rules was not necessarily in their members' interests would dawn only gradually on the union's leadership.

By now, though, awareness of the dispute had spread beyond the music profession. Margaret Thatcher had been elected prime minister on 4 May that year, and for journalists at both ends of the political spectrum any story involving trade unions had a wider significance. This was a story of enterprise and individual freedom against the dead hand of organised labour. There were letters to *The Times*, and the dispute featured in *Private Eye*. 'Musician Attacks Union' was the *Guardian*'s headline on 5 November, over a report that quoted Hogwood's own response to attempts to strong-arm him into joining the collective: 'I've many reservations about joining the Musicians' Union. I do not agree with the closed shop and I do not agree with barriers to free movement of musicians within the EEC, and the union has not done anything to assist chamber music and soloists.'[24]

In the *Spectator*, Christopher Booker took up the Academy's cause: to his eyes, 'as bizarre a tale as can ever have unfolded in the musical life of this country':

> For all sorts of reasons, Mr Hogwood is extremely reluctant to accede to this sort of pressure to join the union. For a start, he is not just a soloist and conductor. Mr Hogwood, in this instance, is also the employer. The Academy of Ancient Music is entirely his own creation. He subsidises the orchestra quite substantially from his own pocket, from his earnings as a soloist. Above all, he is extremely anxious about the growing threat to his freedom to choose foreign performers where they are musically essential.
>
> In all these arguments the union expresses no interest whatever . . . the real irony of the situation is this. Mr Hogwood's skill, dedication and reputation are such that he would have no difficulty in earning a living without the Academy. He could even set up a similar group overseas tomorrow if he so wished, and continue to play concerts all over the world. For the union members who make up the Academy themselves, however, it is a different matter. Thanks to Mr Hogwood's personal subsidies, they already earn more than the union rates for their work. For many of them, playing with him has not only been musically extremely enjoyable, but has provided them with a substantial part of their income.[25]

The MU's General Secretary John Morton fired back in the letters page: Booker's account was a 'fairy story' and 'our union's rules and policies on membership reflect the collective will of the vast majority of British musicians.'[26] Booker responded at length:

> Three general issues have been raised by this affair, each of which, unless it is resolved, could have a devastating effect on the thriving serious music of this country. The first is whether non–union members like Christopher Hogwood, Daniel Barenboim, Antal Dorati or Pinchas Zukerman will be permitted to lead an orchestra composed of union members while playing their own instrument (whether keyboard or violin).

The second is whether union members will be allowed to play chamber music with non-union members – as the late Cecil Aronowitz used to play with non-union Amadeus Quartet, or as the late Benjamin Britten (non-union) used to play with members of the English Chamber Orchestra (union).

The third, particularly relevant in the growing field of 'authentic' performances of eighteenth-century music and earlier, is the question of whether a foreign (i.e. non-union) musician may be hired, as and when he or she happens to be the best performer available in that particular style for a particular job. On all these points, the union remains so vague at the moment that one cannot help wondering whether Mr Morton and his officials really understand what the issues involve.[27]

The correspondence eventually petered out. Compromises were found, and after an extraordinary MU branch meeting attracted more than two hundred musicians, overwhelmingly supportive of change, the union conceded that the rules should be applied more flexibly in future. But during those angry weeks in the second half of 1979, the Academy of Ancient Music had found itself at the centre of a debate that would, over the next decade, reshape the economies of the Western world. It was an unlikely position for an early-music group. The musicians of the counter-culture were now at the cutting edge of the market revolution – operating without subsidy on their wits, their talents, their energy and their initiative. Confronted with this new and self-evidently popular phenomenon, the dinosaurs of the sector responded first with incomprehension, then with brute force, and finally with evolution. At the start of the 1980s, though, the paradox was inescapable. Hippies had become entrepreneurs and the purveyors of ancient music had become – slightly to their own surprise – the classical music industry's most dynamic modernisers.

6

REVOLUTION AND COUNTERREVOLUTION

While Christopher Hogwood and the Academy of Ancient Music were busy making history, the record industry entered the 1980s in a state of transformation. On 1 January 1979, Decca's engineers took their own specially built mixing desk to the golden hall of the Musikverein to record Willi Boskovsky and the Vienna Philharmonic in the annual New Year's Day concert. The double LP set that resulted was Decca's first ever digital recording, and the first commercial digital recording ever made in Europe. Meanwhile, like the rest of the industry, Decca was working towards the introduction of a new universal system for reproducing music digitally. The compact disc was a joint project of Philips and Sony; when its imminent launch was announced to the world in 1981, it was designed to contain 74 minutes of music – a length specified (or so an enduring legend has it) by Sony's president Norio Ohga in order that Beethoven's Ninth Symphony might be recorded on a single CD. The new format was also, apparently, indestructible. In March 1983 a presenter on BBC TV's *Breakfast Time* spread honey and poured coffee on a CD, before inserting it in a player to demonstrate that it still played perfectly.

Since Decca (and with it, L'Oiseau-Lyre) had been bought by Philips's parent company Polygram in 1980, the AAM stood ready to benefit from this revolution in recording technology. The Academy of Ancient Music made its first appearance on compact disc in 1983, with a special release of Mozart's 40th and 31st ('Paris') Symphonies taken from the tail end of the Mozart cycle. *Messiah* was re-released on CD in 1984. Meanwhile the combined effect of these two new technologies was to inject steroids into the market for classical recordings. Record collectors began to replace their cherished LP collections with re-releases (or new releases) on CD. And digital sound – particularly when reproduced with Decca's legendary warmth and finesse – offered an unheard-of quality and clarity of listening experience. You're a classical music buff in the mid-1980s, and you've just invested in a state-of-the-art new stereo. Your favourite Handel, Mozart and Vivaldi LPs have yet to be released in the new format, so you turn to the critics and the record shops to see which of the latest crop are the must-have alternatives. More often than not, you'd be pointed towards a new L'Oiseau-Lyre release featuring Christopher Hogwood and the Academy of Ancient Music.

There's an irresistible synchronicity about the digital revolution in classical recording and the boom years of the AAM. It's been suggested that the sonority of a period-instrument performance of seventeenth- or eighteenth-century music – especially when played with the rhythmic energy and meticulous precision of a Hogwood interpretation – was particularly suited to digital sound (and to audiophiles with expensive new equipment to show off). Vibrato-free strings, the bright, clear singing of a Bowman or Nelson or Kirkby, the boyish purity of an Oxbridge choir, and the pungent, tactile sonorities of valveless horns or period oboes – they all sounded fabulous in digital, especially when competing for market share with the slow tempi and sometimes muddy analogue sound of the symphony orchestras on many classic recordings of the LP era. 'The glassy, transparent, rhythmic and exciting clarity of the period instrument perfectly suited the sound-world of the new CD,' observed Nicholas Kenyon.[1]

The AAM was not the only British early-music group to benefit, of course. But it was the one with the highest profile and the largest recorded catalogue, playing in a digital-ready style at precisely the moment in history when classical-record buyers were most willing to invest in something new. By now, even Decca's most conservative managers were beginning to accept that L'Oiseau-Lyre was more than just Peter Wadland's pet project. 'For ages, their offices were kept well away from what was the "main label",' remembers Michael Haas.

> After PolyGram's purchase of Decca, the L'Oiseau-Lyre offices were closed and he [Wadland] was moved in with the rest of

the producers and made part of Ray Minshull's A&R staff. Ray could not stand the idea of 'original instruments' or 'authentic performances'. In retrospect, it seems extraordinary that it took the top executives and sales representatives across the globe to point out that Christopher Hogwood was outselling Riccardo Chailly, Christoph von Dohnányi, Charles Dutoit – indeed, nearly every conductor Decca had under contract, with the possible exception of Solti. Even when Minshull was confronted with the figures and royalty statements, he simply would not have it and continued with his insane policies of signing conductors to expensive orchestras and just letting them record whatever they fancied. There was one month when I believe four of the Decca house conductors recorded the same Bruckner symphony. I produced at least two of them.

The AAM's success as a recording orchestra was real enough. That, in turn, led to concert engagements, which in turn drove record sales. *Messiah* picked up an Edison Award in the Netherlands and a Caecilia Prize in Belgium. The year 1980 took the orchestra to Germany and Switzerland, 1981 to Italy and Poland, 1982 to Portugal, 1983 to Austria and back to Germany and, in June, a first appearance in Scandinavia, at Finland's Naantali Music Festival. In February 1984 a classical-sized orchestra toured Japan and Taiwan, and in September that year, a chamber-sized baroque group, featuring Hogwood at the harpsichord, began the Academy of Ancient Music's first ever tour of the USA.

Classical audiences in the USA seemed, by then, to be experiencing a mild form of Hogwood mania. The Mozart discs had made a significant impact on the specialist classical market, and *Messiah* had become a calling card of enduring value – with or without the AAM to perform it. It was almost like missionary work, and Hogwood's favourite soloists suddenly found themselves in demand. His guest-conducting fees, meanwhile, enabled him to subsidise the AAM. 'One of the things Christopher did soon after the *Messiah* recording was offer *Messiah*s, done his way, to a lot of American symphony orchestras,' remembers Emma Kirkby.

American orchestras played *Messiah* every single year, and for many of them it was just a chore. Some of them may love it

– who knows? But, anyway, Chris managed to make some really good relationships with various people in Los Angeles, Detroit, Montreal and in St Louis.

We did *Messiah* tours where we went to two or three orchestras at a time and spent four days in each place. It was fun: Chris would have the orchestra for a couple of days before we all arrived, and start shocking them by asking for less vibrato and all that sort of thing. And then when we arrived, he wouldn't say anything. He would just stand us up and switch us on. And it was quite funny because as we got going, they'd begin to look more and more amazed.

They either loved it or hated it: it wasn't a hundred per cent successful. What mattered more than anything, really, was the attitude of the leader. If the leader was behind it, then we were fine. In most cases, we had a pretty good time. But there was a very angry leader in Detroit. He was a very fine player, but he *knew* how *Messiah* went – which was that in 'I Know that My Redeemer Liveth' he always played that gorgeous tune as a solo. It was 'his' piece. Chris said, 'Well, I'm sorry. It was never played that way, so you can't.' The leader was not happy, and finally, in the middle of the rehearsals, he suddenly exploded and just said, 'Maestro, this is ridiculous. This is absurd. What do you expect me to do? It's completely . . .' And he just went on and on and on.

And Chris just sat back on his chair with that beaming smile and his head slightly on one side, and just listened. Didn't say a word. The whole orchestra was stunned and terrified about what was going to happen. What happened was that while Chris was just sitting there quietly listening, the leader began to run out of words and to hear himself. He suddenly heard how he sounded and just petered out. And that was the end of it. But where they liked it, it was a joy.

With vast new audiences ready for a first taste of 'authenticity', Hogwood was willing to stretch a point. In July 1984, as part of the Los Angeles Olympics, he conducted a 400-performer *Messiah* with the Los Angeles Philharmonic at the Hollywood Bowl. Ostensibly based on a late eighteenth-century performance at one of the great Westminster

Abbey Handel commemorations, it was spectacular proof that historically informed no longer had to mean small-scale. 'I think we had sixteen oboes,' remembers David Thomas. 'The Hollywood Bowl is extremely daunting, and Chris was terribly worried that the audience would start rolling bottles down from the back. The auditorium holds about 17,500 people and normally, if the people at the back got bored, they'd start rolling their wine bottles down the steps to make a noise. That was the last thing you wanted.' But no bottles rolled, and if proof were needed that Hogwood was now one of classical music's glitterati, the Philharmonic's CEO Ernest Fleischmann took him out for coffee with Leonard Bernstein and David Hockney.

By the time he brought the AAM across the Atlantic in September 1984, Hogwood was probably the single biggest name associated with early music in the USA. AAM recordings hurtled up the *Billboard* charts, and Terry McEwen, Decca's extrovert, no-bullshit chief in New York, took to describing Hogwood as 'the Karajan of Early Music'. (Herbert von Karajan, in the 1980s, was probably the world's most commercially successful conductor: a blue-chip celebrity, hugely prolific in the record-ing studio and known, as much in envy as in awe, as the 'general music director of Europe'.) The hype, in some cases, was luridly at odds with the scholarly seriousness that underlaid Hogwood's approach to music-making. It was at this point, in 1984, that Nicholas Kenyon asked him whether the record companies had not 'oversold the whole business of authenticity':

I reminded Hogwood that one of his recent records is marketed in the United States with the sticker 'Authentic Edition: the famous Kanon as Pachelbel heard it'. 'Hmm, that's just a piece of patent commercialism, now we've made it into the big time they have to extract their world killings. But I'm rather ambivalent about that approach because of course in the eighteenth century there was masses of hype and self-advertisement. And with a record like that you do make so many converts and persuade people to listen in a way that they might not have thought of.'

The AAM's first concerts in New York certainly set out to make converts. On 12 September 1984 at Lincoln Center's Alice Tully Hall, the Academy took part in a televised joint concert with the Chamber

Music Society of Lincoln Center. It was billed as 'Bach to Bach', though some called it the 'Battle of the Bands'. The host set the scene – and set the bar high:

> We're in the middle of a whole week devoted to the music of Johann Sebastian Bach. And at this midweek point, the Chamber Music Society has chosen to give us a unique television opportunity to compare the playing of Bach's music in the way that it would have been heard in his own time in the early part of the eighteenth century on the instruments of that time with contemporary interpretation of the same pieces.
>
> I can say that the Chamber Music Society scoured the world to find the best group to play in the ancient manner, but the truth of it is there was precious little scouring required because it's well understood that the most exciting group in the world today committed to playing the music out of that extraordinary fruitful period we call baroque is Christopher Hogwood's Academy of Ancient Music from London. And so the Chamber Music Society has brought Mr Hogwood and the Academy over here for this evening's concert, for this week as well. It's a kind of antiphonal concert, except that the two voices separated by just a few feet on the stage are also separated by about 250 years in time.[2]

The idea was to demonstrate the ideas behind historically informed performance by pitting the two ensembles against each other, in turn – with Hogwood offering explanations of why the AAM did things the way they did, and engaging in friendly discussion with the host and the American performers. The men of the AAM wore white jackets; the modern-instrument players wore black. 'Chris introduced it all in a very frilly shirt, as I recall,' says Simon Standage, who was playing that night. And the whole concert was broadcast out coast to coast on network television – completely live. 'It left its mark on me,' recalls Standage. 'Our friend [the US harpsichordist] Kenneth Cooper, too, was playing. Apparently his nails suffered somewhat from nerves.'

The broadcast as a whole is fascinating for the good nature of the discussion, for Hogwood's lucid explanations ('You're going to love it because he talks so purty,' predicted the host), and for the performances

– with a full-blooded Bach Brandenburg Concerto (complete with the organ of the Alice Tully Hall) giving a vivid illustration of the modern-instrument way of doing things to set against the AAM's seven-player period-instrument version. But at least one observer was uneasy about the implication, however collegial, that the two approaches were in competition. The musicologist Richard Taruskin (1945–2022), then a member of the faculty of Columbia University, and later a contributor to *The New York Times*, noted Cooper's slightly defensive remark that 'we're no less concerned with Bach's intention than Chris is.' Taruskin would later develop his ideas about authenticity rather more forcefully at Hogwood's expense, but for now he noted that all of the performers present offered something distinctive and, on its own terms (if not, perhaps, those that Hogwood would have accepted) authentic. In an essay written in 1988, he recalled:

> We have got our purposes, all right, and our stylistic prefer-ences, and they are well and truly represented – authentically represented! – in our performances of music of all ages. This was quite dramatically illustrated at that much touted Battle of the Bands in September 1984, when the Chamber Music Society of Lincoln Center and the Academy of Ancient Music faced off on the stage of Alice Tully Hall. It was – despite the advance publicity and the differences in the ways Messrs Cooper and Hogwood expressed themselves at intermission time – by no means the expected case of the Schleps vs the Prigs. One heard dash and vigour from the British fiddles, and poise and clarity in the New Yorkers' playing. Both groups started their trills from above and neither eschewed string vibrato. Simon Standage played with the panache of the Galamian pupil he is, and Kenneth Cooper brought down the house with the unforgettable glitter and drive of his splendiferously embellished Fifth Brandenburg (replete with sixty-five-bar 'cadenza'). This was first-rate modern Bach from all hands. All of it was fleet, buoyant and eminently geometrical. And it was not simply a matter of 'convergence', nor one of the 'mainstream' aping the 'historians'. The geometrical Bach, as we now know, was in place before the 'historians' ever began to ply their wares.[3]

The problem was that Hogwood did indeed believe that the historically informed performance had a superior claim on authenticity, and he'd been saying as much, very publicly, for some time. 'I'm a bit afraid of being made out to be a very severe evangelist for only authentic performances,' he told one journalist in one of many interviews intended to promote the *Messiah* recording:

But I do worry when you get, say, 58 performances of Handel's *Messiah* on record that bear no relation to the sound or the work that Handel knew and wrote, and, until recently, not one that attempted a version that Handel might have recognised. It's just the proportion of the thing: I reckon that people should merely be given fair evidence to make up their own minds.[4]

For now, though, the question was moot, and authenticity, AAM-style, was carrying the day. Wadland pressed on with a vigorous recording schedule. In April 1981, at the Royal Festival Hall, the AAM gave the first performance in modern times of Handel's *La Resurrezione* – 273 years to the day since its last performance at Easter 1708, as Hogwood noted with evident satisfaction. A recording appeared the following year. There was more Purcell theatre music, Handel and Telemann concerti, and (a special favourite of Hogwood's) two of Haydn's 'London' symphonies (1984), taking early music into the 1790s. There were discs to delight Decca's accounts department: Handel's *Water* and *Fireworks Music* (1981), a Mozart *Requiem* (1984) and the disc of Pachelbel and other baroque 'lollipops' (1981) that had proved so embarrassingly marketable in the USA. In August 1982 the AAM provided a period-appropriate soundtrack for a BBC television adaptation of Sheridan's *The Critic*. And, of course, in 1983 there was Vivaldi's *The Four Seasons*, performed with irresistible zest by four of the AAM's own violinists – Christopher Hirons (Spring), John Holloway (Summer), Alison Bury (Autumn) and Catherine Mackintosh (Winter).

After two and a half centuries of relative neglect Vivaldi's four programmatic concerti had been one of the main beneficiaries of an earlier phase of the early-music revival. Neville Marriner's 1969 recording with the Academy of St Martin in the Fields, featuring Alan Loveday as soloist (and Simon Preston on continuo) had sold over half a million copies, and won the ASMF its first gold record. If Wadland and Hogwood had any doubts about whether the record-buying public was ready for a period-instrument alternative, they can't have lasted long. The 1985 BRIT Awards ceremony was held at the Grosvenor House Hotel, London, on 11 February 1985, hosted by the Radio 1 DJ Noel Edmonds, and Hogwood and the AAM were shortlisted. Back then, the BRIT awards didn't distinguish between classical and pop records; Hogwood found himself in a crowd that included Prince, Madonna, David Bowie and the team behind the motormouthed puppet star of breakfast TV, Roland Rat. The broadcaster Richard Baker read out the nominees and announced that the AAM had won the classical category.

'One of the interesting things about this disc is that it's actually sold more on compact disc than on normal LP and cassette together,' announced Edmonds, as a smiling and evening-suited Hogwood picked his way through the assembled rock stars and bounded up to the glitter-covered podium to accept the prize. 'Apart from my total surprise, I should also mention Vivaldi's total surprise at being included in something where he is easily 250 years older than anybody else present,' he began. Seizing the moment, he saluted Decca's – and Wadland's – commitment over the preceding twelve years:

I think one ought to say, if one's going to mention something slightly serious about BPI, is that without the patronage of this industry in this country there really could hardly have been the revival there has been in the performance of early music authentically. What most people are looking for nowadays of course is the sort of patron that existed in the eighteenth century. To our great surprise, when we first had the idea of putting together an orchestra of what most of my friends call stone-age instruments, a record company, Decca, was brave enough to say 'meet for the first time' at one of our recordings. From that it went on. We're very grateful for that form of patronage. Long may it continue – on Vivaldi's behalf as well.[5]

A month later, on 16 March 1985, the AAM's *Four Seasons* entered the top 100 of the UK album charts – just above the Eurythmics' *1984* and immediately below the *Ghostbusters* soundtrack album. A week later, they'd moved up to No. 85. 'I ain't afraid of no ghost,' insisted Ray Parker Jr, but he'd just been bumped off his perch by a Venetian violin teacher who'd been dead since 1741.[6] There seemed to be no worlds that the early-music movement – or at any rate, Hogwood, Wadland and the AAM – couldn't conquer. Later that spring, they recorded the first disc in the first Beethoven symphony cycle ever to be recorded on period instruments.

Doctor Death

To challenge success – to question the status quo – is simply human nature. For the Academy of Ancient Music and its hard-working director, the journey from first session in an empty church to international chart-topping phenomenon took little more than a decade: an unexpected, near continual escalation of activity and fame that can have left little time (or energy) for reflection. In 1973 the AAM had been a scratch assembly of pioneers from a lively but still very much marginal countercultural fringe. As late as 1980 Howard Mayer Brown, in an article on performing practice in *The New Grove*, had concluded that although Beethoven on period instruments was – in theory – a fascinating prospect, 'the practical difficulties of assembling and equipping such an orchestra would be almost insuperable'.[7]

The AAM was now winning international awards, appearing on prime-time TV, breaking America and preparing to record a Beethoven symphony cycle on a major label. It's unlikely that Hogwood saw himself as part of a mainstream – still less an orthodoxy – but equally unlikely that the artistic principles expounded by the leaders of the early-music scene could have been accorded the benefit of the doubt indefinitely. As early as February 1984, in the magazine *Early Music* (and at the invitation of its editor, Nicholas Kenyon), Richard Taruskin had started to question the entire aesthetic and moral basis of the notion that Hogwood would own so proudly at the 1985 BRIT Awards, 'the performance of early music authentically':

> The line we draw between our idea of the historical realities and our present-day performance practices is never determined solely by feasibility. There is always an element of choice and taste involved; but that is often, indeed usually, left unmentioned or

even hidden behind a smokescreen of musicological rationalisation, in the name of 'authenticity'.[8]

Taruskin didn't mention individuals, but the single most prominent name in musical 'authenticity' in the USA at that time was Christopher Hogwood and his orchestra. The 'Battle of the Bands' would shortly make it even more prominent. Hogwood's willingness and warmth as a public speaker, broadcaster and educator made him an obvious figurehead for the movement, as well as for his own often expressed belief that a conductor of eighteenth-century music should be if not invisible, then certainly 'transparent'. He'd lost none of the fluency or missionary zeal with which he'd expounded his scholarly and artistic principles on *The Young Idea*, or talked to new audiences in Hong Kong or King's Lynn. Taruskin, for his part, slammed early-music devotees who 'heard the sound but not the music', and who used scholarship, period instruments and historic playing techniques as a fig leaf for a failure (or inability) to engage with the music on an emotional level. With Decca's Terry McEwen giving the AAM the hard sell across the USA, it's difficult not to suspect that Taruskin had Hogwood in mind when – with the academic's eternal disdain for the popular – he bemoaned the fact that

> even as the authenticity movement has begun to achieve the technical proficiency that is at last gaining it credibility and acceptance in the music world at large, it is unfortunately taking on some of the less attractive characteristics of that world. We now have our own star system, our personality cults and fan magazines, our hype machines and our beautiful people. And above all one encounters self-congratulation and the heaping of scorn upon the mainstream artists from whom we still have many lessons – and some of the most basic ones at that – to learn. What entitles us to our airs of moral superiority? Our commitment to authenticity? Not if our authenticity is as spurious as I have come to believe, in many ways, it is.[9]

Hogwood had, of course, predicted the demise of the 'anachronism' of playing Bach on the piano; in interviews about *Messiah* he'd suggested that his recording, alone in the catalogue, represented something that

Handel might have recognised. But as Taruskin returned to the subject over the next decade, developing his argument into a powerful critique of the whole conceptual basis of authenticity in musical performance, his commentaries took on an uncomfortably personal tone, reflecting an Anglophobia that also, on occasion, distorted his writing on Russian music. He would refer to Hogwood as 'Dr Death';[10] 'the authenticity ringleader'.[11] Reflecting on the debate some years later in *Text and Act*, Taruskin accused Hogwood, Decca and the AAM of calculated dishonesty:

> I am well aware that many 'Early Music' viewpoints are upheld not seriously at all, but altogether cynically. Yet I have always considered it important for musicologists to put their expertise at the service of 'average consumers' and alert them to the possibility that they are being hoodwinked, not only by commercial inter-ests, but by complaisant academics, biased critics and pretentious performers. Thanks to Nicholas Kenyon, I can cite Christopher Hogwood's words in confirmation.[12]

It's unrecognisable as a description of Hogwood or his motives. Hogwood had merely conceded, in that 1984 interview with Kenyon about Pachelbel's Canon, that some of the metaphors he'd used to explain his methods to the uninitiated were not meant to stand up to logical scrutiny. 'Taruskin was very, very unfair, because Chris had said that with a little bit of a smile,' says Kenyon.

Taruskin never used a sledgehammer to crack an argumentative nut when he could detonate a dirty bomb instead. But two of his arguments, first articulated in 1988, found their mark, with a lasting philosophical and aesthetic impact on the early-music movement. One was his observation that what he called the 'sewing-machine style' in historically informed performance – transparent textures, clipped rhythms, swift tempos – rep-resented the projection of a modernist aesthetic onto the music of the past, rather than any serious attempt to recreate the emotional experience of baroque listeners or performers: something that was in any case impossible.

The other was his deconstruction of the very idea of authenticity. Taking one of Hogwood's own favourite metaphors – of restoring an old-master painting, stripping away the grime – he dismantled its basic assumptions to arrive at a devastating conclusion:

In musical terms, neither what is removed nor what remains can be said to possess an objective ontological existence akin to that of dust on a picture. Both what is 'stripped' and what is 'bared' are acts and both are interpretations . . .

What is thought of as the 'dirt' when musicians speak of restoring a piece of music is what people, acting out of an infinite variety of motives over the years, have done with it. What is thought of as the 'painting' by such musicians is an imaginary rendering in which personal choices have been 'reduc[ed] to a minimum' [Hogwood's words] and, ideally, eliminated. What this syllogism reduces to is: people are dirt.[13]

For Taruskin, the tendency of early musicians (and Hogwood in particular) to 'sterile restoration', was where '"authenticity" turns ugly'. It was rooted in an impulse that was at best false, and at worst dehumanising. He didn't hesitate to call it 'evil'. We've travelled a long and very dark road from Hogwood's youthful enthusiasm, or Emma Kirkby singing Handel on a Hampstead summer afternoon, while the orchestra smiles at how right it feels and how lovely it sounds.

Academic squabbles have little bearing on record sales and only rarely impede the purchase of concert tickets. It'd be naive to suggest that the AAM's continuing commercial success was significantly affected by Taruskin's ideas, or the debate that surrounded them. Ideas are most likely to attract challenges when they are at their most dominant: debate is healthy and Hogwood, a scholar to his bones, was well equipped to argue his corner. But Taruskin's demolition of 'authenticity' does seem to have shaken his confidence. The varnish-stripping metaphors disappeared from his published interviews, and the 'A' word itself had been ruled permanently out of court. In an interview with Kenyon for *The New York Times* in 1988, Hogwood hedged and back-pedalled: 'I think we inherited a shorthand term like authentic when it should probably have been spelt with a "k",' Mr Hogwood says.

I think all that 'early musicke' and 'authentick' has mercifully gone, and in its place we have this shorthand: a pursuit of an interest in certain historical relevancies, and a guarded absorption of those into what we think of as a correct modern performance style.

That's probably a circuitous way of saying that we invent it as we
go along and look for back-bearings to the post.[14]

And yet the promise of musical liberation through scholarly diligence had
been Hogwood's primary motivation in parting company with David
Munrow and Neville Marriner, and founding the Academy of Ancient
Music in the first place. 'Now the question was, well, is that scholarly
basis any more reliable and is it genuinely reinventing the past? Or isn't
it? And I think we have to say that Chris had become the poster boy for
the authenticists' notion that what they were doing was reinventing past
performance practice,' says Kenyon.

Wadland didn't mind; the AAM's huge record-buying and concert-
going public certainly didn't mind, and Taruskin, in turn, would find
his position under attack. 'If consumer values are the issue, surely the
remarkable prosperity of Taruskin's bête noire, Christopher Hogwood,
must be strong evidence: someone must have bought all those records,'
commented the harpsichordist and scholar John Butt in 2002.[15] But the
concert and recording scene was evolving too; major changes were afoot
much closer to home. By the mid-1980s, the pioneering days – when
Hogwood and the AAM had taken on the world and won, defining the
sound and the direction of historically informed orchestral playing in the
English-speaking world – were numbered.

The Age of Enlightenment

It all began with a cancellation. Or at least a proposed cancellation.
The Academy of Ancient Music (AAM) were due to perform a
concert on 30 November 1985 at St Margaret's, Westminster.
The circumstances of the concert were somewhat unusual: for
once Christopher Hogwood, founder and conductor of the AAM,
was not directing. He had a date elsewhere and the orchestra's
manager, Judith Hendershott, in response to the players' enthusiasm, had booked Flemish baroque violinist Sigiswald Kuijken
instead. As the concert date approached, it became clear it was
going to make a loss: the funding had fallen through. Catherine
Mackintosh, leader of the orchestra, did not want to lose the

opportunity of performing with Kuijken and took matters into her own hands . . .[16]

The founding of a new orchestra is a moment of optimism. As told in Helen Wallace's official history, *Spirit of the Orchestra*, the founding of the Orchestra of the Age of Enlightenment was a matter of a bright idea, a golden opportunity and a group of the right musicians and their supporters being in the right place at exactly the right time. That it emerged from the Academy of Ancient Music, in a brief instant when Hogwood was preoccupied elsewhere, is almost incidental.

What actually happened was a little more complex, but also – in retrospect – inevitable, at least from a certain perspective. As 'The Class of '73' flourished, and groups such as Roger Norrington's London Classical Players and Caroline Brown's Hanover Band staked out their corners of the concert scene, it was evident, by the mid-1980s, that the UK now possessed a critical mass of skilled and committed historically informed orchestral musicians. Players moved between different freelance ensembles; there were still overlaps and (if diaries were not sufficiently well managed), occasional clashes. But what could be more natural in London – where four major symphony orchestras had long been managed on a freelance basis – than the idea of a self-governing freelance period-instrument orchestra, run, like the London Symphony Orchestra, as a musicians' collective?

'It didn't only emerge out of the Academy,' remembers Catherine Mackintosh.

> It emerged out of all the groups, really, that were run by one director. There was Christopher Hogwood, Trevor Pinnock, Roger Norrington, John Eliot Gardiner – all those four had been what we used to call the 'robber barons'. And I think a lot of us musicians at that time were getting the feeling that we weren't really developing. We were all doing lots of work and concerts and touring, but obviously with the same director, you'd tend to have a house style. And we were desperate to get some input from completely different sources.

Orchestral musicians enjoy gallows humour: the idea of Christopher Hogwood as a 'robber baron' at a time when he was paying his players from his own earnings shouldn't be taken literally. The courteous, collegial Hogwood was an unlikely figure to be cast as a monomaniacal podium tyrant: the early-music scene, then as now, contained individuals far more deserving of a player rebellion. The source of the difficulty around this particular concert seems to have been that the overworked Hogwood had briefly taken his eye off the ball. By 1985 Heather Jarman had moved on, and the day-to-day management of the AAM was not in good shape – outsourced to an individual (apparently recommended to Hogwood by the Lord Mayor of London) who exported armoured Land Rovers to Africa out of his bachelor pad on Welbeck Street in London.

'The office was actually a flat with a bedroom and a bathtub and all kinds of stuff,' recalls Judith Hendershott, a former teacher from Portland, Oregon, who was recruited after Jarman's departure to assist with administration. 'A rather strange setting for an orchestra office, I thought. But anyway, that's where I was installed to assist the manager who was being paid by Chris to run the orchestra. But there were some very strange things going on. This manager told me that I must not say "Academy of Ancient Music" when I answered the phone. I opened the post, and at some point I noticed that there was this huge overdraft – that the orchestra was £33,000 in debt.' The AAM's concert and recording work at this time was contracted directly through Hogwood – who in turn paid the players and met the running costs of this minimal back office.

'So I blew the whistle, Chris and Jasper Parrott saw the manager off and on 1 June 1984, I moved all the stuff out of Welbeck Street to my flat in Blackheath. We put it in my bedroom, and that's where I started running the Academy of Ancient Music.' With coaching from Jarman, Hendershott booked the players for the 1984 US tour.

> I was thrilled to be asked to do the job, but nobody ever gave me a contract. I was using my bedroom, and they nickel-and-dimed me. I had to invoice them for postage and phone calls. It was ridiculous. Chris didn't run it at all – he was always away, always off on tours doing other things. I was mainly getting directions from the leading musicians. People like Simon Standage and Cat Mackintosh would say, 'Well, try this person, or that person.' And that was how it went.

For the players, as Mackintosh remembers, it was simply that the opportunity to work with, and learn from, a virtuoso of Kuijken's calibre seemed too good to turn down. When the funding fell through, a group of them took matters into their own hands and approached Michael Rose, the Head of Sponsorship at the American Bankers Trust Company to underwrite the concert. And so an AAM concert went ahead without Hogwood, and a group of players – on a high – met after the concert for a drink, as Wadland and Hogwood had done a decade and a half earlier. And just like Hogwood and Wadland, they fell to talking about the business of running an orchestra on their own. It might even have been the same pub. Violinist Marshall Marcus had started playing with the AAM in 1984, and was present that night.

I never heard this from Chris, but I was always told that he was angry that a concert was being organised for the AAM without him conducting. But I remember very distinctly sitting in the pub – I think it was the Marquis of Granby – having a drink after the concert. Those of us there were all agreeing and saying, 'That was a really interesting concert' – because, actually, we'd just worked with somebody who had a completely different kind of palette and approach. We suddenly realised how interesting it was to open the door to this influence from the Continent. I was absolutely fascinated, as a violinist, by the way Sigiswald was directing from the violin. The way that he played, the way he held his instrument, the way he talked, the way he looked at phrasing, was all completely different. I remember thinking, 'This is amazing. We could have lost this really easily.' And I don't remember who it was – it might have been [bassoonist] Felix Warnock – but somebody said, 'Look, why don't we make our own orchestra and we'll decide which directors to have, instead of the directors deciding which players to have.' That was the birth of the OAE.

We didn't think in any way whatsoever that we were doing anything against Chris. It wasn't that we were saying that the AAM needed to have other directors. On the contrary, we accepted the fact that the AAM was Chris's baby. We weren't interested in trying to control what a director did with his group. We were interested in a far more radical revolution, which was having our own group – a player-run group. It was the same idea as the founding of the London Symphony Orchestra: a group of players wanting to run the thing themselves. I can't have thought there was any reason why that should have been a problem for Chris. I carried on playing with the AAM after that. It didn't provide any kind of problem for me, but I think Chris was pretty pissed off about it.

In fact, many founder members of the new group – originally called The Age of Enlightenment, with the word 'Orchestra' coming later – continued to play as members of the AAM with little sense of conflict or tension. There was enough work to go around and, after all, the early-music movement had been built on that kind of pragmatism. Behind the scenes, the story was less tidy. The official OAE history mentions that Hendershott was 'already working out her notice with AAM'. 'Well, I had quit – mentally,' says Hendershott. In fact she worked on AAM projects in 1986 while simultaneously assisting the breakaway OAE players in raising funding and planning – arguably on the AAM's time, although Hogwood had only himself to blame for her lack of a formal employment contract.

Understandably, her working relationship with Hogwood deteriorated. 'He was pretty prickly by that time,' she recalls. 'He didn't show much appreciation at all. I think he resented me particularly because I had got sponsorship for this new orchestra, and maybe he felt it should have been directed toward the AAM. But I did the job for him that I was supposed to do.' She parted company with the AAM before the OAE's inaugural concerts, in Oxford and London in June 1986. Sigiswald Kuijken conducted, and the 'robber barons' of the UK period-instrument scene took their seats in the audience: curious to see what their long-term players could accomplish under their own steam.

'All the period-instrument conductors came to that concert,' says Hendershott. 'John Eliot Gardiner was there. I can't remember if Trevor Pinnock came. But Chris definitely came. It was quite a stellar audience.' The OAE's next venture, five months later, was a programme of Weber – music far outside the AAM's core repertoire – under Roger Norrington. 'I thought what they were doing was important,' he says. 'They carefully hired foreign conductors to begin with, and I was the first English conductor who was allowed to conduct them, which was a great honour.

I remember saying to them at the first rehearsal, 'You didn't need to start an orchestra. If I'd known you'd wanted one, you could have had mine.'

With hindsight, the foundation of the Orchestra of the Age of Enlightenment changed the UK early-music scene for the better: a collective coming of age, almost as significant as the AAM's first recording. It's not unreasonable to view the OAE as yet another product of the revolution started by Hogwood and Wadland back in 1973. But any revolution has its casualties, and history is full of ostensibly democratic utopias that have rapidly become less stable – and a great deal less tolerant – than the monarchies they supplanted.

'There were power-games,' recalls one early member of the OAE. Within two years, Hendershott herself had been defenestrated by the player-managers.

> One Saturday morning in August 1988 they came to my door and presented me with a piece of paper that I was supposed to sign, resigning from the orchestra. It was all a huge surprise, and I asked, 'What are the reasons? Can we have a meeting?' They wouldn't talk about it at all: I was just supposed to sign this thing. But I didn't. I chased them out my front door and got legal advice, and in the end I got some compensation – which was a hell of a lot better than with Hogwood, I have to say.

Hogwood largely kept his own counsel throughout the whole process – he'd never seen himself as an autocrat, and he valued his relationships with his musicians. It was not in his nature to pick a fight in public. The AAM players who formed the OAE overwhelmingly continued to play in the AAM too (a barely established orchestra with three concerts in six months was in no position to ask its players to refuse the frequent well-paid tours and recordings that the AAM could offer). Few can recall any instance of being made to feel uncomfortable by Hogwood. But very occasionally, Hogwood's collegial nature buckled and it became impossible to maintain a facade of good sportsmanship. Marshall Marcus remembers one such moment:

> I don't remember him ever showing any kind of irritation or anger over the fact that we'd started this orchestra. But there was

a tour to the States with the AAM, which included a concert in Cambridge, Massachusetts. I have a memory of Chris giving a speech at a drinks reception after the concert, with everybody present, and saying some quite unpleasant things about the OAE. He used a rather unpleasant phrase about the orchestra: he called it 'The Age of Embezzlement'. I couldn't work out what it was about, to be quite honest.

Possibly Hogwood was mentally conflating the OAE's genesis with the earlier difficulties over the AAM's Land Rover-dealing manager, or with his perception that the OAE had been founded on the AAM's time, by an AAM employee, in partnership with a potential AAM sponsor.

Of course, nothing unlawful had occurred. Hogwood, like most great conversationalists, occasionally let his wit override his discretion. Heather Jarman returned to work as Hogwood's personal assistant in 1987:

What we were upset about wasn't the OAE's existence: what we were upset about was that we paid for it to be founded. It wasn't the existence of the OAE itself, because there were always other orchestras around, and you collaborate, you don't compete. The way you keep ahead of the competition isn't by beating them up, it's by having new ideas and better ideas. We were very envious of Roger Norrington, who did themed weekends at the Southbank. They were fantastic. We were just . . . 'Damn it, why didn't we think of that?' We weren't against him. We were admiring.

But what the founding of the OAE made unambiguously clear was that 'The Class of '73' no longer had the field to itself – and that the early-music scene was evolving beyond the control of idealistic Cambridge graduates and their one-man bands. Hogwood and the AAM had done more, perhaps, than any other single conductor–orchestra partnership to give a mass classical audience a taste for the sonority and style of historically informed performance, but it was no longer about the sound alone. As soon as more than one period-instrument recording existed of a given work, it became a question of interpretation, of taste, of all those messy, intangible, non-Urtext emotions that Taruskin seemed so keen to discuss.

Roger Norrington and the London Classical Players were also beginning a Beethoven symphony project. The OAE was lining up guest
conductors from the mainstream: artists who had fallen in love with the
recordings of Hogwood, Harnoncourt, Brüggen and Pinnock and were
now eager to apply the lessons of historically informed performance for
themselves. Would the public continue to choose historically informed
Mozart or Beethoven from Hogwood when they could get it from Simon
Rattle or Sir Charles Mackerras? The changing professional environment,
as well as the backstage conflicts surrounding the birth of the OAE, seem
to have taken an emotional toll on Christopher Hogwood.

'The OAE did feel like some sort of betrayal,' says Hogwood's former
partner, Anthony Fabian. 'This conductor-less idea, many of his players
going over to the other side, as it were. No, he loved people to be loyal to
him. He wanted his people – his singers, his players, his boyfriend – to be
loyal to him and anybody leaving for whatever reason was a big betrayal.
That was just who he was. He was highly competitive. Everybody that
wasn't in his team was competition.' And competition – by the second
half of the 1980s – had become the new spirit of the age.

7

A NEW-CREATED WORLD

For its first decade and a half, the story of the Academy of Ancient Music is the story of something unprecedented. After the mid-1980s – the period of Taruskin's attacks on the early-music ethos, and the foundation of the Orchestra of the Age of Enlightenment – the picture changes. Inspired by Halley's Comet, which blazed on its once-a-lifetime path across the night skies in the spring of 1986, Judith Hendershott had chosen a star as the logo for the breakaway OAE. In truth, the AAM had dominated the firmament of British and American early music since the mid-1970s, as Hogwood and his orchestra sped towards their early-1980s perihelion. By the late 1980s, though, the heavens were more crowded, and no one star dazzled quite so brilliantly. True, the AAM still held an enviable position – with a globally recognised name and an unrivalled discography. But the original band of pioneers had evolved into a major professional orchestra, with the concomitant (and often mundane) problems and responsibilities.

And as events had demonstrated, the AAM urgently needed to start organising its affairs as a professional outfit. No more word-of-mouth hirings or management by contact book; an end to scripts thrown in taxis or payrolls signed off in a spare bedroom. Jasper Parrott's agency HarrisonParrott had been handling Hogwood's conducting and solo career. On the back of the AAM's successes, he was in high demand and, in 1986, Hogwood was appointed Artistic Director of the Handel and Haydn Society in Boston, Massachusetts – one of the USA's longest-established societies for the performance of ancient music. It was proof of the reputation he (and the AAM) had established in the USA, and the extent to which historically informed performance had entered the mainstream in North America. The AAM, however, was starting to show the strain of years of ad hoc management. Parrott appraised the situation:

> Chris was quite conflicted about the fact that the AAM was an expensive thing to run. The money needed to run it depended upon profits from touring – which varied from year to year. Chris was very reluctant to put his royalty income into the business. And so there wasn't a flow of financial support which enabled one to build and grow the whole company, and it sort of waxed and waned. And then it got into quite serious trouble. Chris and I talked about it, and I offered to take the management in house, into HarrisonParrott. And I introduced Paul Hughes to the group.

Paul Hughes was one of Parrott's younger agents. The idea was that, while remaining an employee of HarrisonParrott, Hughes would take charge of the AAM's day-to-day management, becoming, in effect, its first full-time manager. At the end of January 1986 Hendershott moved all the AAM's papers out of her bedroom and Hughes arrived in a taxi to take them back to the HarrisonParrott offices. 'So Paul Hughes became the manager of the Academy out of our basement offices in Penzance Place,' recalls Parrott. 'The whole principle was that we would consolidate – we would be able to reduce the costs, and when the business had recuperated the idea was to float it off as an independent operation. Which is exactly what we did, although there were various hiccups along the way.'

Hughes approached the task without preconceptions – or much in the way of advance knowledge. 'I'm not entirely sure that they had told Judith,' he remembers.

> She was nice, but it was slightly awkward to begin with. I mean, I didn't know a period instrument from a period pain. I'd never managed an organisation before, of any sort, so it was a leap of faith. There was a loosely structured Board with Heather [Jarman] and Chris and some other people. We used to meet in Cambridge, which was nice because it meant I got out of London. It was a little bit unstructured – let's put it that way. For me, it was a very steep learning curve. I was constantly having to call on Judith Colman, who was running The English Concert, and who was very kind

and generous to me: 'How do I put a recording contract together? How do I negotiate with a trumpeter? How do I do this?'

We started to put things a little bit more in order – a little bit more structured, planning ahead. It shouldn't have been that complicated, and it wasn't really: you book the players when you need them, you do the budget, you raise the money, and you do the project, whether it's a recording or a tour or a Barbican concert. And I really enjoyed working with Chris. He was very warm and open, though occasionally he would bristle and say, 'That's not very helpful.' That was one of his expressions when he didn't like something: he would say it wasn't very helpful.'

One thing that Hogwood found particularly unhelpful was his sense that he and the AAM had become too inextricably linked. He'd started to perceive that for either party to flourish in future, they needed to be able to work with other people.

The problem was that the public disagreed. A magazine cartoon of the period showed a speech bubble coming from a radio, 'And that was the Academy of St Martin in the Fields . . .' – to which a parrot in a nearby cage responded, '. . . conducted by Neville Marriner.' The same could have applied to the Academy of Ancient Music and Christopher Hogwood. The orchestra was difficult to sell as anything more than an adjunct to its director. The promoters of a 1988 Australian tour even made it a contractual stipulation: 'The Artists shall be billed as Christopher Hogwood and the Academy of Ancient Music.'

'Chris was always pushing against that,' says Hughes. 'He'd say, "You need to find somebody else to take it on. I've done it for nearly fifteen years – I can't be doing it any longer." And yet selling them without him was very difficult. I pushed it to one side and thought – if we are going to grow the AAM, put it back on the tracks and see it through its fifteenth anniversary, it really needs to be rock solid, with Chris at the heart of it.' For Hughes, the fifteenth anniversary of the group, in 1988, provided a useful focal point. A professional designer was engaged to smarten up the orchestra's logo and general image: 'We wanted to have a new logo, a new look, something that was a bit more contemporary. It felt good, it felt successful. It felt like we were slightly shaking off the cheesecloth and yoghurt, hand-knitted look.'

A more sophisticated image might, or might not, have been a response to the heavily promoted launch of the OAE, but it also aligned with the sheer scale of the AAM's international profile as it approached the 1990s. At the heart of it all was the ongoing relationship with Peter Wadland at Decca. The Beethoven symphony cycle took shape from 1983 to 1989, although the first disc was released only in 1986, when the landscape was already changing. No matter; with the release of the Ninth Symphony, in 1989, plans were announced for a complete cycle of Haydn's symphonies – one of Hogwood's favourite composers, and an obvious sequel to the Mozart and Beethoven cycles.

Naturally this was to be the first period-instrument Haydn cycle (in fact, only one complete cycle had ever been recorded – the Philharmonia Hungarica's set, under Antal Doráti). The Cornell University Haydn scholar James Webster was to be the musicological adviser and, as with Mozart, Hogwood intended to explore beyond the 104 canonic numbered symphonies. In the commercial climate of 1989, that did not seem over-ambitious. The Beethoven cycle had been heralded with an extensive feature by Hogwood in *Gramophone*. For the Haydn project, the whole orchestra flew to the palace of Eszterháza in Hungary to perform three early symphonies for an ITV *South Bank Show* special. Filmed in April 1989, it was broadcast across the UK in January 1990.

Meanwhile, on the back of *Messiah*, *Alceste* and *La Resurrezione*, the big Handel projects continued, including (in 1984) the Academy's first encounter since 1731 with *Esther*, the oratorio *Athalia* (1985) and in 1989–90 the opera *Orlando*, with a cast that matched AAM veterans Emma Kirkby, James Bowman (in his final recording with the AAM) and David Thomas with Arleen Augér (1939–1993), the peerless American coloratura soprano, then best known for working with mainstream conductors including André Previn and Riccardo Muti. She'd taken a special interest in period performance, working with Hogwood in Boston and collaborating on several AAM recordings, including, in September 1988, Beethoven's Ninth Symphony. *Orlando* went to the BBC Proms for a semi-staged performance on 30 July 1989 (Lynne Dawson took Augér's role of Angelica): almost a curtain call for the team that had been at the heart of so much of the AAM's work for so long. 'We acted it out at the Prom on a sort of podium thing, which was a very strange sensation,' remembers Thomas. 'I remember James making silly faces at me when I was singing my aria. James was quite a character to work with.' Bowman, too, remembered it fondly: 'Chris was really at the peak of his powers.'

In May 1985 Wadland had given his single most spectacular demonstration of his command over the Decca stable of artists – and of the AAM's stature in the wider musical world – when he lined up the Australian soprano Dame Joan Sutherland, the boy soprano Aled Jones, tenor Anthony Rolfe Johnson and a classic AAM team of Kirkby, Bowman and Thomas to record Handel's *Athalia*. A cast like this was the stuff of dreams, and for no one more than the diva-loving Wadland. Aled Jones, then aged fourteen, was already the subject of a BBC documentary (shown shortly after the sessions in June 1985) and his recording of Howard Blake's song 'Walking in the Air' from *The Snowman* would hit No. 5 in the UK singles chart that December. His mother attended the sessions with him. Sutherland, meanwhile, was, at fifty-eight, approaching the end of a career as one of the most celebrated opera singers of the century, a *prima donna assoluta* known as 'La Stupenda' for her diamond-like high notes and outsize stage presence.

'A good example of [Wadland] managing to charm people into the studio and keep them there was when he asked Joan Sutherland to work with Hogwood,' says Michael Haas. 'She took a lot of persuading before recording *Athalia*.' Bowman remembered some initial discomfort when Sutherland arrived at St Jude's, Hampstead, to find herself expected to sing at the lower baroque pitch. 'Chris always used A = 415. The harpsichord was tuned to that, and everything else went from there. She wasn't keen because she had perfect pitch, and also, her husband Richard Bonynge was hanging around and he felt he had perfect pitch, too.' But Wadland had finally brought a singer he revered together with an orchestra and conductor that he knew better than anyone alive. His tact, and his determination that the moment should live up to its potential, carried the day.

'So, anyway, Sutherland turned up for the first session,' remembers Catherine Mackintosh, who saw it all from the leader's seat. 'Peter came in front of the orchestra and said, "This is just a wonderful moment for me – for years I've been wanting to invite Dame Joan." And she said to us, "Well, yes, Peter, you see I'm an ancient instrument as well.""* Some

---

* Michael Haas recalls it as 'I guess many would call me an "old instrument" as well.' David Thomas remembers her saying, 'Well, I think I'm the oldest instrument here.'

adjustment to the world of ancient instruments, clearly, was still necessary. 'I remember that she said that we spent all our time tuning up. She sat in the control box doing her tapestry or knitting – she couldn't believe how long it took us to get things in tune.' But with Wadland at the top of his game, Haas recalls, 'Everyone got on famously well. He could switch from consummate diplomat to matron in a second. If things got heated, he was excellent at turning himself into a Jean Brodie character and getting everyone to "move along".'

Road Stories

Mackintosh stood down as leader of the orchestra in November 1987, becoming an active member of the OAE (though she continued to work as an adviser to the AAM). In a sense, it was a reflection of the AAM's maturity. Founder members had been playing under Hogwood for nearly a decade and a half, and craved variety. 'The Academy of Ancient Music continued to thrive, but the OAE was just different,' she says. 'It was made up of quite a lot of people who had been founding members of those other groups. It was stimulating, actually, to have different conductors and directors coming in. We had to relearn our craft every time. Whereas we'd spent the past fifteen years just doing it in the style of Hogwood or the style of John Eliot Gardiner.'

Working for the AAM at this point certainly meant spending a great amount of time working with Christopher Hogwood, and often overseas – a lifestyle that did not always suit musicians with parental responsibilities. For players with the energy and the capacity, the touring schedule in the late 1980s was dizzying. In May 1985, they took Handel's *La Resurrezione* to Milan, Hamburg, Vienna and Rome. In March 1986 a USA tour included Chicago, New York, Washington DC and Northwestern University's campus in Evanston, Illinois. Shortly afterwards they were in Paris and Lyons, and in May 1986 they were in Spain: Barcelona, Madrid and Bilbao. Less than a month later they performed at the baroque palace at Schwetzingen, near Mannheim; then it was a return to France for a summer festival in Divonne before an autumn tour of the USA with Vivaldi's *L'estro armonico*.

1987 found the Academy performing *Athalia* in Spain, appearing at Le Châtelet in Paris, participating in the Ansbach Bach Week in Germany and – in June – taking part in a Europe-wide midsummer broadcast of extracts from Monteverdi's *L'Orfeo*, filmed in Mantua with the orchestra in seventeenth-century costume. There were dates in Paris and Cologne, and in October 1987, a series of concerts in São Paolo, Brasilia and Rio de Janeiro. The fact that their first ever South American tour then rolled over into a return visit to the USA hardly seemed remarkable. But the sheet of advice that was issued to the touring musicians before their departure for Brazil on a subsequent tour (in 1990) suggests that it was still possible to take the AAM out of its comfort zone:

> NEVER travel around the streets alone but preferably in groups of at least three.
>
> In Rio particularly do not wear any jewellery or valuable watches when walking in the streets and especially on the beach – this includes rings, ear-rings, cameras and handbags.
>
> CAMERAS are best left in your hotel in Rio but should be okay everywhere else. ALWAYS carry a ten-dollar bill with you so that in the unlikely event of your being mugged you can hand that over and get away fairly lightly.
>
> LOCK your suitcase and instrument case and bring spare keys.

And so the unending tour rolled on. In 1988: France, Austria, Germany, Switzerland, Finland, Italy and Belgium; California; Japan and Hong Kong; and an invitation to participate in the Australian bicentenary celebrations – the only UK orchestra to do so, and the AAM's first visit to the Antipodes, although Hogwood was already something of a regular. 'I'm welcomed here without having to push someone else out of the way . . . there's a terrible oversupply of musicians in Europe,' he told the *Canberra Times*.[1] The sound of a full-sized period-instrument orchestra (the programme featured music from the year of Australia's foundation, including Haydn's Symphony No. 90 and Mozart's 'Jupiter' Symphony) came as something of a jolt to the critic of the *Melbourne Morning Daily*:

> Intonation was a disturbing feature of this concert. It began with a resounding unison: the start of Haydn's 90th Symphony in C major, which was, in fact, a collection of Cs of various pitches, which made one wonder momentarily if the conductor should not have scrapped that one and started again. But certainly things got better and apart from some occasional ensemble lapses one was

able to listen to the performances as performances of the music
and not as performances on original instruments.[2]

From 1988 the AAM also found itself, with increasing frequency, in
the schedules of the more exclusive (and affluent) European venues – in
January 1988 it was the first period-instrument ensemble to appear as part
of the Salzburg Mozarteum's concert series, and the later stages of the
Beethoven cycle took the orchestra to the Lucerne Festival. A touring
period-instrument Beethoven Ninth (played at Lucerne in September
1988, where it was described as 'a shock for modern ears') was now the
sort of project that the AAM took in its stride.

It was even possible to contemplate splitting the workload, such was
the demand for AAM performances. In the summer of 1987 Hughes
announced the foundation of the 'Academy of Ancient Music Classical
Chamber Ensemble': a conductorless group comprising Monica Huggett
and Pavlo Beznosiuk (violins), Jan Schlapp (viola), Timothy Mason (cello),
Barry Guy (bass), Anthony Halstead (horn), Antony Pay (clarinet), and
Felix Warnock (bassoon). The Chamber Ensemble had already made
its first disc: the Mozart horn and clarinet quintets and oboe quartets
recorded at Abbey Road and produced by Michael Haas in June that year.
The following autumn, Wadland produced a disc of Schubert's Octet and
the group toured the USA and Canada in its own right, with a broadcast
appearance on Minnesota Public Radio.

Four further discs of Schubert, Beethoven, Haydn and Mozart would
appear at infrequent intervals up to 2002. But it was evident, early on, that
a Hogwood-less AAM was not as compelling a proposition for promoters.
More seriously, for Decca, the economics of recording chamber music as
if it were an orchestral recording session – with musicians' fees calculated
as if they were simultaneously soloist and ensemble members, and the
AAM charging a management fee on top – simply didn't add up. 'In many
ways, I think it could now be argued that the early-music players are now
asking for the best of both worlds,' grumbled Paul Myers, a senior producer at Decca: the sums involved were, he argued, 'irrational'.[3] A private
backer got cold feet; the momentum spluttered. If the Chamber Ensemble
never crashed, exactly, neither did it ever fully get off the ground.

But the intensity of orchestral touring continued under Hughes's suc-
cessors Christian Rutherford and Timothy Calnin well into the early 1990s:

▲ David Munrow (1942–1976), the inspirational founder of the Early Music Consort, whose performances exploded onto the early music scene.

▲ Xris: the young Christopher Hogwood at the harpsichord. 'Very beautiful, with lots of long hair', remembered the late James Bowman.

▲ Peter Wadland (1946-1992). The visionary Decca producer and co-founder of the AAM revolutionised the global audience for early music through his record label L'Oiseau-Lyre.

▲ 1978: Jaap Schröder (left) and Christopher Hogwood (right) celebrate the launch of the AAM's complete Mozart symphony cycle for Decca.

▲ 'The nut-cutlet brigade'. AAM string players and luthier Rowland Ross (left) at St Jude's Church, Hampstead, during the *Messiah* recording sessions, 1980.

◄ 1979: Hogwood and the AAM at Kedleston Hall, Derbyshire, while filming the BBC2 documentary *Come Back Mozart*.

Handel at the Concertgebouw, Amsterdam. The global success of the 1980 recording made Handel's *Messiah* a calling card for Hogwood and the AAM.
▼

▲ 1981: Hogwood and the AAM record Handel's *Music for the Royal Fireworks* at St Jude's Church, Hampstead. Even four years earlier, a period-instrument orchestra of this size would have been unthinkable.

▶

Milan, 1985: the Academy on tour with Handel's *La resurrezione*. Christopher Hogwood (left) and bass player Barry Guy (right).

◀ Vivaldi's *Four Seasons*: (L–R) John Holloway, Catherine Mackintosh, Alison Bury and Christopher Hirons. The AAM's 1982 recording with soloists drawn from the orchestra became a worldwide bestseller.

February 1985: Noel Edmonds looks on as Christopher Hogwood accepts a BRIT award on behalf of the Academy of Ancient Music and Antonio Vivaldi, who was unable to be present.

The Academy on tour in the USA, November 1986. Audiences were enthusiastic and hotels were sometimes luxurious, but Hogwood's hard-working players rarely stayed for long in any one city.
▼

◀ The 1980s were like an endless tour for Hogwood and the AAM. On 31 January 1988 they perform Schubert, Mozart and Beethoven at the brand-new Philharmonie in Cologne.

◀ Back to the source: the AAM at Esterháza, Hungary in April 1989 while filming an ITV *South Bank Show* special about the Decca Haydn symphony cycle.

▶ 1993: the sky's the limit. Decca's promotion of the AAM in the 1980s and 1990s was energetic, but by the millennium the CD boom had come tumbling to earth.

◀ Swansong of the Lyre-bird: Hogwood and the AAM record Bach with harpsichordist Christophe Rousset at Henry Wood Hall, London in August 1994.

Paul Goodwin directs the AAM. During his time as Associate Conductor, he startled the early music world by commissioning and premiering new works from living composers.

Emma Kirkby sings and Andrew Manze (right) leads the AAM while Christopher Hogwood (left) conducts. The two men took very different approaches to period performance style.

The Triumvirate. (L-R) Paul Goodwin, Christopher Hogwood and Andrew Manze, pictured in 1998 for the AAM's 25th anniversary.

▲ In 2009, Richard Egarr and the AAM perform Purcell's *Dido and Aeneas* in the ancient Roman theatre at Sabratha, Libya.

▶ 2017. Richard Egarr (left) with the pianist and Mozart scholar Robert Levin (right) – whose Mozart concerto cycle with the AAM spanned three decades from 1993 to 2023.

▲ Happy, glorious and wet: on 3 June 2012 the AAM and Richard Egarr perform Handel's *Water Music* on a rainy River Thames during Queen Elizabeth II's Diamond Jubilee river pageant.

▲ Richard Egarr bows out at the Barbican Centre, June 2021. During the COVID-19 pandemic, the musicians were obliged to stand two metres apart.

◀ Unfinished business, 2022. Robert Levin plays Mozart's Church Sonata No.17: one of the final recordings in the AAM's long-postponed, three-decade Mozart keyboard concerto cycle.

Laurence Cummings began his music directorship of the AAM with extrovert, innovative performances of Haydn's oratorios *The Creation* (2021) and *The Seasons* (2022).
▼

Eszterháza, Paris, Lyons, New York, Tampa, Los Angeles, Pasadena; *La Clemenza de Tito* in Japan in 1991, and in May 1992 a televised concert at Prague Castle in honour of the first president of the newly democratic Czechoslovakia, Václav Havel. In November 1994, by way of Hogwood's Boston contacts, the AAM began the first of several collaborations with the New York-based baroque dance expert Catherine Turocy – a choreographed staging of Purcell's *The Indian Queen* – and took it on tour to Japan. The list of destinations visited is so extensive that one might wonder how the group had time to do anything other than rehearse and record while in the UK. In fact, in February 1989 the AAM inaugurated the first major UK-wide education project by a period-instrument orchestra: a three-year programme of workshops drawing on experts from across the early-music sector and based around universities in Bath, Belfast, Birmingham, Glasgow and Keele.

Orchestras of all sizes thrive on touring. It's a bonding experience, as well as a chance to see the world (even if, on a tight schedule, that means little more than the view from the airport bus and the walk from the hotel to the concert hall). A tour supplies variety – a stream of fresh and receptive audiences. And when programmes are repeated over the duration of a tour, interpretations are refined and details are honed to an extent impossible on a UK working schedule. Technical problems, tackled nightly, fall into place, liberating conductor and orchestra to make music together. Artistically, as well as socially, a good tour tends to bring an orchestra to a high pitch of unanimity; and of course the tales of mishaps and surprises along the way provide material for tea-break banter for years to come. With a presiding spirit as congenial as Hogwood, the atmosphere on AAM tours was enjoyable. Paul Hughes escorted the players on tour and saw it for himself:

Chris was a very kind and generous man, and very often, if we had a meal after a concert or on tour, he would very quietly, without any fuss at all, sneak away and pay the bill. He did it time and again. That kindness, I think, is enormously telling – many conductors have very short arms and very deep pockets.

Touring is always a learning experience: no amount of planning can prepare for all contingencies – or, indeed, misunderstandings. 'We were setting up the Australian tour in 1988,' recalls Hughes.

In those days, everything was done on telex — it was before fax machines had really got going. And I remember this great long telex to our travel agent, Christina: who were smokers and non-smokers and vegetarians and all the rest of it. Who was going to be in which hotel, and who was going to be seated where, and all the rest of it. I said, 'So that's all kosher then, and I'll talk to you later.' Well, Christina didn't know that expression, and so she booked all the food kosher on the entire tour. So we were sitting on the British Airways flight to Australia, and the steward asked, 'Who are all the kosher meals?' Nobody said anything. And I thought, 'Oh shit.'

. . . But it was an extraordinary tour. One player — I think he played second oboe — bought a didjeridu on day one, which he then had to carry around the entire rest of the tour. And [clarinet-tist] Tony Pay bought some kind of stuffed snake at a stop-off on the way down, and then wasn't allowed to bring it into Australia and had to sacrifice it.

Like trench warfare, orchestral touring often combines the tedious with the shockingly unexpected. As a violinist, Andrew Manze toured with the AAM and Hogwood in the 1990s:

I learned — touring with Chris in the States, where we did the same programme fourteen times — that the boredom factor can be very difficult to fight against. One time we were in a plane, we landed somewhere and all the passengers got off except for the Academy of Ancient Music. Everyone was just sitting there, saying, 'No, let's not get off. Can we just stay here and have a rest and fly on to the next place?' Everyone was so tired. But we got off, we did a concert, and you knew that on stage everyone would give their absolute all, day after day.

. . . On another American tour Emma Kirkby sang Handel's *Silete Venti* and Bach's Wedding Cantata; we were doing a Handel concerto grosso and I was playing a Bach violin concerto. We were in New York, on a free day in March and I went for a walk in Central Park, literally in a T-shirt because it was freakishly warm. Anyway, we met at four o'clock, to get a bus to Cornell

University in Ithaca, and the weather closed in. We got on the bus and started driving – it's only about 120 kilometres – but the weather closed in, the snow started falling and we got stuck. We were on the bus for twenty-four hours, apart from four hours where we got off, and we found a motel to stay in for a few hours. The bus driver's name was Larry: we called him Saint Larry because he sat there all night with the engine going to keep us warm. People from other trapped cars were knocking on the door to come and use the toilet in our bus.

We were there all through the night and the day – stuck. Emma Kirkby sat with a hydrating face mask so that she could preserve her voice – the air was so dry. She was on the bus, Chris Hogwood was on the bus; we were all there, literally, for twenty-four hours on this bus. All we had with us was a video of *Casablanca*. So we saw that quite a few times. Eventually we got to Ithaca and had a couple of hours for a shower and some food. Then we did a concert and it was fantastic. Emma sang wonderfully, Chris was full of life. The orchestra was amazing. It was incredible, and I thought, 'What a group of people. They will not let the audience know what has just happened. They have such pride in what they do.' That, for me, summed up the Academy of Ancient Music – there's something very special in the spirit of the Academy.

Shared experiences like this forge enduring professional and personal relationships. Tours provided many long-term members of the AAM with their first taste of professional life in a major period-instrument ensemble, as Hogwood cast his net wider to replace regulars whose circumstances prevented them from touring. Violinist Pavlo Beznosiuk, fresh out of college and intrigued by his flautist sister Lisa's involvement with the early-music scene, was intensely frustrated by the gigs he was getting as a modern violinist on the London scene.

Without wanting to be too negative about the Orchestra of St John's Smith Square, it was another pick-up band, basically. It was all very nice, but it wasn't going to change your life. Neither, frankly, was the London Symphony Orchestra – they had just moved to the Barbican and were losing money hand over fist. It was an old orchestra, full of old men. It was a great experience for the few concerts that were worth doing, but it wasn't buzzy.

Beznosiuk was starting to walk more and more openly on the baroque side, but it was a booking to play in the second violins on the AAM's first ever Japan tour, in 1984, that swung his career decisively onto a different path.

> The Academy had much more of a buzz: it was full of interesting people, for a start. Playing early-baroque instruments was and is a tightrope walk. There was an element of risk about the whole enterprise, and the people taking those risks are the people that one remembers. It was the first time a period band of that size had gone to the Far East and, for many players, it was the first time we had been in Japan. We saw Kabuki theatre for the first time, and played in the incredible Suntory Hall. It was a momentous experience.

For violinist Maya Homburger and bass player Barry Guy, the January 1988 European tour – the one that took the AAM to the Salzburg Mozarteum for the first time – proved even more significant. Guy had been playing with the Academy since the late 1970s; the Swiss-born Homburger had arrived on the London circuit in 1986 and was working principally with The English Concert and the English Baroque Soloists: 'I was asked several times to do something for AAM, but I was never free. Then I found out that they were going to Salzburg to play in the Mozart Week in January 1988. My parents, in Switzerland, always went to this festival, so I did the unspeakable thing: I rang up Christopher and said, "I will be free in January, and I would love to be on this concert."' She didn't realise that it would entail a three-week tour.

> Well, it was amazing. We all had great fun and the musicians were constantly playing tricks on each other. At one concert I came on stage and there was one of those big forestry saws with huge blades, just sitting on my stand. I had to put it on the floor; it would have been obvious to the audience. Also, whenever I turned the page, my desk partner Brian Smith – a really long-term

member of the Academy – put a Mon Chéri chocolate after each page turn. It was hilarious – I almost wasn't capable of making the next page.

Guy remembers her first rehearsal:

Maya made her first appearance at the pre-tour rehearsals in Rosslyn Hill Chapel: I was sitting on the opposite side of the orchestra on bass and Mandy McNamara was my faithful number two. So I asked Mandy, 'Who's the new bird over there?' I was a very enthusiastic, if not terribly talented, squash player, and Mandy happened to mention that Maya played squash. So in the first tea break, I scuttled over and said, 'Don't forget to bring your squash racquet on tour.'

One of the things about tours is that as soon as you get anywhere, you go to a restaurant, then possibly eat too much for lunch and possibly snooze in the afternoon till the rehearsal. That kind of routine over a three-week period is pretty bad, so we decided that as soon as we got into town, we would look up the nearest squash court. And so we avoided all these extra big lunches before rehearsals; we were sparkling and healthy and feeling good, and we got to know each other.

Homburger continues the story:

The tour started in Munich, Cologne, Salzburg and Linz, then went to Sicily and came back via Milan. And during that three-week tour, Barry and I fell in love. The amazing thing was that everybody was delighted – because we were both single so it wasn't a scandal like normally happens on orchestra tours. Paul Hughes, the manager, was wonderful. He even re-arranged the hotel bookings to get us a double room in Sicily. To cut a long story short, we came home from the tour and four months later we found a thirteenth-century cottage in Cambridgeshire, which we bought that May. That was quite close to Cambridge, where Chris lived, and obviously he knew that thanks to him and his group, we had found each other. He was our first guest at the cottage.

We'll never forget that. He brought us a fantastic bowl – he had a wonderful taste in glassware and porcelain – and we treasure it to this day.

Representations of Chaos

When Christopher Hogwood and the Academy of Ancient Music finally recorded Haydn's *The Creation*, it was never likely that it would be anything other than a special occasion. Haydn occupied a special place in Hogwood's musical life; as early as 1980 he'd written a short but lovingly researched book about Haydn's visits to London in the early 1790s (he dedicated it 'To My Father'). *The Creation* is the point at which the musical worlds of baroque London and late-classical Vienna intersect; its dark, unstable opening *Representation of Chaos* prefiguring the coming romantic era as poetically as the great choral blaze of C major – as God creates light – embodies the crowning glory of the musical Enlightenment.

Handel had defined the Academy's early years; now they had recorded Beethoven's Ninth Symphony and, with their Haydn symphony cycle gathering momentum, Hogwood planned something spectacular. The forces assembled at Walthamstow Assembly Hall in the middle of February 1990 filled almost every square foot of the floor. Dunkerley's Decca team divided the 80-voice chorus (the choir of New College Oxford, and a specially convened AAM Chorus trained by Simon Rattle's brilliant young Birmingham chorusmaster, Simon Halsey) into two banks of 40 singers, with the soloists – Emma Kirkby, Anthony Rolfe Johnson and Michael George – and continuo players grouped between them. They were all positioned behind Hogwood and a 120-piece orchestra: more instrumentalists than most symphony orchestras would use for a Haydn oratorio. The string section alone numbered more than 70 players. There was a scholarly logic to these vast forces. It was the first recording of the work in a new performing edition by the musicologist Peter Brown and was (as the cover of the CD declared), the 'First recording, with 120 players and 80 singers, to recreate in sound, scale and disposition the performances conducted by Haydn in Vienna. The English text is that authorised by the composer.'

'I think that was the largest ensemble that Chris had ever conducted,' says Dunkerley. 'To be honest, I thought we would end up having problems, but in the end it just worked.' Emma Kirkby, too, overcame her initial misgivings.

I was a bit jealous of David Thomas at that moment because he went and did it with Simon Rattle. They did a 50-player version and we did this multi-multi-player version, which freaked me out until I consoled myself with the thought that the soprano arias are really chamber pieces. There's one moment which always terrified me, when I was supposed to sock out a top C – never my forte anyway. But otherwise, I really enjoyed that intimate, beautiful process of sharing my solos with just a handful of instruments; whether it was images of birds, or of herbs and flowers.

Barely a week after the sessions, the entire army squeezed into the quire of Gloucester Cathedral to film the whole thing. 'They shot that in complete takes, because there was no time to have it edited,' recalls Dunkerley, although it's impossible to tell from the finished product. The *Creation* project – if, inevitably, it lacked the sheer, revelatory shock value of *Messiah* a decade earlier – was a landmark on its own terms: a reading whose communicative warmth (Kirkby was not wrong about its chamber-like qualities) and sense of joy gave the lie to the increasingly frequent critical taunts that Hogwood was a technician first and a musician second.

'The cracking of thunder and the rush of rain are created anew in dry, rattling timpani and strident brass; the descending minor chromatics of the *stile antico Chaos* thrill again in muted, vibrato-less strings; the piping of the transverse magic flutes is evocative at an almost atavistic level,'[4] wrote Hilary Finch in *Gramophone*; for the American critic David Hurwitz (no Hogwood cheerleader), 'This extraordinary recording of Haydn's *Creation* may just be Christopher Hogwood's best release of anything.'[5] Its release, in 1991, was proof that the Academy of Ancient Music still operated in an expanding musical universe.

Whether Hogwood saw it like that was another question, though it wouldn't have been his way to express uncertainties in public. Self-evidently, the business of wrangling a 120-piece orchestra through a major recording, filming and touring project was a substantial effort. Even with dedicated professional management, pressures mounted and strains sometimes showed. Tours were not all sunshine and muddling through: a breakdown in travel plans led to a concert at Cuenca, in Spain, being cancelled at the last minute in April 1987. 'It was inexperience on my part, I would say,' recalls Paul Hughes.

We had had lots of delays, and it was a long, awful, horrible journey. The orchestra were due to do a concert when they arrived, and they refused to play. They said they were exhausted, and I had to tell the promoter that it couldn't happen. That would be unthinkable now: you would just find a way of making it work. But I remember being bullied by one or two of the older players, who were saying, 'Well, this is ridiculous. You can't expect us to play after we've been sat on a bus for ten hours.'

Barry Guy saw it as symptomatic of a deeper problem in the expanding orchestra: a culture clash between committed early-music veterans and new players who were crossing over from the symphony-orchestra scene, and bringing its cynicism with them. Bus late? Tea cold? Yell at the manager. Guy expressed his concerns in a letter to Hughes:

At present too many people see the AAM as a convenient money-making machine as and when they are free to pick up the work. As a member for many years, I am anxious that the dreadful musicians' inertia and negative attitudes be kept to a minimum, otherwise we may sadly see the day when Chris might wind up the whole operation. The past days have brought to the fore this very attitude in its worst form.[6]

If anything is likely to have demoralised Hogwood, however, it might have been his awareness that a small but increasingly vocal body of critical opinion remained unmoved by or actively hostile to his work. Audiences at the AAM's Salzburg debut in January 1988 were enthusiastic, but the critic of the *Süddeutsche Zeitung* – even this late in the day – openly doubted the artistic value of the entire exercise:

According to the programme notes the aim of the AAM of London is to perform baroque and classical music on period instruments as it must have sounded when originally written. There is little point discussing the issues raised by these intentions any further. If men wish to dress as slaves and row the Aegean or send their mail by messengers on horseback, well, let them . . .
    Period instruments, valveless trumpets and horns are very difficult to play. The generally accepted theory is that for every ten

notes played in performance, five will burst. In other words the player has a 50–50 chance of getting a clean note. This is not a problem in recording studios, but presents a gross disservice to composer and work alike in live performance. This dilemma must have been obvious to the discerning listener, if not to the keen devotee of authentic performance, in the concert given by the AAM under the direction of Christopher Hogwood in the Herkulessaal.

In the USA, Taruskin led the academic baton charge, but individuals in the UK press were starting to take aim too. Hugh Canning, in the *Guardian*, had opened the attack in February 1986 under the headline 'The Star Who Failed the Academy'.

Whatever happened to the Academy of Ancient Music? Ten years ago this pioneering band of 'authentic' instrumentalists stood at the vanguard of Britain's burgeoning early-music movement making award-winning records of all the Mozart symphonies, while today with or without their director Christopher Hogwood at the keyboard they invariably sound undernourished and ill-prepared in concert.[7]

His main criticism of the AAM ran along the lines of the old saw: what dreadful soup, waiter, and so little of it! Canning took issue with the infrequency of the group's UK performances, as against Hogwood's busy schedule in the US, and gleefully cited a US critic's description of Hogwood's 'frantic determination to become an international celebrity'. A forthcoming AAM tour was dismissed as a mere 'promotional tour'. As a picture of Hogwood as an individual, it's barely recognisable. Music critics are rarely well informed about the economics and logistics of the classical music business, and the fact that Hogwood's US income was effectively underwriting the group at this point was not widely known. Six AAM players, including Standage and Mackintosh, wrote to the paper in Hogwood's defence:

Over the last thirteen years Christopher Hogwood has been the catalyst in probably the most energetic and wide-ranging explosion of interest in eighteenth-century music anywhere in the world. From this countless musicians have benefited, and some, not surprisingly, have gone on to develop their own successful careers.[8]

More damagingly, Canning singled out the AAM's incipient Beethoven cycle, damning Hogwood's 'manifest lack of a striking musical personality'. It was an idea that would gather traction, and which Taruskin – when he finally brought his guns to bear on the AAM's Beethoven – would express with brutal force:

> I must declare fraudulent both the claim of accuracy and that of novelty for the recordings of the Hanover Band and the Academy of Ancient Music. They have no right to the privilege they assert. Their endeavours must stand or fall by the same standards as everyone else's. And as sure as pride goeth before them, they fall.
>
> Hogwood's do so for the usual reasons: his performances are dull run-throughs, devoid of detail, with nothing at all to impart to anyone who is really listening. One cannot hear his 'Eroica', in particular, without mounting irritation. That such a job is foisted on the public, accompanied moreover by such a clamour of hype, must set a new standard for chutzpah.[9]

The Hanover Band had completed the first period-instrument Beethoven symphony cycle; Roger Norrington and the London Classical Players, working at around the same time as Hogwood, had produced the most compelling. Or so the consensus has evolved: posterity has relegated Hogwood and the AAM's Beethoven to a place in the middle – which, on the AAM's own pioneering terms, meant obscurity. *De gustibus non est disputandum*; but it's arguable that Hogwood had, indeed, come up against the outer limit of his selfless, 'transparent' approach to interpretation. Beethoven did not respond in the same way as Handel, or even Mozart. Jasper Parrott believes that Hogwood found himself 'boxed in', artistically. Anthony Fabian is in no doubt that the experience scarred him:

> I attended the recording sessions for Beethoven Nine. He was very excited and would come home in a state of euphoria and adrenalin, absolutely energised. Then the recordings came out

and they were not popular with the press. It wasn't the kind of Beethoven that people were used to. Again, his principles of being transparent were felt to be inappropriate for this composer – critics found it bloodless. And he was so hurt by that that he basically never performed Beethoven willingly again.

He denied absolutely that it was because of the criticism, but I'm certain that it was the reason. He said, 'Oh, I don't get on with Beethoven.' But actually I was there, witness to him absolutely adoring the process when we were recording. And I think it's very unfair that there was that reaction, because if you listen to those Beethoven recordings now, they're really wonderful. They stand up extremely well against any of those other conductors and orchestras.

It's difficult to say for certain, but it's tempting to conclude that around this time the AAM set a chronological limit on its artistic ambitions. The OAE, by 1992, had recorded Schubert, Weber and Mendelssohn. Norrington's London Classical Players were pushing forward into Berlioz, Schumann, Brahms and by the mid-1990s (unthinkable to the early-music pioneers of the 1970s) Bruckner and Wagner. In 1989, John Eliot Gardiner expanded his empire with the foundation of the Orchestre Révolutionnaire et Romantique, 'to provide bold new perspectives on the music of the nineteenth and early twentieth centuries': Fauré, Verdi and a rival period-instrument Beethoven cycle were now within Gardiner's sights. In 1992 the New Queen's Hall Orchestra was launched, with an explicit agenda of giving period-instrument performances of music by Holst, Elgar and Vaughan Williams, some of it premiered within living memory. 'Authentic performance practice can be said to have come full circle,' commented the composer and critic Anthony Payne.[10]

While the rest of the early-music movement (or, at any rate, its orchestral wing) surged forwards mob-handed, securing its territorial gains, Hogwood's AAM planted its flag in the late-classical period and resolved to stand firm. A cut-off date of 1827 – the death of Beethoven – has since become part of the AAM's collective culture. The scholarly impulse reasserted itself: better to consolidate what has been achieved, and to strive for excellence within parameters that are thoroughly understood. The aim was depth and sincerity rather than breadth and sensation; an ever richer engagement rather than the quick (and often unsustainable) thrills of conquest. While other period-instrument groups hurtled headlong into competition with established symphony orchestras, the AAM concluded that the seventeenth and eighteenth century still offered limitless worlds to explore – and that two decades into their adventure, they had never been better equipped to explore them.

But the AAM's world was changing. On 30 June 1992, Peter Wadland died a few weeks after his forty-sixth birthday. He had been too ill to work for several months before his death, and had reluctantly let go of the AAM Haydn symphony cycle. 'Most people within the company knew that it was AIDS – which at that point meant a death sentence,' remembers John Dunkerley. Wadland's musical interests had been gloriously catholic, and friends and colleagues from across the industry mourned his death. James Jolly remembers, 'We had an incredible party at Henry Wood Hall, with a really spectacular line-up of guests. Shura Cherkassky was there; Ioan Davies, Iestyn Davies's dad, who played in the Fitzwilliam Quartet – he was there – Emma Kirkby was there. Christoph Croisé was there – Peter had been one of the first people to record him.' For Michael Haas, 'I can safely say that since Peter's death, I have never met another person who could reduce me to tears of laughter, or talk so sensibly about art, music, performance or sex. His view of the world was different to everyone else's, and that was his genius.'

Wadland's vital role in the founding of the AAM and his constant, enabling presence at Hogwood's side had created an irreplaceable trust between the two men. 'Peter belonged to the last great phase of the classical-recording business, where the producers were more or less on the artist's side, and finagled their way through the management,' remembers Jasper Parrott. Nicholas Kenyon watched Wadland steer and shape Hogwood's ambitions with a light but pragmatic touch: 'Peter Wadland was no fool – for instance, when the AAM went into Mozart opera, he didn't let Chris run away with that. He did *Seraglio* and *Clemenza*' – recordings (made in 1990 and 1991 respectively, with the latter featuring Decca's latest superstar *prima donna*, Cecilia Bartoli) of operas that would not put Hogwood into direct competition with more extrovert conductors.

'Peter protected us from the seamier side of the record industry,'[11] reflected Hogwood, years later. Chris Sayers, the harpsichordist turned record producer who took over at Decca after Wadland's death, remembered the Wadland era as a time when 'we were allowed to dream something up, cost it out and put it forward . . . and as often as not, to our surprise, it got accepted'.[12] Volume six of the Haydn symphony cycle, released in 1994, incorporated some of Wadland's last recordings alongside Sayers's work: a reassuring sign of continuity. 'He [Sayers] was a very good producer, but it was never the same kind of hands-on leading that Peter always gave. It was less personal,' says Dunkerley.

Still, a commercial partnership is bigger than any one individual, and even in Wadland's absence, the AAM and Decca were committed to their relationship, with the massive Haydn cycle in full flow and another landmark project on the slipway. In August 1993, at Walthamstow Assembly Rooms, Sayers produced the first disc in a complete Mozart piano concerto cycle with the American pianist and scholar Robert Levin – an artist whose combination of profound historical knowledge and daring, improvisatory performance had won the admiration of even Richard Taruskin.

'I'm actually rather proud to say the initiative for my collaboration with the Academy of Ancient Music began with me,' says Levin. 'My relationship with Chris Hogwood was principally that of a great admirer of everything that he did – I'd bought his Mozart symphony cycle.' When Levin was asked to take part in a Channel 4 TV series on the history of improvisation, an orchestra was required. 'I said, "Why don't you get the Academy of Ancient Music and Christopher Hogwood?" At that point, Chris was rather charmed by the whole idea, and he went to the people at Decca and said maybe we could do a disc of Mozart concertos. Decca said, "No, we don't want to do a disc. We want you to do the whole set." I said that it would be a dream come true.'

> So we did a few concerts together with the AAM, we toured a bit, and Decca started to set up a schedule of recordings. We would take the pieces on the road and then come back to London and go to St John's Smith Square, or to Walthamstow, or to Henry Wood Hall. And that's how the project got underway.

The musicologist Cliff Eisen provided the scholarly underpinning, and for much of the 1990s, Mozart piano concertos would become a regular part of the AAM's programmes. As Levin recalls, that led to some historic encounters:

Mozart's own piano was for many years kept in Mozart's birth-place. Then it was moved across the Salzach river to the residence house, the *Wohnhaus* on the Makartplatz. In 1997, it was proposed to have a performance of three of the piano concertos, and one of the concert rondos, and since the Academy of Ancient Music and Christopher Hogwood had been invited to come and play those two concerts [No. 15 (K.450) and No. 26, the 'Coronation' Concerto]. I thought, 'This is a fantastic opportunity. Instead of finishing our tour and then going back to London and recording there, why don't we actually record in Salzburg?' Fortunately, I have very good relations with the Mozarteum, and meanwhile Unitel got interested, so they ended up filming all of these per-formances. That was a very exciting moment.

It wasn't as simple as he makes it sound. The logistics of moving any key-board instrument – let alone one as fragile and irreplaceable as Mozart's own 1782-vintage Walter fortepiano – are delicate.

You have to be terribly careful about it, and of course this was in February, when there was a fair amount of snow on the ground. We had to be sure that when the instrument was moved from its repository at the *Wohnhaus* to the large hall at the Mozarteum, every possible precaution was taken. There was heating and some natural humidity, but of course, everybody was a little bit heart-in-the-throat, because things can happen. People were worried, as you can imagine.

Oboist Lars Henriksson had started playing with the Academy in 1995. The Salzburg Mozart sessions were an early landmark of his career. 'We were in Salzburg for a week, but we also travelled to Slovenia, and we went down to France, and we played in Nice and in Paris.' He remembers facing similar problems from the lack of humidity in the sub-Alpine air. 'Salzburg is horrifically dry: as an oboe player, I knew that from playing there with other orchestras. You come well prepared, with good reeds, and nothing works.' But the historic fortepiano paid the heaviest price: 'I think on the third day of the sessions the soundboard cracked. It was a horrific sound. We were able to finish the work of the day, but it was a chilling experience.'

And yet it's impossible to listen to that recording without feeling that the results outweighed the risks: there's a euphoria, and an almost tangible sense of delight, to the two concerto performances. 'I remember when we came to the first session and we were going to rehearse with Mozart's piano, it was really quite emotional,' says Henriksson.

I remember the first sounds we heard from that fortepiano were really quite shrill. It wasn't immediately effective, but the instrument warmed up until at the end of the project, it sounded wonderful. In the concert we played in the Mozarteum, Robert played an encore, a Mozart sonata slow movement. People were very moved in the orchestra – there were tears and sniffling all over the place.

Levin's spontaneous ornamentation and spur-of-the moment cadenzas generated a David Munrow-like sense of excitement and creative risk. 'Chris used to talk about this a great deal,' Levin recalls –

addressing the audiences and pointing out that, for instance, it was normal for eighteenth-century audiences to applaud, not only between movements, but *during* movements when they heard something that they liked. Chris would talk about the risk of improvisation. When we performed, say, at Lincoln Center in New York, and we got to the moment where the cadenza should begin, the silence in that room – the concentration, the sense of expectation – was extraordinary. When I got to the end of it, you could hear the audience exhale: somehow I had shot the crossbow from one side of the valley to the other, and walked across it and actually survived to tell the tale.

Hogwood and the AAM were once more thinking big and living dangerously. Their relationship with Decca had survived Wadland's death, and if the AAM's place in the wider musical landscape was not what it had been, a clearer sense of the group's long-term needs was beginning to emerge. The Haydn cycle was making good progress and the Mozart series would move steadily forward throughout the 1990s at the rate of a disc a year. There was no reason to suppose, in the mid-1990s, that Christopher Hogwood and the Academy of Ancient Music would not see either of them completed.

8

BUILDING TO LAST

Simon Standage is self-deprecating about his four years as Associate
Director of the Academy of Ancient Music. He'd first played with
Christopher Hogwood while still in his teens, he'd been there in 1973
at the inaugural Arne sessions and although he dropped in and out of
the AAM violin roster throughout the 1980s, he was best known as the
leader of his own period-instrument Salomon Quartet, and of another
orchestra: Trevor Pinnock's The English Concert. From the leader's seat
he had noticed the accelerating drift of the early-music movement away
from the baroque repertoire that had initially fired his enthusiasm. In 1989
he recorded Vivaldi's Op. 9 concertos with the AAM, and in the summer
of 1990 he teamed up with Hogwood and the AAM again for a set of
Mozart violin concertos – the first on period instruments. *Gramophone* was
enchanted: 'His pure, slender tone (with vibrato reserved only for specific
expressive effect), delicate, precise articulation and rhythmic subtlety make
for fresh and inspiriting performances of music that has so often been
drenched in an excess of opulence and sophistication.'[1]

That same year, with the conductor Richard Hickox, Standage
founded his own ensemble, Collegium Musicum 90 – a bid to recapture
the small-scale spirit of the 1970s early-music scene. 'I started CM 90
because as the early-music movement moved forward in time, increasingly
it became like orchestral playing again. The attraction of baroque music
is that it was chamber music – one player to a part, largely,' he says. 'And
then Chris asked me to be Associate Director of the AAM. I imagine
it was because he wanted somebody to do the concerts that he was not
going to do, because he'd got something better.'

By now, Hogwood's international conducting career was on full thrust. The Los Angeles Philharmonic, the Chicago Symphony, New York's Mostly Mozart Festival, the Accademia Nazionale di Santa Cecilia (Rome), the Lausanne Chamber Orchestra, the Paris Opera, Sydney Opera House, the Czech Philharmonic – these were engagements to excite any conductor, in addition to Hogwood's standing commitments to the AAM, the Handel and Haydn Society, the Saint Paul's Chamber Orchestra (from 1987 to 1998) and the Australian Chamber Orchestra (1989–1993). Looked at from Hogwood's perspective, the logic of sharing the direction of the AAM with a skilled and seasoned colleague – one whose enthusiasms lay, moreover, with the kind of repertoire for which Hogwood and Decca had increasingly little time – made perfect sense.

It also opened out an early vision of a possible future. In January 1993, Standage and the AAM recorded a disc of symphonies by Johann Christian Bach for the independent label Chandos. Decca's relationship with the AAM was primarily a relationship with and through Hogwood. The Chandos partnership spluttered, but it was a first acknowledgement of a future in which the AAM might no longer be a Decca house band. More significantly, this was the first time in the history of the AAM (other than the temporary, project-based relationships with Simon Preston and Jaap Schröder) that anyone other than Hogwood had held an official artistic leadership position with the AAM. It was the first serious intimation that there might some day be an Academy of Ancient Music without Christopher Hogwood.

Not yet, though. If Hogwood was starting to contemplate his own exit strategy, he seems to have decided that Standage was not the solution to that particular problem. As Standage recalls:

> It was hoped that the Academy could continue recording for Chandos, but it didn't come to fruition for a variety of reasons. That was just about the time when the record industry was starting to shrink. So, unfortunately, that didn't go any further. I directed various concerts in Europe and an American trip. But I was increasingly involved in CM 90, and I dare say I was not going to be the person to step in to even one pair of Chris's shoes.

Standage served as Associate Director of the Academy of Ancient Music until 1995, when Hogwood – with characteristic courtesy and tact – quietly drew the line:

> He came to a concert I was playing at in Cambridge, then invited us round to his house in Claremont. I said to my wife, 'I think I'm going to get the sack.' In my experience, sackings are usually shirked or done brutally. But not in Chris's case. He did it very nicely, and I absolutely accepted it. I'd known Chris for a long time, and he was always a friend.

Not all partings were quite so amicable. Accounts differ of the break between Hogwood and his long-term agent Jasper Parrott. Heather Jarman was now working as Hogwood's personal manager from a rented house at 11 Brookside, Cambridge – directly adjacent to Hogwood's own newly bought home at No. 10. She recalls a growing sense that the agency was letting the AAM's affairs slide. 'I got quite fed up with them because the accounts were a mess. Jasper's one of these big-picture people and he always said that I couldn't see the wood for the trees. But Jasper sold only the wood, never the trees – I was the one who was checking up on those,' she says. Parrott remembers it as a case of Hogwood and the AAM failing to appreciate the full extent of HarrisonParrott's work on their behalf, with finances as the flashpoint:

> We had a good understanding for very many years. And then, sadly and unnecessarily, there came a moment when Chris's big master recording contract with Decca had run out or was near to running out. We were fully authorised to renegotiate it, and we had negotiated a great contract renewal, complete in every detail. But it needed Chris to sign off on it and, very sadly, Chris decided that he wanted to cut us out so that he would save the commission on the next three years of the contract. In retrospect, it was the most foolish thing he ever did, because it was just at the cusp of the decline of sales in the classical-recording business. He delayed. He did not sign off, and during that period of two or three months Decca reviewed all of its business and cancelled the contract.

And so he lost – and the Academy lost – the substance of the next three years of support for their big projects. It's a very sad story, after all of the incredibly good years. In the end we got into a legal conflict. It went pretty much up to the line, and then Chris's lawyers advised him to settle on what was, to me, a financially acceptable basis. But what was left of the contract was a fraction of what was originally arranged, and it broke the relationship completely. I'm not even sure that he and I ever spoke again.

The ending of a three-decade professional and personal relationship will have been distressing enough, but it reaffirmed two increasingly urgent truths. Post-Wadland, a long-term relationship with Decca – the central constant of the AAM's commercial existence up to this point – could no longer be relied on. And the AAM urgently needed to establish a permanent organisational structure in its own right: a concrete artistic and administrative footing that would shockproof it against a changing musical marketplace and the potential future absence of Christopher Hogwood.

'I don't like what the players rudely call the "owner-directed orchestra" syndrome,' he told *Early Music Quarterly*.[2] Standage's associate directorship had been a first step towards diversifying the AAM's top table. Now, in January 1996, it was announced that the AAM would have not one, but three artistic leaders. Hogwood was to be joined by the oboist Paul Goodwin as Associate Conductor, and the virtuoso baroque violinist Andrew Manze as Associate Director and Concertmaster for an initial term of three years. *Gramophone* magazine promptly dubbed the new team 'the triumvirate'.[3] Goodwin remembers the moment:

'Chris was thinking, well, now what is best for the orchestra? I've been doing this for a long time. There are these young people coming up. What would help the development of the orchestra would be to get other people involved in it. So how's the best way to do that?' Goodwin was thirty-nine and had been playing with the AAM since the *Fireworks Music* sessions in 1981 – one of the young freelance players who'd been called in to make up the numbers back in those days of improvisation and stretched resources. He'd studied with Nikolaus Harnoncourt's oboist Jürg Schaeftlein as well as the great Swiss virtuoso and composer Heinz Holliger, and by the early 1990s he had performed across the British and European early-music scene, working with Gustav Leonhardt, Sigiswald

Kuijken, Frans Brüggen, John Eliot Gardiner and Trevor Pinnock as well as playing as principal oboe on Norrington's Beethoven symphony recordings. Goodwin had been directing ensembles since his student days, and by the mid-1990s he had decided that conducting was his future. Hogwood was sympathetic.

> I'd always had a close relationship with him, and we'd spent quite a lot of time together. Chris was always very generous towards me, not just as an oboe player, but also as a quasi-academic and as a conductor. Throughout his life, when he couldn't do something, he would always come to me, because he knew that I would be a good caretaker, and that I wouldn't oust him – I would help him out. That happened on a number of occasions, and it worked very well. So he invited me to conduct the orchestra in various things.
>
> I'm an all-or-nothing person, so I decided to give up the oboe and study conducting: I wanted to do it properly. I arranged to have end-of-term concerts with the various orchestras: I played a whole lot of concertos at The English Concert, gave my last concert with Roger Norrington, and stopped, just like that, and went off and studied conducting in Helsinki. And while I was there, Chris asked me to direct the orchestra. I remember having dinner with him and his partner Tony Fabian at their home in Cambridge – Tony was a fantastic cook – and it was at one of those that he said, 'Look, I'd like to have you have a position.'

Andrew Manze remembers that 'Christopher approached us and told Paul that he either had to start his own orchestra or take over someone else's. "Why not have mine?" he suggested.' His own appointment, he believes, had a pragmatic aspect: 'Christopher wanted to have a violinist closely associated with the orchestra in order to get the strings more unified.'[4] Manze, at thirty-one, commanded the respect and excited the enthusiasm of players, audience and critics – who'd christened him 'the baroque terrorist' for his wildly inventive, fearlessly virtuosic playing. Like Hogwood, he'd studied Classics at Cambridge – Clare College – though he was initially interested in contemporary music. Simon Standage taught him baroque violin at the Royal Academy of Music: 'It was the first time anybody had come with a piece of Berlioz to a baroque violin lesson,' remembers Standage.

Never a natural rank-and-file player, Manze had led Ton Koopman's Amsterdam Baroque Orchestra and since 1989 had made occasional guest appearances as leader of the AAM, including their 1995–6 recording (with Cecilia Bartoli) of Haydn's opera *L'anima del filosofo*. If Hogwood was looking for a fresh and inspiring new face in early music, it was sitting directly next to him in the leader's seat. 'It was very much Chris's idea,' says Manze:

> Chris was always on the lookout for someone to share the Academy with, with a view one day to passing it on. I wasn't by any means the first. I believe he had been in conversation a long time ago with Robert King, but nothing came of that. I even heard rumours of Hogwood talking to Reinhard Goebel.

Goebel, who had founded Musica Antiqua Köln, was nicknamed 'the ayatollah of the baroque' for his uncompromising scholarly and interpretative rigour. Manze observed the near miss.

> I remember going to a concert at St James's, Piccadilly, in the London Festival of Baroque Music, where Reinhard Goebel brought his ensemble from Germany and played Brandenburg Concertos at breakneck speed. Chris was in the second row there, the idea being that he would speak to Goebel. Maybe they did talk, but I think they realised they didn't really sit very well together.

'It's fair to say that Chris Hogwood was never a megalomaniac in the sense of wanting his own kingdom and wanting to be the supreme ruler,' says Manze. That was never a given in the early-music world. 'He was looking to share, and so he brought in me and Paul Goodwin, simply to be able to increase its viability – its future strength – by sharing the workload.' As Decca's interest in the Academy entered its terminal phase, Manze brought an existing relationship with another record label, the early-music specialists Harmonia Mundi. Christopher Lawrence, who became the AAM's General Manager in 1997, appraised the situation on his arrival: 'You'd have Paul doing the choral and vocal stuff. You'd have

Andrew doing the violin-directed baroque stuff. And Chris might do the bigger opera projects,' he remembers.

The establishment of the AAM's artistic triumvirate was a statement of creative intent. Both Goodwin and Manze belonged to a younger generation than the fifty-four-year-old Hogwood. And each had a specialism that, taken together with Hogwood's interests, would enable the AAM to advance across a range of artistic fronts as it headed towards the day – now dimly visible on the horizon – when Hogwood would take a major decision about his own future and, by implication, the future of his orchestra.

New Foundations

It's difficult today to grasp just how dependent on Christopher Hogwood the Academy of Ancient Music had been, and for how long. Obviously, he was the group's artistic leader and the face of its international brand. But it went deeper. The orchestra's management had been handled by HarrisonParrott as an extension of its relationship with Hogwood. The Decca contract had been with Hogwood, not with the AAM; he, not the orchestra, received the royalties. Day-to-day administration had been handled by Jarman and a handful of freelance assistants (principally, since Hughes's departure, the horn player Christian Rutherford, who rented a house near Hogwood's on Brookside in Cambridge and was paid to book and organise players on an ad hoc basis). The Academy had been run, effectively, as an extension of Hogwood's personal diary.

There was no agenda in play, because there was no real plan at all. Few early-music owner-conductors have been less like the 'robber baron' of band-room gossip than Hogwood; in fact, it had seemed at times as if there was no upper limit to how much of his income the AAM might devour, if permitted. The AAM's rise had been so swift and its subsequent career had been so busy that no one had any time (or any great motivation) to set its management on a more formal footing. It was simply how things had evolved and how – crises apart – they had more or less successfully functioned. But it was no foundation for a future. In 1997, the AAM advertised for and appointed a general manager – the first salaried, full-time executive on the orchestra's (as opposed to Hogwood's or HarrisonParrott's) payroll. Christopher Lawrence – a Cambridge Classics graduate and keen tuba player, then working as a business manager at the BBC Symphony Orchestra – got the job through a characteristically Hogwoodian process.

'Paul Goodwin was a personal friend,' says Lawrence.

He alerted me to the vacancy and I jumped at it. I remember being interviewed in Chris Hogwood's house by Heather Jarman. For some reason I had to sit in a rocking chair, so I did the interview at a funny angle. It was a panel of Heather! Chris trusted her completely. Anyway, having passed the Heather test I was lined up to meet Chris. There was a recording session in London the following week at Henry Wood Hall – Mozart piano concertos with Robert Levin – and it was arranged that I would meet him there. I introduced myself as we were queuing up for food in the canteen, and Chris turned to Robert and said, 'Oh, meet Chris Lawrence. He's the new General Manager of the Academy of Ancient Music.' So that was my interview.

'My musical knowledge started with the invention of the tuba, which is 1835 – so my repertoire was Berlioz onwards. Whereas some parents might take their children to a Mozart *Requiem* early on, my very first concert had been *The Rite of Spring* and my first opera was *Lulu*.' Lawrence's on-the-job education in the ways of early music would be speedy and comprehensive. An even more pressing priority, however, was governance. The search for knowledgeable and supportive advisers brought Hogwood into contact with Christopher Purvis – though the introduction, in a manner of speaking, came via another old friend, one George Frideric Handel. 'At that point I was just leaving my career as a banker at Warburg's,' says Purvis. 'Stanley Sadie had this long-standing dream of making 25 Brook Street [Handel's former London residence] into a museum. In the early to mid-1990s, he formed a charitable trust and persuaded various great and good to join him on the Board.' Purvis was recruited in 1996 via a mutual business acquaintance.

So I joined the Board and I found Christopher Hogwood was one of the trustees. Cutting to the chase, he and I found ourselves agreeing on a lot of things. He was a very practical man. He didn't mince words, and he didn't like things that drifted, and the Handel House project was drifting. So Hogwood and I got to know each other, and we began to talk about the Academy of

Ancient Music. He just wasn't sure what to do about it: founded in 1973, and here we were, twenty-five years later.

We began to talk. My recollection of our conversations runs along the following lines: I said to him, there are three things that you can do, and two of them are respectable and one is not. The non-respectable one – the one that you absolutely mustn't do – is not make a decision, and to let the bloody thing drift. So you have two choices. You can kill it off. At that point the AAM had quite a meaningful amount of reserves – I seem to recall there was £200,000 in the bank – so we can take those reserves, we'll book the Festival Hall, we'll invite all our friends of the last twenty-five years, we'll have the most marvellous concert, and we'll say, 'We've done it, and now having taught everybody else how to do it, we don't need to be blazing the trail any longer.' And we go out with a blaze of glory and that would be absolutely fine.

I'm a great believer that organisations of any kind need to stop – let's say every five years – and say to themselves, 'Do I still need to exist? And, if so, do I need to exist in my present shape, or do I need to change?'

Hogwood, it became clear, wanted his creation to live on.

Notwithstanding his pragmatism, he also had a soft spot for the concept of the Academy of Ancient Music and a soft spot for its players. But I like to think – and possibly this is wishful thinking on my part – that he and I between us had developed the thought that there was more to be done. In a funny sort of way he had been getting there himself. The idea of diversifying away from Hogwood was very much alive already, but we decided that we needed to take that step, because simultaneously the whole business model was changing.

We were at the end of that great era when record companies had money and actually paid you to do things. And we were also at the end of the time when people would ring up and say, 'Will you come and do a tour of America and we'll pay you zillions of dollars?' And you do the Brandenburgs every night for thirty nights and you fill your coffers for the next year. Two factors were going on here: the change in business climate for orchestras, and the change of Hogwood's own ambitions, his move to Martinů.

Hogwood's guest-conducting interests were starting to draw him away from the AAM's core repertoire – towards Elgar, Stravinsky and the Czech tradition.

The AAM was incorporated as a registered charity on 17 November 2000, its stated objectives, 'To advance the education of the public in the art of baroque and early-classical music and the allied arts'. It was a practical decision. Charitable status greatly simplified the process of soliciting donations – unthinkable and unnecessary in the profitable boom years of the Decca contract, but now essential to the orchestra's long-term survival.

'Up until then, the Academy of Ancient Music was not a charity – it was a for-profit company of which I think Christopher was the only shareholder,' recalls Purvis. 'In a nutshell we were trying to institutionalise ourselves – to take the AAM away from being just Hogwood, or even just Hogwood and Jarman and Lawrence – and making it an institution, which meant getting a Board, getting people to give money, and building up a group of supporters so that there would be life after Hogwood.' Lawrence recalls that it was all done 'with Chris's absolute blessing and encouragement'. Purvis was by now fully on Board; as Chairman, he would head the newly constituted charity until 2013.

A plan was taking shape; Lawrence's task was to make it work. The first step was to spread the gospel of the triumvirate. 'There was a hell of a lot of work for me to do, to persuade promoters around the world that the AAM appearing without Chris Hogwood was a valid concept,' he recalls. The second task – which went hand in hand with the first – was to build a viable calendar of events for the AAM in the UK.

I said to the players, 'OK, I've arrived. Tell me what I need to know, tell me what you want from me.' And they said, 'We want as much work as possible.' The brass players said, 'We want more classical rep. There's too much baroque stuff. We want bigger bands.' But there were also some really important messages: 'We would love to do some concerts in the UK.' I remember counting and finding that in the previous year, over 90 per cent of the concerts had been abroad. These are musicians that live in the UK. They've got families in the UK, they'd have their rehearsals in London, but then they'd practically be living at Heathrow.

There was no concert series in the UK, and there were, in fact, very few concerts in the UK, full stop. There was a time when the AAM was so busy with recordings and foreign touring that no one really thought there was a need to start getting UK appearances as a priority. But as I arrived, Japanese touring was starting to slow down – Japan had been a very big market, but the Japanese economy had gone in the wrong direction. There had been an American tour, possibly the last under HarrisonParrott, that had not quite washed its face. So, there were cracks starting to appear in foreign touring. And there were cracks starting to appear in the future of recording as well.

To Hogwood's lasting distress, Decca cancelled the Haydn symphony series, incomplete, in 2000. Lawrence recalls 'difficult conversations'. 'Chris had been quite canny in leaving many of the later symphonies to the end – which is where they might have started to sell more,' recalls Lawrence. The cycle never got that far: 'I managed to get two unreleased symphonies released on a *BBC Music Magazine* CD, as a freebie, just to remind the world.' Decca's interest in making new recordings with the AAM ended altogether after 2002. The Lyrebird had sung its swansong.

Instead, Lawrence continued to lay the foundations for the AAM to thrive in the concert hall. One opportunity seemed like an open goal.

I arrived in 1997, and the AAM was about to have its twenty-fifth anniversary in 1998, but there was nothing planned at all. So, I wanted to establish two things early on. First: there's this new triumvirate running the AAM, and also, we do appear in the UK occasionally! It happened that, in 1998, we had a booking at the City of London Festival conducted by Paul Goodwin, a concert in the York Early Music Festival, directed by Andrew, and Chris appearing at the Proms. So, I retrospectively made that look like it was planned. And I produced a little postcard with pictures of the three conductors. My market for this message was the profession, not the public – this went out in every copy of *Classical*

Music magazine. The message was: the AAM exists, it has got three people directing it, and it's doing some concerts in the UK.

Then I thought: right, we need to do something to mark the twenty-fifth anniversary. So we promoted a concert at St John's Smith Square. It was on 19 April 1999, so it was in the 1998–99 season. [The question of whether the AAM's age should be dated from the 1973 Arne recording session, or the first public concert in 1974, was discreetly fudged.] The whole musicological/ historical aspect of Chris's approach to the AAM meant that he collected historic programmes from the early eighteenth century. We decided to combine with the Coram Foundation, which used to be the Foundling Hospital, because Handel had done a concert for the Foundling Hospital on 10 May 1749. So, 250 years to within a month of that concert, we got in the choir of New College, Oxford, and replicated the whole programme. In fact, for the programme book we actually just reprinted the original eighteenth-century listing.

It was exactly the kind of project to reignite Hogwood's enthusiasm: a playful, historically faithful reminder of the AAM's connection to its eighteenth-century predecessor. That heritage had been on Hogwood's mind: a few months earlier he'd edited, and the AAM had published, a modern edition of Sir John Hawkins's 1770 *An Account of the Institution and Progress of the Academy of Ancient Music*. The twenty-fifth anniversary concert included excerpts from *Solomon*, the *Fireworks Music* and the *Foundling Hospital Anthem*, the work whose premiere in 1749 had cemented the iconic status of the 'Hallelujah' chorus (Handel, in one of his more inspired moments of self-plagiarism, had lifted it from *Messiah* and incorporated it into the new work). 'There's a general tendency to laugh gently when people see an eighteenth- or nineteenth-century programme, the same way people laugh when they look at an eighteenth- or nineteenth-century cookbook,' Hogwood told *Early Music Quarterly*. 'I find myself very bored by many modern concerts. It's not because it's a historical recipe; we do it because it actually works.'[5]

'And so that was the AAM promoting its first concert in recent memory,' says Christopher Lawrence. It worked: a spate of newspapers and musical magazines ran features and interviews on the Academy's twenty-fifth anniversary, with Hogwood taking pains to mention the tri-umvirate and the new artistic direction. Lawrence surfed the momentum:

I decided to start a London series at St John's Smith Square. It's a lovely building and it's really appropriate for a lot of the repertoire the AAM does. But back then it was no good at marketing, so we had to do our own thing. The very first concert season that I promoted in London, in 2000–2001, had three concerts: one by Andrew, one by Chris and one by Paul, which was another way – again – of emphasising the trio. Andrew's concert was Handel, Bach, Purcell, Wassenaer and Geminiani. Chris's was an all-Mozart programme. And Paul's was J. S. Bach, C. P. E. Bach and Telemann – but also a piece by David Bedford, because we'd started commissioning new works for old instruments. So our 2000–2001 season at St John's Smith Square had a princely three concerts. But for an organisation that had no staff, no sponsors and no history of promoting, even that was quite a big step forwards.

We decided to come back to St John's the following year, with a more colourful brochure, and slightly more concerts – we went from three to five. We began with Andrew Manze direct-ing Locatelli, Corelli and Vivaldi. Then the second one was Chris Hogwood, in December, doing the Bach *Magnificat* with Christmas interpolations. By this time, Chris was already saying, 'I will never, ever conduct *Messiah* again.' He was happy for the AAM to do *Messiah*s, but not with him. The third concert was Paul conducting a baroque programme, with arias for soprano and tenor. Then there was another Chris Hogwood one with Robert Levin: Mozart with Levin improvisations. And finally a chamber programme at the end, led by Andrew doing Tartini and Locatelli.

We'd worked out how to promote concerts by this point. So, for the 2002–3 season, we continued in London at St John's, but I was also thinking about how to make the AAM appear in the UK more. Here was an orchestra that everyone had heard of: it was on Classic FM several times a day. But the opportunities for British listeners to hear the world-famous Academy of Ancient Music in their own country had been very limited. So there was a PR rationale to that: an out-of-sight-out-of-mind issue that I needed to address. We could have just focused on London for promotions, but in London, there was The English Concert, the King's Consort, the English Baroque Soloists, and so on. None of those had a base outside London. Chris had lived in Cambridge forever, the office was in Cambridge, I was living in Cambridge. I knew the Cambridge musical market, and I reckoned that there was an opportunity to start something at West Road Concert Hall, Cambridge.

Lawrence brokered a deal for a joint series with another Cambridge-based ensemble – the modern-instrument Britten Sinfonia. Its manager, David Butcher, was an old friend: 'I said, "I will, if you will," and he said, "I will, if you will." The Britten Sinfonia and the AAM both decided to establish concert series in Cambridge at the same time, and we co-marketed from a standing start.' Andrew Manze launched the Cambridge series on 7 October 2002. 'The concept was that these Cambridge concerts would always be a subset of the London concert series,' says Lawrence. 'So, if we were doing five in London, three of them would be repeated in Cambridge.' The twin concert series – London and Cambridge – established a pattern of self-promoted concerts that still forms the basis of the AAM's annual planning, allowing artistic and commercial growth from a twofold base. Not every initiative succeeded. An attempt to launch a third new series, in Norwich, survived for only three concerts between October 2004 and March 2005.

It did, however, form part of a tour that brought the great Japanese Bach specialist Masaaki Suzuki to the UK for the first time. 'It somehow came as a shock to see this fifty-year-old conductor mounting the platform of St John's on his British debut tour and looking, well, exactly like his photographs. Compact build, immaculate white hair, bouncing down like waterfalls towards the shoulders,' wrote Geoff Brown in *The Times*, when the programme was repeated in London. He noted that 'this venerable group' seemed 'stocked with youngish players' and concluded that this

was among the daintiest period-instrument Bach performances these ears had ever heard: no heavy accenting, no raw edge, a bantam-weight sound and dynamic. The minuet movement saw Suzuki's subtlest interpretative touch, with the middle section despatched by the AAM in a quiet honeyed legato, gorgeous to hear.[6]

Here was a refreshed-sounding AAM that was capable of springing surprises and setting the agenda even without Hogwood or his fellow triumvirs. As the group marked its thirtieth anniversary in 2003, Lawrence was able to note, with some satisfaction, that the ratio of overseas to UK concerts in the AAM's diary had shifted from around 90:10 in 1997 to something closer to 60:40. The AAM's emergence as a UK concert promoter did carry an increased element of financial risk – it's a truth, universally acknowledged, that classical concerts do not make money – and here, too, Lawrence started to build. In the autumn of 2000, for the first time in the group's history, the AAM applied for and was granted a subsidy from the Arts Council of England (ACE)'s National Touring Programme: a one-off £27,000 grant to support a six-concert tour with Paul Goodwin in March 2001.

Several more would follow, though never (in Lawrence's time), a regular revenue grant. 'It irked me that we weren't able to access any core Arts Council funding. And there's my best mate, David Butcher, running the Britten Sinfonia – also in Cambridge – and getting maybe £400,000 a year.' Arts Council funding, however, can represent a Faustian pact for an ambitious and independent arts organisation. The ACE's bureaucracy could have been designed by Kafka: the mere process of applying for funds (and later, compiling, reporting and – where necessary – fudging statistics on how the funds have been used) can impose a punishing burden on an organisation that carries no excess fat. Long-term recipients of ACE cash often become dependent on subsidy, and face insolvency or extinction when – in response to some new shift of the political wind – those funds are slashed or withdrawn outright. The Academy has always had a clear sense of its artistic purpose, and has prized its autonomy. If it was to rely on any external funders, Lawrence preferred it to lean on its most committed friends.

'Very early on, Heather Jarman and I established the Academy of Ancient Music Society. This was our group of well-to-do individuals who wanted to support the AAM.' Jarman had previously established a Friends organisation for the AAM in the early 1980s. It had foundered in the choppy waters surrounding the establishment of the Orchestra of the Age of Enlightenment in 1985–6. This time, explains Lawrence, they built to last:

> The moment the AAM went from being Chris's private company to being a charity, the concept of charitable giving and gift aid became a possibility. Because the AAM had never really been doing many concerts in the UK, there had been no supporter base. But the setting up of a London and Cambridge concert series created a sort of virtuous circle: we'll put on concerts and drinks receptions for you to come to, but we need your money to make it happen. There are a lot of people who really enjoy the close association with the group, who feel they know the players, who will come to the pre-concert talks and receptions, and even follow them abroad or come and sit in on a recording session. The Academy of Ancient Music Society has been a real success story for the AAM.

That the AAM was able to make that transition – from raising almost no funding on its own account prior to 2000, to a proficient and highly effective fundraising operation less than a decade later – was an object lesson in the value of making and cherishing friends. 'Unlike the major London orchestras the funding did not come from corporates,' recalls Christopher Purvis. 'It came mainly from private individuals: an amazing group of people who gave generous support.' By 2011 one-third of the AAM's annual expenditure – some £360,000 – was covered by donated income. 'People from other arts organisations used to come and ask me what the secret was,' says Purvis. 'Well, the secret was that between us all – including and especially Chris Hogwood, as well as Heather Jarman, Chris Lawrence and successive CEOs – we developed this sense of an AAM family to which donors were committed. They were first and foremost loyal friends – and they gave significant money.'

Lawrence recalls,

> The two things went hand in hand: building up of a financial support base, combined with the promotion of concerts in two centres, London and Cambridge. Because we were still doing fully funded foreign tours, we'd rehearse in London, we'd go on tour,

and we'd come back and do a concert in London for which all the set-up and rehearsal costs had been covered by the tour. And so therefore the costs on the day of the London concert were one fee per musician, plus marketing and venue hire, plus the costs of keeping our donors engaged. If it was a Chris thing, we would pay him a rock-bottom fee – one of his personal ways of supporting the AAM was to conduct for something like a quarter of his normal rate. And Andrew and Paul would always be very flexible. They understood that our promotions in London and Cambridge were wafer-thin financially.

The art – as usual in the classical music world – was to convey an image of trouble-free assurance and quality on a break-even budget.

We'd always produce very glossy programme books for London and Cambridge, and I gave them out for free. I wanted the people who came to these concerts to leave these nice programmes on their coffee tables at home. And when their mates came round, they'd say, 'Oh, what's that?' I wanted the association to be with something successful and classy.

And so the AAM, belatedly, but always on the most realistic of financial assumptions, transformed itself into an autonomous entity and equipped itself for a future without a constant stream of Decca recordings, without endless and lucrative overseas tours and (it was increasingly obvious) without the permanent leadership of Christopher Hogwood. Lawrence hired a pocket-sized team of staff: Fiona Seers – 'she doubled up as tour manager, librarian, all sorts of things' – and, as an orchestral fixer, the bassoonist Noel Rainbird. Lawrence's management team eventually expanded to (but never exceeded) four people.

Reaffirming a historic AAM strength, new recording and concert partnerships were forged with the two pre-eminent Oxbridge chapel choirs: Stephen Cleobury's Choir of King's College, Cambridge, and Edward Higginbottom's Choir of New College, Oxford. Rather than gamble sparse resources on a loss-making in-house record label, Lawrence sought to nurture the new partnership with Harmonia Mundi – which, unlike Decca, paid royalties directly to the orchestra, rather than its director. For things to stay the same, they have to change and if the future of the Academy of Ancient Music was starting to look very different from its past, it was for the best of reasons. Belatedly, but determinedly, the orchestra was laying the foundations for long-term survival.

9

TRIUMVIRATE AND SUCCESSION

Christopher Hogwood's 1999 recording of Handel's *Rinaldo* was the last hurrah of the long relationship with Decca. Produced by Chris Sayers and recorded in Henry Wood Hall, London, in November 1999, it was the final AAM–Decca project in the grand Wadland manner: a full-length Handel opera with a superstar diva, the flamboyant Italian mezzo Cecilia Bartoli, heading a cast that included the tenor Mark Padmore, the bass Gerald Finley, soprano Catherine Bott and in the title role (on loan from Virgin Classics for what was unarguably a prestige project) the fast-rising American countertenor David Daniels. Sayers, in the great tradition of Decca opera recordings, went all out to create theatrical atmosphere: mixing live birdsong into Act Two and adding thunder courtesy of the eighteenth-century thunder machine from the baroque theatre at Drottningholm, Sweden. *Gramophone* magazine found it 'irresistible': 'For all-round standard of performance and production it currently wins hands down. This is an important Handel recording, and it will take some beating.'[1]

Another creative force was present in the *Rinaldo* sessions. In his new capacity as concertmaster, Andrew Manze was at the front of the violins, bringing an energy that was entirely his own. 'We did it over two projects,' he recalls, 'meaning we met and did some concerts, and then we met and did some more concerts, and then we recorded it. So the recording – for once – was the end product of about seven performances.' Two performances took place at the Barbican, London, in the week of the first recording session on 17 November 1999. Audience members queued for returned tickets, and Edward Seckerson, reviewing for the *Independent*, noticed the new interpretative dynamic:

Resourceful playing from the Academy of Ancient Music gave full rein to Handel's elaborate orchestral effects from airy birdsong to martial trumpets (four of them upstanding) and drums, though I could not help but think that the amazing Andrew Manze, leading very much from the front, generated more energy from his body language and thrilling violin pyrotechnics than anything communicated by the conductor Christopher Hogwood.[2]

Manze's extraordinary creative dynamism – and by implication, the contrast with Hogwood's transparent, carefully rationalised precision – was impossible to ignore during his time with the AAM.

'He was one of the great violinists of all time, and the great musicians of all time,' says Richard Egarr, who had begun a close musical friendship with Manze during their time together as students at Clare College, Cambridge. 'He brought a sense of freedom and inspiration, particularly to the string players, which has hardly ever been equalled.' 'He was totally amazing,' says the oboist Lars Henriksson. 'He had such energy, and such dynamism. You could look out in the audience and see that people were just sitting on the edge of their chairs. He had that quality.'

For flautist Rachel Brown,

There's a lot to be said for people directing from the violin. That's not to say it's not good when they conduct, but it's a different dynamic when they're actually involved, and you're committing to their sound as well. I loved that with Andrew. I've done hundreds of performances of Bach's B minor Suite, many of them with lovely people, but I remember one particular one with Andrew Manze where there was such a degree of spontaneity between us that something special really happened. There were things that happened that we never discussed – that happened because we were on a different level of communication. That was absolutely wonderful.

It's impossible to escape the conclusion that artistically, Hogwood and Manze were polar opposites – mutually respectful colleagues but completely different musical animals. The contrast was relished by the players. For Manze, though, the *Rinaldo* sessions, coming at the end of a thrilling series of concerts, simply reaffirmed their temperamental difference.

After seven performances, a piece has evolved. You've developed things which you cannot put into words, but it's achieved a depth. And then – this is a rather sad story – when we came into the studio to record it, I felt that Chris then undid all the good things that seven performances had given us, and took it back to its pristine, pre-performance state. I was rather disappointed at that – that he didn't carry on with what we'd achieved in those seven performances; where they had taken us. He didn't take it on to the next stage. He rather undid all those things that had developed. He wasn't comfortable with them.

I liked Chris very much and I am very grateful to him. I owe him a lot. But there were some things about his attitude that I didn't really agree with. For example, he told me with great pride that by lunchtime on the very first day the Academy ever sat down together, they'd finished recording a symphony.

Hogwood was remembering – possibly through the rosy lens of memory – the inaugural Arne sessions, back in 1973.

He was very proud of this fact, and I was a young idealist to whom the idea of sitting down with people you've never met, most of whom had never played their instruments before, and by lunchtime, making a recording . . . well, that was awful to me, just awful. I'd be ashamed of that attitude. When I became Associate Director of the Academy of Ancient Music, I already had contacts with Harmonia Mundi and because of the reputation of English players – that London freelance scene, just throwing recordings together – the lady at Harmonia Mundi's Los Angeles office, Robina Young, said to me, 'I want to do recordings with you, but I want you to show me, orchestrally, that you have performed all the music you record for us, and I want to see the orchestra lists, so that I can see that they're the same as the people recording it.'

She wanted to know that what she was being given was something that really existed, and wasn't just being thrown together. Of course, they're American, and for them, time is money in recording terms. I think it was the best thing that Harmonia Mundi did for the Academy. They made the Academy much more responsible for its end product, and said, 'Look: be an orchestra, stick with the same players, raise the standards, and make each concert the stepping stone to the next concert, so you can build on quality.' I think we did, and I think it was quite an important change.

If Manze's concerts with the orchestra set both players and audiences buzzing, the recordings that he made with the AAM for Harmonia Mundi were like a shot of adrenalin for the group's critical reputation. 'Andrew got to mould the string section he wanted, and they were very loyal to him in return,' says Christopher Lawrence. 'We had a very established and consistent string section under Andrew. So the more work I could give them, the more it would be the same set of players on the night.'

The results can be heard, at maximum spontaneity, in one of Manze's first discs with the AAM: Handel's Concerti grossi, Op. 6 (1998) recorded with a footloose and flamboyant team of thirteen players led by Manze from the fiddle in the acoustic of St John's Smith Square. Manze, wrote *BBC Music Magazine*, 'is irrepressible. His imagination, puckish wit and total absorption in the spirit of Handel is enthralling. He too omits wind, and also argues effectively for having no separate continuo instrument when soloists play alone: the textural contrasts with full orchestra are all the stronger. He plays constantly to the limits but, to my mind, never beyond them.'[3]

Later discs told colourful stories, playing to Manze's flair for the theatrical – an all-Vivaldi programme inspired by a concert given in Venice in 1740 in honour of the Prince of Poland (2002), and a musical 'Grand Tour' of Vivaldi, Bach, Handel and Geminiani (2002). 'These wild young things play Vivaldi like they're Italians – and a greater compliment I can't give,' wrote the German early-music magazine *Alte Musik Aktuell*; *BBC Music Magazine* spoke of 'a veritable pageant of colour'. Small ensembles and dazzling recordings made for good touring prospects too, and the AAM's Californian US touring agent David Rowe wasted no opportunity to promote a rejuvenated AAM under a director whom *BBC Music Magazine* described (in a review of Manze's 2003 release of Bach violin concertos with Rachel Podger) as 'the Grappelli of the baroque'. In 1998, Richard Taruskin himself admitted to being impressed by Manze's playing:

What early music has been needing even more urgently than other branches of classical music has been a new infusion of old-fashioned – truly old-fashioned – performerly values: not self-elimination but self-asserting, crowd-pleasing exhibition-ism and vulgarity, the kind for which Mozart was famous, and Handel, and Vivaldi . . . [Manze's] is the most convincing 'period performance' I have ever heard.[4]

While Manze liberated new realms of chamber-scale baroque perform-ance, Goodwin staked out his own, very different territory. 'Obviously I had my own ideas of projects I wanted to do,' he says. 'One of those was to sort out the choir.' An 'Academy of Ancient Music Chorus' had been con-vened on an ad hoc basis at various points over the years, most notably for the supersized Haydn *Creation* project. But it lacked any permanent form.

> Until I sorted it out, it was an amorphous group that Chris asked various fixers to assemble as required. And that worked very well when he was doing stuff with Simon Preston, or with Edward Higginbottom or Stephen Cleobury – these wonderful directors, with their fantastic university choirs. But when he needed to do a bigger project with singers, it was simply whoever happened to be around, and whoever the fixer had as their friend. I didn't think it was working very well, so therefore I wanted to form an elite choir.
>
> Which is what I did. I headhunted a small core group of sing-ers, which we toured with the earlier music. I used them when I needed choruses for later small-scale repertoire – Haydn or Mozart. And for bigger things, I used the same fixer and the same basic choir, and just added on.

Under Goodwin's direction, the Chorus would become a regular fea-ture of the AAM's BBC Proms appearances between 1999 and 2004. 'We did Handel's *Acis and Galatea* with a big choir and John Tomlinson singing Polyphemus from the rafters, which was wonderful.' That was in August 2001.

> And then we did a Biber project for the 300th anniversary of Biber's death in 2004. I don't know whether it had been done in this country before, but we did the *Missa Bruxellensis*, a much more interesting piece than the normal Biber masses that get done.

My other idea was to do earlier seventeenth-century music with the orchestra, because I felt that had been lacking. So I did Praetorius and Monteverdi: the *Vespers*, and the instrumental music, which I loved. I brought in sagbutts and cornetti. One of the things that stuck was this record of Schütz and Gabrieli Christmas music, which Harmonia Mundi thought was a nice commercial idea.

'The music is so satisfying, its range so admirable, as to make for compelling listening,' declared *Gramophone*.[5]

New Sounds for Old

One of Goodwin's projects was rather more startling – so startling, in fact, that for some observers it seemed to mock the entire basis of historically informed performance. Between 1999 and 2006, at Goodwin's instigation, the Academy of Ancient Music commissioned and premiered a series of new works from some of Britain's pre-eminent living composers. Ultra-modern music, in other words, written specifically and intentionally for the techniques and timbres of period instruments. The idea, on the surface, was radically counter-intuitive. For Goodwin, it was simply a matter of following his artistic instincts:

> I've always found in early music that the audiences were, if you like, anti-romantic audiences. They don't want to hear Puccini operas and *La traviata* but they're very happy to hear both early stuff and new stuff. And certainly a lot of the early pioneers of the early-music business – people like Tony Halstead, Tony Pay and myself – also played a lot of contemporary music. I'd always had a love of both ends of things and wanted to show the skills of early-music players, and also the timbres, which are so different to those of modern instruments. I discussed the idea with Chris Hogwood and he was very supportive. So I used my connections within the contemporary music world to commission a series of pieces for the AAM.

The first was *Eternity's Sunrise*, a setting of William Blake by John Tavener (1944–2013) – a leading figure in the late-1960s classical counterculture who had converted to Greek Orthodox Christianity and found a huge new audience for his music after his *Song for Athene* was performed at the funeral of Diana, Princess of Wales, in September 1997. 'I wanted to find someone who would have an obvious synergy with early music,' says Goodwin.

> I'd met John and we talked a lot about Purcell and Handel, and with his music being based on Gregorian chants and Greek myths and all the rest of it, it seemed like a clear way to bring early music and modern music together. I discussed it with his agent, Jill Graham – she was very enthusiastic – so I went over to his house and he said, 'OK, I'll have a think about it.'

'My first ideas for *Eternity's Sunrise* came to me in January 1997, soon after my father's death,' wrote Tavener.

> These ideas were taken up again in September the same year, in response to a commission from the Academy of Ancient Music, which happened soon after the death of Diana, Princess of Wales. There is no such thing as accident or coincidence, so I dedicated my piece to the memory of the Princess. The concept of solo soprano (representing earth) at ground level, handbells (representing the angels) at an intermediate position, and the main baroque ensemble at a high level (representing heaven) fitted exactly with the Blake text which I had decided to set . . . The music should be played with quiet joy, as a day of sunshine and calm, full of gentleness and radiance.[6]

Goodwin conducted the premiere at St Andrew's Church, Holborn, on 1 July 1998, with Patricia Rozario singing the solo soprano part. Tavener was taken with the Academy's sound, and the following year, Goodwin (with Manze leading the orchestra) recorded *Eternity's Sunrise* for Harmonia Mundi along with a sequence of Tavener works, none of which was originally conceived for historic instruments. Tavener, however, was eager to hear them performed with the Academy's uniquely transparent sonority, and this initial engagement with Goodwin and the Academy was only the first of several increasingly unexpected collaborations. The AAM recording of *Eternity's Sunrise* would find a global audience in 2006 when it was incorporated into the soundtrack of Alfonso Cuarón's blockbuster movie *Children of Men*.

Goodwin had adapted several other Tavener works for the Harmonia Mundi disc, so in the summer of 1999, when Tavener was approached to provide some suitably fantastic ritual music for the BBC's large-scale dramatisation of Mervyn Peake's *Gormenghast* – a Millennium project, and one of the most expensive and ambitious single drama series that the Corporation had ever produced – he enlisted Goodwin's help.

> Basically, he wasn't really interested in it, but he said, 'Why don't you do it for me, Paul?' I spoke to the producers of *Gormenghast* so I had an idea of what they were going to be doing. I wanted to create a secondary piece, if you like, that used early instruments and would fit in with *Gormenghast* – I was a fan of the Peake novels anyway. So I used John's existing music and went along to him and showed him what I was going to do and said, 'Look, can I use cornetti, and sagbutts doing trills and this, that and the other,' and he just said, 'OK, go for it.'

The creative decisions were all Goodwin's and the AAM's contributions took their place in the score representing ritual music from within the story's fantastic feudal world – an entirely different sound from Richard Rodney Bennett's main symphonic score.

The Academy's colours clearly intrigued Tavener. In 1999 he completed *Total Eclipse,* a 40-minute work for chorus, vocal soloists, solo saxophone – in this case, John Harle – assorted modern percussion instruments plus 'baroque orchestra' that was premiered by Goodwin and the Academy, with Edward Higginbottom's New College Choir, in St Paul's Cathedral on 20 June 2000. 'The music should be performed in a "petrified ecstasy",' commented Tavener. 'My use of period instruments is deliberate. I favour their more sober and hieratical sound. Also the combination with modern instruments, such as the saxophone, heightens the inner ritual of *metanoia* and the ikonic nature of the music.'[7]

By now, the relationship with Tavener was two way: players remember being intrigued and engaged by the rehearsals and recording sessions, and Tavener's taste for a post-session bottle of bubbly helped lubricate the partnership. Timpanist Benedict Hoffnung remembers that '[trumpeter] Dave Blackadder and I went to the pub opposite the Temple Church, where we were recording. We'd ordered a pint. And John Tavener came in and sat near us and ordered a bottle of champagne. We chatted to him – he certainly didn't offer us any champagne, though.' Blackadder was more fortunate: having had to rush to reach the AAM's *Rinaldo* sessions after playing the shofar in Tavener's *Fall and Resurrection*, Tavener 'suddenly turned up at another recording with a bottle of champagne for me, which was really nice of him'.

The Tavener projects were only the first of Goodwin's new-music commissions – although it's fair to say that no later collaboration would prove quite as close, or as fruitful. *Like a Strand of Scarlet* by David Bedford (1937–2011) was premiered in March 2001 and taken on a six-date national tour. 'I've always loved David's music since playing his more galactic pieces in youth orchestra,' recalls Goodwin.

> He was the most modest, sweet man and very knowledgeable about the early-music world, so he was absolutely thrilled. My idea was to have a piece that could go in a programme with the Bach oboe and violin concerto. Because it was an anniversary of Schütz, he wrote the piece using Schütz themes, but with orchestration for solo oboe, solo violin and strings. It has the most exquisite slow movement – very reminiscent of the Bach slow movement – so I put it in programmes with that, partly because I wanted to use Frank de Bruine playing the oboe. I love his playing. Pauline Nobes played the violin. And, once again, David was happy to come along to rehearsals and to adapt it to what worked. To this day I think it's a fantastic piece.

Fiona Maddocks, reviewing for the *Observer*, heard 'a refuelled verve'[8] in the AAM's performance.

The next commission, premiered on 1 March 2003 on tour at Symphony Hall, Birmingham, was John Woolrich's *Arcangelo*. Woolrich explained his process to the *Guardian*:

> This year is Corelli's 350th, and in order to write a piece for the Academy of Ancient Music to mark that anniversary, I have

listened again to the music of Corelli, trying to identify the things in his work that resonate with mine. As Stravinsky said: 'The one true comment on a piece of music is another piece of music.'[9]

'John Woolrich was someone I had worked with at Dartington,' says Goodwin.

> I asked him to write a piece that would work in a programme where we were doing Telemann baroque orchestral suites with very strong parts for three oboes and bassoons. And so therefore you have this connection between themes and textures in the strings, like Corelli, and also an orchestration that has a really powerful oboes and bassoon sound as well, exploding all over. It's a dramatic piece – acerbic, but very, very dramatic. I did that in a programme with Corelli and Telemann.

The following season found Sir Peter Maxwell Davies (1934–2016), then the Master of the Queen's Music, being approached to write something for a very different kind of line-up. Attentive to concerns that the AAM's virtuoso brass players were being under-utilised under the triumvirate, Christopher Lawrence used Arts Council touring funds to assemble a tour featuring no fewer than eight baroque trumpets. 'It's one of the programmes I was most proud of,' he recalls, and it was directed jointly by violinist Pavlo Beznosiuk and David Blackadder, placing brass-heavy music by Biber against Maxwell Davies's new work for four trumpets and timpani, *Telos 135*. Even for a composer as seasoned as 'Max', the art of writing for period brass provided a steep learning curve, as David Blackadder recalls.

> The piece was called that because it was commissioned by a couple who had a connection with the Wallace Collection [Sir Nicholas and Lady Judith Goodison, both committed long-term members of the AAM Society] and 135 was their joint age. They'd specifically requested that he use valveless trumpets. The first thing that happened was that I got a call from Max saying, 'Let's have a chat about how to write for natural trumpets,' because he hadn't really ever done that. We had a lot of correspondence and he ended up

writing it for trumpets in different keys. Max decided to use two trumpets in C, one in B flat and one in D, with the timpani tuned to C and F sharp. It was quite a complex piece, to put it mildly – even though I'd told him the limits of what we could do, he wrote pretty much on those limits. Towards the end, it got louder and it got more complex and there were sextuplet semiquavers flying up and down the scale. It was a real test.

But he was very interested. He came to the first full rehearsal, and sat there listening. We played it through and he very quietly came up and said that he'd noticed that we were occasionally using the finger holes to adjust some of the notes. 'No,' he said, 'I don't want you to do that. I want it earthy, I want it really earthy – I want it as nature intended. Let me hear it through it again.' And all of a sudden this magical effect happened because it's like quarter-tones – the eleventh harmonic, neither an F sharp nor an F. And the same with the thirteenth harmonic, which is somewhere between an A and a G sharp. So when we suddenly stopped adjusting those by using the finger holes, the hairs started coming up on the back of your neck. It was jarring, but in a good way.

Telos 135 was premiered on 24 June 2004 at the Spitalfields Festival; the first date of the AAM's 'Sound the Trumpets' tour. For Blackadder, it was a memorable night:

In the concert it was particularly difficult, and all I can remember is that we did it. It went really well. Chris Hogwood was in the audience. He came to see me afterwards and congratulated me, and next thing I can remember is going to the pub over the road, when the European Cup was on. I think England must have just won, because everyone was cheering. It was quite a memory.

Telos 135 was played, at its commissioners' request, at Sir Nicholas Goodison's memorial service at St Martin in the Fields in September 2021.

The idea of playing new music on old instruments seems to have been an education for all concerned and, overall, composers, performers and listeners seem to have taken it in a constructive spirit, with some – Tavener in particular – finding that it opened new creative avenues. What better way to demonstrate that early music was not an antiquarian cult, but a vital and creative element of the twenty-first century's musical ecology? Taruskin's accusation that groups such as the Academy were imposing a modernist aesthetic on the music they performed had been taken up, acknowledged, and turned entirely around.

Which is not to say that there was no scepticism, or that every commission was comparably successful. Blackadder recalls that passages in Tavener's *Total Eclipse* were unplayable on a valveless instrument – 'simple as that. And even after I had all those conversations with him.' Pavlo Beznosiuk remains unconvinced by the whole exercise:

How relevant it was, I don't know. What composers tend to do is just write the same music they would've done if it was modern instruments. Unless they actually start writing with old compositional techniques in mind, or looking at music's historical function. Which they never do, of course. They just carry on getting involved in their own personal psychodrama.

Nonetheless, Goodwin feels that the project was its own reward:

The players were very happy to try new things and they loved the process of collaboration. They loved the fact that a composer would come along to our sessions. We spent lots of days, for instance, on one of the albums we did in the Temple Church with John Tavener. He came along to all the sessions, and we had had John Harle playing the saxophone and lots of antiphonal effects using the triforium of the church. Tavener was completely involved in this, and I knew from the orchestra how much they loved that. It was very much like a baroque collaboration. Handel wrote for the singers that he knew, and John wrote for players that he knew – and was happy for them to say what they wanted to add.

One final commission remained. In the words of its composer, Thea Musgrave, *Journey into Light* 'was commissioned as a possible companion piece to Mozart's *Exsultate, jubilate* and the decision was quickly made to write something as a complete contrast'. As Goodwin recalls,

I'd known Thea for years, because she writes a lot for oboe and I love her music. So I got in touch with her and she, of course, is one of the world's most enthusiastic people – she's adorable and crazy and will try anything. I met up with her and her husband at their home in California and we talked through lots of themes and ideas. As opposed to all these baroque-inspired pieces, I wanted to do something that would fit in with the classical programme. Thea was interested by Mozart's orchestration for two oboes, but she had them doubling on cor anglais, with strings and soprano, and a medieval Scottish text. A very dark text, in a thick Scottish dialect that [soloist] Carolyn Sampson had to use. It was an incredibly atmospheric, dark, slow piece.[10]

Too dark, and too atmospheric, for some. Goodwin conducted the premiere of Thea Musgrave's *Journey into Light* in Southampton on 25 May 2006, before taking it on tour the following season. 'The Academy of Ancient Music has in recent years become a propagator of new music as well,' wrote the critic Erica Jeal, in the *Guardian*, after the London premiere that December:

> Musgrave revels in the plangent sonorities of the AAM's oboes and bassoon, but elsewhere the music falls into rich Wagnerian harmonies that suggest she would have been equally happy scoring this work for modern orchestra, had a commission been forthcoming.

Goodwin, however, remains proud of the series of commissions, and hopes, some day, to conduct a concert in which each of the new works is performed alongside the baroque or classical piece that inspired it – 'So it would be Purcell and *Eternity's Sunrise*, Telemann and Woolrich, Bach and Bedford, and Mozart and Musgrave. I think it would be a wonderful concept.' By the time of the Musgrave premiere in 2006, however, the triumvirate had dissolved and the Academy of Ancient Music had set out on a wholly new chapter.

The Long Day Closes

From one perspective, the success of the triumvirate sowed the seeds of its own dissolution. As 'The Class of '73' turned thirty, the early-music landscape was undergoing a generational shift, and Trevor Pinnock announced his intention to step down as director of The English Concert in July 2003. The group, naturally enough, looked for an inspirational and dynamic new leader to replace their long-serving founder and, naturally enough, they lighted on the new millennium's most inspirational and dynamic baroque violinist. The only problem was that he was currently the Associate Director and Concertmaster of the Academy of Ancient Music.

'I'll be completely frank about this,' says Andrew Manze.

I'm not sure I did the right thing. At that time, the idea of being number one with a successful operation like The English Concert was something I felt I couldn't say no to. I sat with Christopher Hogwood – I remember we had lunch together – and I said, 'I've been offered this position as number one at The English Concert. I'm tempted, and I want to go.' Chris said, 'Well, I'd rather you stayed with us.' He was very kind: he offered to pay me more, and I said that it wasn't about money, it was about being my own boss.

What Chris didn't say was, 'Well, maybe in a few years' time, I'll be finishing, and then the Academy will be open.' Maybe at that point he wasn't ready to hand it over. I now rather regret that I left the Academy, because I enjoyed it so much: it was a great group of people. On the other hand, my leaving and then spending a few years with The English Concert was a catalyst for doing more conducting. Within a few years, I'd stopped playing the violin completely and was a full-time conductor. I wouldn't be doing what I'm doing now if I'd stayed at the Academy.

Manze resigned his position with the AAM and took up his role as Artistic Director of The English Concert at the start of the 2003–4 season. Four years later, he stepped down, subsequently abandoning his career as a baroque violinist – and as an early musician – to focus on symphonic conducting. 'I don't want that to be a reflection on the Academy of Ancient Music,' he says.

If I'd stayed with the AAM longer, I think I would have loved it. With The English Concert I was up against a very English style of music making, and I couldn't really do anything about that. So I felt a little pigeonholed: I was being defined by my playing. That was always important to me, but my playing was being packaged as the saleable commodity: so long as I did Vivaldi's *Four Seasons* in a concert, then I could do whatever I liked. I felt I was no longer in charge, and I felt I wasn't able to go in new directions.

He also regrets that his departure might have distressed Hogwood – though Hogwood certainly never said as much.

He was such an English gentleman that he wouldn't betray his feelings. It could well be that I am on that list of people whom he felt had benefited from what he'd offered, and then had said, 'Thank you, I'm off now.' It could well be. I haven't thought about it in that way, because I feel I did contribute to the Academy as well as benefit from it. It was a mutually beneficial relationship. But Chris could, at times, be very touchy. We once arrived in Charleston, South Carolina, and there was a big poster saying, 'Sir Christopher Hogwood, conductor'. He looked at this poster and he said, with a slightly wry expression, 'Oh, yes – when will someone tell The Queen?' It was a joke, but you sensed that he was also a bit hurt that, for whatever reason, it hadn't come his way.

By then there was Sir John Eliot Gardiner, and Sir Roger Norrington; Christopher maybe felt he'd done just as much for music in Britain, and for early music. I think that hurt him. He was hugely successful – not to put too fine a point on it, he was very rich from his recordings and concerts – and in early-music terms he was a household name. But somehow he felt he'd never quite made it to early-music royalty, in the way that Nikolaus Harnoncourt or Gustav Leonhardt or any of those people had.

Whatever Manze's motivation for moving to The English Concert, he left a gap in the AAM's artistic plans, taking his relationship with Harmonia Mundi with him, and opening – once again – the question of how the AAM might function in a post-Hogwood world. By 2003, that question was becoming pressing. Hogwood would turn sixty-five in 2006, and he was increasingly preoccupied with the question of artistic succession.

'He wanted it to be as cooperative as possible,' says Christopher Lawrence.

> He definitely didn't want any sort of cliff edge. So there we were: we had this triumvirate of Chris, Andrew and Paul, which was a way of introducing the world to the concept of the AAM with someone other than Chris – but then Andrew leaves. That created a little hiatus. So, in that hiatus, I explored working with multiple guest directors. I brought in Masaaki Suzuki and Giuliano Carmignola, invited Edward Higginbottom to conduct his own choir with us for a change, and asked Pavlo Beznosiuk to do some directing. We started casting the net a little wider. That was a gentle way of exploring whether there was someone whom we might want to bring closer to the AAM.

From October 2004, the process involved the entire Board and artistic leadership – all acutely aware that the choice of Hogwood's successor would define the future prospects of the entire organisation.

'There was a process and quite a lot of homework,' says Christopher Purvis.

> We had long lists of possible candidates, and people went off to hear them. We had debates about the type of person we wanted: a mainstream conductor, someone directing from the fiddle, someone from the keyboard? The process was tied up with the debate about the type of orchestra we wanted to be.

As Lawrence saw it, one possible candidate led the field:

> Now, I knew Richard Egarr because, again, he was a contemporary from Cambridge. He had played there with Andrew, and we'd done a recording of the Bach harpsichord concertos for Harmonia Mundi with Andrew sort of directing from the violin but of course – really – Richard directing from the harpsichord. So there was already something tangible in existence that said Richard Egarr plus the AAM. It had always struck me that Christopher Hogwood had started the AAM directing from the

keyboard. Andrew had been very successful directing from the violin. It was very clear that the AAM's core strengths began with Handel, and spread outwards from Handel, and having a player-director either from the violin or possibly – even better – from the harpsichord, was the obvious way to go rather than bringing in a conductor. Economically that wouldn't have worked. We couldn't find a year's worth of work with a band big enough to warrant having a conductor.

So in that regard, Richard was the natural person to get involved. Andrew's job title had been Associate Director, Paul was Associate Conductor, and we brought Richard in to fill that Associate Director vacancy.

Egarr became Associate Director in 2005. 'Then we took the decision to make Richard the sole Music Director. And at the point of making Richard the Music Director, Paul's role had to go.'

There was a logic to the decision:

The reality was, there were fewer and fewer projects that we could do with Paul standing up in front of a large band. If we were having Paul conduct only one project a year, that didn't really justify a titled post. European touring was getting harder and harder, both for economic reasons and competition reasons. I can't quite remember our thought process, but we probably thought we had to give as many opportunities as possible to Richard to establish the concept of Richard as our new Music Director.

Still, the end of his eleven years with the AAM came as a personal blow to Goodwin.

In retrospect, it was very clear that if you have a new director with the ideas and enthusiasm and talent of Richard Egarr, then he's going to want to do his own thing and he's going to want to draw a line. Chris Lawrence has been a friend of our family for years. He did a fantastic job; he was very supportive of me all the way through, and I still had lots of ideas lined up to do. At the time, it wasn't very comfortable. But in retrospect, I can understand.

Crucially, though, a decision had been taken. Richard Egarr would succeed Christopher Hogwood as Music Director – and having commenced serious succession planning in the mid-1990s, Hogwood was not inclined to delay the handover. As Lawrence recalls, 'We'd actually set a date further in the future, but Richard was already working well as Associate Director. We'd suffered the loss of Andrew to The English Concert and we couldn't afford to run the risk of losing Richard the same way. So we decided to bring the offer forward by a year.'

The announcement was made at the start of May 2006. Hogwood would step down as Music Director at the end of that season, and would take on the title of Emeritus Director. From 1 September 2006, Richard Egarr would be sole Music Director of the Academy of Ancient Music, while Hogwood would continue to pursue less frequent – but still regular – projects with the group. The transition was noticeably low key: in fact, at the point where the decision was made, Hogwood had already – unremarked, because unknown – conducted his last concert as Music Director. The 2005–6 AAM season in Cambridge and London featured concerts directed by Richard Egarr, Pavlo Beznosiuk, Paul Goodwin, Giuliano Carmignola and Stephen Layton (with his chamber choir Polyphony).

'Chris was available to do one big project each year,' says Lawrence.

So we set up a Handel opera project to be done in the Barbican and elsewhere for three years, with an opera from each of three formative decades, the 1710s, 1720s and 1730s. So they were anchored in the diary for three years, and the Barbican was going to co-promote them. And after that Chris would have carried on appearing with the AAM once a year, because it was important for all of us to maintain that. It wasn't a cliff edge.

Hogwood toured with a concert performance of *Amadigi di Gaula* in the spring of 2007, *Flavio, re de' Longobardi* in 2008 and *Arianna in Creta* in 2009. 'The Academy was looking for a project to span the three years prior to Handel's anniversary in 2009, and I wanted to do something coherent – all my career, I've been working to try and bring some coherence to our picture of Handel,' Hogwood told the current author, in an interview for *Metro* in April 2008. 'A lot of modern directors who stage the operas don't really trust Handel's music, it seems to me. So they fill the stage with guns, helicopters and nudity. But it's not TV opera – it has to have a certain studied formality. And it needs great singers.' No problems on that score: with casts that included Klara Ek, Miah Persson and the countertenors Lawrence Zazzo and Iestyn Davies, it's easy to imagine that Peter Wadland would have been thrilled. Tony Fabian is convinced, nonetheless, that Hogwood was making a conscious change in the pace of his life and career:

> One of the qualities that I most admired about Chris was that he did take a long view about these things. Too many people die without a will or don't think about legacy. He was always aware that he had to make preparations for his demise, and he started early in that process. There were two factors involved. One was for the Academy to survive him – planning how that could be done and doing it stage by stage and then eventually stepping down altogether. That wasn't too painful for him because he understood why he was doing it. But the other factor was that for the entire first thirty years of the Academy, he was subsidising it. I think he really felt he'd done quite enough to bail it out over all those decades, and that it was time for someone else to be responsible. He was aware that working for the Academy was not earning him anything like as much money as working for other groups and other orchestras, and if he was going to continue to bail them out, he was going to have to do more work for other people to make that happen.
>
> I remember that when he turned sixty, he started subscribing to the *Oldie* magazine: he accepted that he was now entering a third age. He was very vital and his mind was absolutely sharp until the brain cancer that took him away. So there was no need for him to consign himself to old age quite as early as he did. But it's almost as though that was all part of his whole preparation for what we know was coming next. And I think stepping down was part of that.

In the later years of his career, Hogwood was in demand – and at liberty – to guest conduct almost wherever he pleased. In 2010, he was appointed Professor of Music at Gresham College in London and, in 2012, he became

Andrew D. White Professor-at-Large at Cornell University. He pursued other musical interests, editing editions of chamber works by Brahms, Elgar's *Serenade for Strings*, music by Mendelssohn and *La revue de cuisine* by his beloved Martinů. He continued to build his collection of eighteenth-century coffee cans (actually cups – although he would correct anyone who used that term) – of which he was a leading collector, amassing well over three thousand. They were, he said, 'a silent source of historical information'. He spent time at his cottage in Tuscany and his fourteenth-century house in Aveyron, France, with his donkeys Paco and Rabanne. He found his voice as a food writer, and planned to write a history of the picnic.

And throughout the years after 2006, he kept a protective eye on the AAM. Conveniently, the Academy was still operating out of the house next door to his own home at 10 Brookside, Cambridge. AAM staff would pop over for a drink and a chat after a day in the office. Simon Fairclough joined the office team in 2007, rising to become Head of Fundraising. He recalls how Hogwood

> would ring at 3 p.m., and it wasn't really a question – it was an instruction – that you were going to come for a drink on the way home, which was always good fun. He had this big kitchen on the ground floor with a nice view out to his beautiful garden, and a dining room next door. There was an absolutely beautiful drawing room on the first floor, full of Georgian furniture. He had a CD library on the second floor. The whole house was like a cross between Sir John Soane's Museum and Kettle's Yard.
>
> He would hold court in his kitchen. We would all stand around the Aga, or sit outside in the garden in summer, and have our G&T, or our English sparkling wine – Chris got into that craze very early. The conversation could be about anything under the sun. He was as interested in the history of the picnic as he was in ancient music. And, very occasionally, drinks would turn into supper. He was not a terribly good cook, but his housekeeper, Anita, would have gone down to Waitrose in Trumpington and bought some quails or something.

Hogwood stepped down from the Board in 2011, but he remained a central part of the AAM's artistic planning. The Decca Mozart piano concerto cycle had spluttered to a halt, incomplete, in 2001: never officially cancelled by the label, it was more the case (in the words of Christopher Lawrence) that 'it didn't quite continue'. But there was no reason why Hogwood's live collaborations with Robert Levin shouldn't continue, and in the spring of 2014 plans were being made for a European concert tour in 2015 that would reunite them for more Mozart. In the middle of the planning process, Hogwood withdrew on health grounds. Levin agreed to direct in his place, and hasty renegotiations were undertaken with the tour venues (which, in the absence of Hogwood, wanted to reduce the engagement fee). Ed Hossack, then Chief Executive, recalls receiving the news that 'Chris had cancer, with a short life expectancy'.

Christopher Hogwood died of an aggressive brain tumour on 24 September 2014, fourteen days after his seventy-third birthday. He was at home in Cambridge. 'He died in the lovely place he'd made for himself,' says Emma Kirkby. A service of thanksgiving was held at St George's, Hanover Square – Handel's church – on 11 March 2015, with music by Handel, Purcell, Byrd and Vivaldi played by the Academy of Ancient Music. Richard Egarr directed, and Pavlo Beznosiuk, Catherine Mackintosh, Simon Standage and Monica Huggett were the soloists in Vivaldi's Concerto Op. 3 No. 1. Alastair Ross played the organ voluntaries, David Blackadder and Frank de Bruine were in the orchestra, Catherine Bott, Christopher Purvis and Colin Lawson all spoke, and Emma Kirkby sang Purcell's *Evening Hymn*. James Bowman, performing for his old friend for the very last time, sang Handel's 'Eternal Source of Light Divine'.

10

RENAISSANCE

Handel's Organ Concerto Op. 4 No. 1 begins with a flourish, but it's far from extravagant: a stately-dance measure, *Larghetto* and in G minor, before the orchestra falls silent and lets the solo organ say its piece. The first music played in public by the Academy of Ancient Music under its new Music Director made no obvious grand statement of intent. Richard Egarr was director and keyboard soloist in three of Handel's Op. 4 organ concertos. There was a pair of Telemann chamber concertos, but only at the end of the programme, perhaps, was there any obvious hint at a celebration or a rebirth, in the form of Bach's Brandenburg Concerto No. 5, with its huge, freewheeling virtuoso harpsichord solo. The programme was heard first at Snape Maltings, Suffolk, on 21 October 2006 and again the following night at Chelmsford Civic Theatre. But when Egarr and his new orchestra brought it home to West Road Concert Hall in Cambridge on 30 October 2006, Brandenburg No. 5 had been replaced with the altogether less demonstrative No. 4. There was no need, among friends, to make a fuss.

Egarr had toured a similar programme with the AAM that January, and together they had taken the Fifth Brandenburg to the York Early Music Festival and to Amsterdam's Concertgebouw as recently as July. The news of Hogwood's retirement and Egarr's succession made headlines on BBC Radio 3 in May but, for the players and staff, the transition had been natural, self-evident and straightforward. Richard Egarr was, in a sense, part of the family already. Born in Lincoln, he'd been a chorister at York Minster and had gone on to study at Chetham's School of Music in Manchester. From there, he had won a place as organ scholar at Clare

College, Cambridge – and what followed almost writes itself. 'I went up to Clare in '82,' Egarr recalls.

I'd never really played a harpsichord until that point, but there happened to be one in the ante-chapel at Clare. I'd seen one before, but never played it. I was curious. My piano teacher in the last couple of years at Chet's was David Mason, a wonderful pianist and singing teacher who opened my ears to early music. He pointed me in the direction of groups like Musica Antiqua Köln. And I remember going into the music library at Chet's and seeing this LP box set called *Music of the Gothic Era*, one of David Munrow's last recordings. And I remember sitting down in the music library and putting these three LPs on and being completely blown away – not just by the music, but also the performance. David Munrow remains a big icon and inspiration: what an incredible communicator and mind!

But it wasn't till I was at Clare that I started playing the harpsichord. I looked for somebody to play with and there happened to be a viola da gamba player at Trinity called Mark Levy – later the founder of the Concordia Viol Consort. So he came along and brought facsimiles of Marin Marais and Bach gamba sonatas, and that was how I started – by being thrown into the deep end, basically. Of course, I'd learned the organ, but that doesn't really help you with harpsichord playing. I'd had that whole discipline of reading figured bass and understanding harmony since I was a choirboy, since I was ten, so it didn't faze me, but finding a continuo style was just something I did by doing it, at that point.

And then the following year, in 1983, a certain Mr Manze turned up at Clare College and the recorder player Robert Ehrlich came to King's College, and we started playing together. Andrew wasn't interested in playing baroque music at all: we played modern music on modern instruments. But I was already playing a lot with Mark and Robert, and I decided that Andrew needed to play baroque violin. I literally put his name on a poster, announcing that he was going to play Brandenburg 4, and said, 'Go and get yourself a baroque bow from the music faculty.' The rest is history – he sort of got into it!

Egarr and his friends formed a baroque ensemble. The tendrils of Cambridge's musical grapevine extend in manifold directions; word spread, and in due course the four students received an invitation to call on Christopher Hogwood. 'I remember it was summer,' says Andrew Manze, 'a lovely day, and we played to him and he gave us some Handel sheet music that he'd edited, which we didn't know and which was suitable for us. We sat in his garden and had strawberries and cream.' But the Dutch school of period performance was what really excited the young Egarr, and while Manze studied with Ton Koopman in The Hague, Egarr travelled to the Netherlands to study with Gustav Leonhardt.

> He was a great teacher in that he really made you listen to what you were doing on the harpsichord – which is the most terrible instrument in the universe. It's the machine that goes ping, as I like to describe it. It does nothing. But he was very good at making you feel real contact with this strange machine, and make a beautiful sound. I had lots of lessons with him and we had coaching with other people in Holland as well, at The Hague and Amsterdam.

Back in the UK, Manze and Egarr dived into the freelance scene. Egarr recalls playing with Pavlo Beznosiuk in the 1990s, though it was Manze, in his post-1996 role as Associate Director, who first invited Egarr to work with the Academy, early in the twenty-first century – principally on his own projects, although Egarr did work once (briefly) under Hogwood's direction. Over and beyond their personal friendship, Manze felt that Egarr's musical personality would bring something vital, new and inspiring to the Academy's sound. Manze points out that Hogwood was big enough to recognise and appreciate a musical personality that was very different from his own.

> Chris Hogwood was a very fine keyboard player, especially given that he didn't play very often. We did some chamber concerts and it was really exquisite what Chris could do – but it was very self-effacing playing. Richard Egarr is much more expressive on a harpsichord. When Richard played continuo for Chris, it didn't really go very well: neither spoke the other's language. But Chris could see that Richard could bring something into the Academy

that was very different. It was a very clever idea to get Richard involved, and then obviously Chris felt that this was someone to whom it was safe to hand the orchestra over.

Richard has the ability to be completely crazy, but he also has the ability to be very sober. He has a very wide range. He can be the most nutty person you've ever met, but he can also play a Bach fugue so that you think that you are inside the mind of Bach. He's got this incredible range, and I think Chris Hogwood could see that. The nutty side wasn't Chris's style at all, but the seriousness was – and also this gift that Richard has, to help musicians play or sing beyond what they should be able to do. I've seen him with an amateur choir, and he can make them sound like they're the BBC Singers. It's phenomenal, and I think he was a very good choice. He has such energy.

That energy made an immediate impact on the AAM's players. 'I'm a number one fan,' says timpanist Benedict Hoffnung. 'Richard was, and remains, a wonderful musical force. Because he never coasts. Richard is always absolutely full on. He's completely focused, and he's out there, in every note, to milk absolutely everything he can out of the score, and out of the musicians in front of him.' For Pavlo Beznosiuk, Egarr was 'a bit of a comedian. He is incredibly lively, unstoppable – borderline-ADHD energy, with a great, sometimes childlike, sense of humour. But there is always something going on. He likes a challenge and a risk. He is always wanting to give people free rein. That was the big characteristic change in the group's sound in his time: more extremes of dynamics. More extremes of tempo. And yes, a bit more risk taking.' Rachel Brown remembers that 'the thing I really appreciated about Richard was the dedication during concerts. While you were playing, he was always in contact, and there was a driving passion there. The concerts could be really exciting – there was an electricity.'

So the approach was made, and accepted, and the transition was smooth to the point of being understated. The group was in good artistic (and improving administrative) health and work had been under way for a decade to loosen the ties between the Academy's collective identity and the personality of its founder. Still – as one harpsichordist-director succeeding another, much more celebrated, harpsichordist-director – it's natural to wonder whether Egarr felt daunted.

'One of the things that the Board felt, certainly, was that they wanted the orchestra to have its own identity apart from the director,' he says.

But I think after the triumvirate, they wanted a single leader again. I'd been working quite a lot in and around London – I was with London Baroque for five years from 1990 to 1995, and then I was doing some guest directing with the Age of Enlightenment and orchestras like that. I lived in Holland, and that's another question mark. But they approached me and I was more than happy to take it on.

The musicians are always the core of an orchestra, and it's interesting to see how that set of musicians reacts to different leadership. The AAM were very flexible: that's part of the English early-music scene, and always was. In the early days, of course, there was a lot of crossover of players between groups. But by the 2000s the orchestras had their own players. There was still quite a lot of crossover with string players for bigger projects, but we had very wonderful wind and brass players, like Rachel Brown and Frank de Bruine and Dave Blackadder. And so the Academy had its own identity as an orchestra, and it was superlatively flexible as well. They could play for Andrew, or they could play for Paul, and the sound would change like any good orchestra, depending on who was in front of them. So, from that point of view, I wasn't afraid of asking them to do naughty things.

In time, Egarr would become more outspoken about his dislike of what he calls the 'bullshit' conventions of the early-music scene. In a 2016 interview with Kate Molleson (and in words that directly echo Richard Taruskin's attacks on Christopher Hogwood), he criticised the historically informed aesthetic of the 1970s and 1980s, 'which was about playing in a post-modern detached way and making everything sound like Stravinsky'.[1] His directorship of the AAM marked a radical stylistic break.

I mean, there had been a necessary cleansing of certain things – but if you cleanse too much, you can throw the baby out with the bathwater. One of the buzz lines from the 1970s was to let the music speak for itself. Well, we're in a different place now. We can, with all honesty, say that, in terms of authenticity, that is utterly the wrong way around. Any musical performance until the twentieth century was necessarily a subjective performance. Composers expected their music to have a subjective element: if Corelli had heard another violinist playing his ornaments, he'd have been appalled. The performer was an integral part of the performance of a piece. Our attitude on that whole question has changed.

I am a musical omnivore, as is Andrew. That's why he's ended up conducting Mahler and Britten and Vaughan Williams. Like Andrew, I always kept on being interested in later, and other, kinds of music, and I've never stopped that. One of my happiest moments in an AAM concert was the Prom we did in 2016: we did the four Handel Coronation Anthems, and I managed to slip in two Stokowski string arrangements as encores. So the idea that music has borders – or that performance has restrictions – is a very difficult one for me.

One field in which Egarr moved swiftly to put his own ideas into practice was choral music. The Academy of Ancient Music Chorus had evolved by fits and starts over the decades. Paul Goodwin had recruited a central core of singers, but the Academy's close relationships with the pre-eminent Oxbridge choirs as well as Stephen Layton's chamber choir Polyphony provided for most large-scale choral projects. Christopher Lawrence recalls that the Academy

had good relationships with New College, Oxford, and King's College, Cambridge, and we did maybe two concerts a year with Polyphony, but I saw relationships with choirs as another route to paid work of one sort or another. Stephen Cleobury [of King's College] was always very loyal: that was a happy marriage between the AAM and King's, and it carried on until Stephen's death. The relationship with New College was less based on recording, and more based on going around Europe in December each year with the choir. But Richard obviously had something in mind for the sound he wanted, combined with the repertoire he wanted to pursue, and he was willing to invest time into choosing voices and working with those voices.

Egarr agrees.

> It's something that was very important to me. When I started, it was very much the usual rent-a-mob phone list. There'd never been any auditions: it was just done by ringing the same people that everybody else was ringing. I had a number of days of auditions, just listening to singers to see what they were about and how they sounded. Being a choir man myself, I have fairly strong ideas about choral sound. And throughout my time, we would always have two or three patches during a year where we'd hold auditions, just to listen to the singers that were around or wanted to come and sing to me – and also for instrumentalists as well. It's important just to keep your ear to the ground and see who's coming along. I remember [tenor] Andrew Tortise and [baritone] Ashley Riches came through as young pros and started singing in the choir. And now they're great soloists.

Egarr saw choral music as an integral part of the Academy's musical personality. Having recruited and fine-tuned a chorus to his own specification, he made sure that choral repertoire was included in each season, not as a one-off project, but as a regular component of the AAM's programming – training and rehearsing the singers in person. 'To have the choir there and have a living breathing part of the orchestra was very important for me,' he says. Two early projects put the AAM and its rejuvenated chorus straight into the international spotlight. The first was the AAM's first ever tour to China (as opposed to Hong Kong under British rule) in October 2008, to participate in the Beijing Music Festival.

Egarr and the AAM performed Purcell's *Dido and Aeneas* – possibly for the first time in China on period instruments – and Handel's *Messiah*, and found, slightly to their surprise, that this most familiar of choral warhorses was suddenly the source of intense controversy. 'It is a must-see performance,' Long Yu, the leading Chinese conductor (and Director of the Festival) told the state-controlled newspaper *China Daily*: 'AAM is one of the world's first and best period-instrument orchestras. Some Chinese fans may have AAM's CDs of ancient music but this is a rare chance to hear them in public.'[2]

And yet, in a paradox baffling to the Western (or, at any rate, democratic) mind, the AAM had been booked and promoted – with the sanction of the Communist Party of China – to play a work that was banned in China. Egarr remembers the confusion. 'So officially the story was that *Messiah* wasn't happening. But in fact, a private performance of it took place for all the great and the good in the Catholic cathedral in Beijing.' The venue was St Joseph's Church, otherwise known as Wangfujing Church, and the doctrinal sensitivities of performing Handel's determinedly Protestant oratorio in a Catholic institution pale beside the complexities of giving it before an audience of atheist – indeed, anti-Christian – state officials. The invitation had been issued prior to the August 2008 Beijing Olympic Games, when the Chinese state had been keen to project a facade of openness. The AAM's performance, however, came after the Olympic crowds (and media) had departed and the ban had been reinstated. The official solution was to make the performance 'invitation only'.

Peter Ansell, who had succeeded Christopher Lawrence – joining the AAM in 2007 from the artists' agency Askonas Holt – was an expert on international touring, but even he was nonplussed.

I only discovered just before flying out that there was going to be no actual public at this performance. It was the sponsors, UBS, plus senior members of the Beijing government because *Messiah*, being religious, couldn't actually be witnessed by the great Chinese public. So, it was a closed concert, which was a bit odd. But *Dido and Aeneas* in the Beijing Concert Hall the next night was a public performance. One of the UK newspapers got hold of the fact that we were going to China to perform a closed concert for senior members of the Beijing government, and they wanted to speak to me about it. I refused. I spoke to Christopher Purvis, the Chairman, and he said, 'No. You did the right thing there – best avoided.'

The second eye-catching project also involved *Dido and Aeneas*, and an unprecedented attempt to stage Purcell's opera in its historic setting – the ruins of Carthage in Tunisia. Well, not quite Carthage: the venue chosen was the restored Roman amphitheatre at Sabratha, across the border in

Libya. In 2009 Libya was still under the dictatorship of Muammar Gaddafi, who was at that point, shortly before his overthrow and death in the 2011 Libyan civil war, pursuing a cautious policy of détente with the West. The UK tour operator Martin Randall specialises in cruises with a cultural twist; they saw an opportunity, and the AAM signed on – twice, in March and October 2009 – for what staff and players privately dubbed 'the War Zones tour'. Richard Egarr's memories are still bright.

> It was hilarious flying into the airport at Tripoli, faced with all these guards, who had no idea what was going on. It took us about three hours to get through customs. We even had a harpsichord with us – it was a major undertaking. And so we all bussed out to the theatre, and rehearsed there in 40 degrees centigrade. Sabratha is simply extraordinary – a huge Roman theatre in this whole Roman city of which apparently only about 30 per cent has been excavated. It was really wonderful. And then we performed it the following day to 270 passengers whose cruise ship had just docked nearby. Everybody was just so high on the experience.

The cruise carried its share of journalists. Sophie Campbell of the *Daily Telegraph* was there in March 2009. 'Even for the well-travelled Academy of Ancient Music, this was no ordinary performance of *Dido and Aeneas*,' she wrote.

> The cellos had cloths safety-pinned under their strings to stop the varnish melting in the African sun. The harpsichord had been impounded by customs and only released at the last minute. And in the middle of Dido's lament there was a buzz of walkie-talkies as two policemen strolled behind the backdrop – the gaping, golden wreckage of the Roman theatre at Sabratha, Libya – dramatically silhouetted against the sky and sea.
>
> As the last note hummed in the stones, it was clear they had a triumph on their hands. Everyone – the 230 passengers on our ten-day 'Romans in Africa' cruise, for whom the performance had been privately arranged, the Sabratha security guards who had abandoned their gate duties and slid into the 1,800-year-old amphitheatre to listen, and the ubiquitous, slightly puzzled small

boys perched along the back walls like swallows – stood up as one
to applaud. Out of the corner of my eye I saw two of our tour
leaders doing high-fives.[3]

A gazebo protected the instrumentalists from the worst of the sun. In
October, *Opera* sent John Warrack to offer a critic's appraisal.

Arranging what was, it seems, the first performance ever of
any modern European work in this theatre must have been no
light feat, but the intransigent Colonel proved no match for
the persistence of the travel agent Martin Randall. There on
5 October was the Academy of Ancient Music and a full team
of soloists and chorus. Only a single Canadian instrumentalist
was denied entry (Libyan bureaucrats apparently feeling that one
North American was as bad as another). Almost any performance would have made an effect in such a setting, but this one
was worthy of it. Directing a dozen players, Richard Egarr leapt
between conducting desk and harpsichord. The chorus was
arranged formally along the stage, occasionally breaking ranks
to produce a witch or two, and there was a breath-taking *coup
de théâtre* when, from high up at the back of the theatre's great
semi-circle, the minatory voice of Mercury suddenly rang out
to the hapless Aeneas . . .[4]

This called for a celebration – in as far as that was possible in Libya.
Pavlo Beznosiuk remembers 'the reception on the boat with no alcohol,
of course'. It's funny how these details stick in the memories of orchestral
players and managers. As Ansell remembers it,

Martin Randall invited all the orchestra and the chorus to the
cruise ship after the performance to have dinner with the audience. But because we were in Libyan waters, alcohol was still
banned, and obviously – musicians being musicians – they could
see all these beautiful bottles of wine behind locked glass cases.
They asked for some wine and they were told no: it was illegal.
So instead, they all ordered the same dessert which was laced with
an alcoholic liqueur.

Back in Cambridge, meanwhile, at 7.30 p.m. on 5 April 2009, Stephen Cleobury conducted his King's College Choir and the AAM, plus a team of bright young soloists (Ailish Tynan, Alice Coote, Allan Clayton and Matthew Rose) in the first ever global cinecast of Handel's *Messiah* – transmitted live to cinemas across Europe and North America. It was a very modern way to mark the 250th anniversary of Handel's death. But one way or another these were all prestigious, satisfying projects, and there seems to have been a new spirit in the Academy. It didn't go unnoticed, especially in the AAM's old touring heartlands in the USA. Reviewing a concert in Boston in February 2008, the *Boston Globe* reported:

> The period-instrument orchestra, formed in 1973, had a penchant for sounding somewhat dry and inhibited under its founder, Christopher Hogwood. Yet the group that came to Emmanuel Church on Friday night – courtesy of the Boston Early Music Festival – demonstrated a rich, well-rounded sound and vigour to spare.[5]

It certainly helped that Egarr was a charismatic and communicative virtuoso in his own right. Orchestral musicians are rarely happier than when sparking off a fellow performer whose artistry they respect. As Pavlo Beznosiuk puts it,

> He might not like this, but Richard is to me, first and foremost, a keyboardist and a consummate continuo player. So for me it's been the smaller stuff – tours of the Bach suites done one on a part. The Brandenburg Concertos. Doing concerts and warming up for the Handel chamber-sonata recordings – these are the things I've enjoyed most with him. His real artistic strengths, I think, lie in his abilities as a flexible and instantaneously responsive continuo player.

A reviewer in Pittsburgh in April 2007 spotted the difference as early as Egarr's first season:

> In the past decade or so, the early-music movement has exploded with musicality, as if the fetters had been torn from these musicians.

No musician has been more crucial in this than Egarr. A fantastic harpsichordist, a more accurate label would just be musician. He has very musical ideas, and the Academy of Ancient Music has soaked them up. This programme of Handel, Bach and Telemann sounded nothing like the old Academy sound. It played with vitality and verve in fast passages and colourfully shaped the slow ones . . . In addition to his strong ideas on dynamics and tempo, Egarr simply has loosened up this orchestra. Conducting as much with his face as his hands, he shot smiles around the group, and lightened the mood with humour in between pieces. He has wrung the remaining bookish and uptight qualities out of the Academy of Ancient Music, and for the better.

'Never', he concluded, 'has the Academy of Ancient Music been less academic.'[6]

Playing through the Crunch

The energy of the new partnership started to generate its own momentum. The recording relationship with Harmonia Mundi had taken a blow with the departure of Andrew Manze, but now Christopher Lawrence saw an opportunity. 'When I got Richard more involved, we were able to reinvigorate the relationship with Harmonia Mundi,' he recalls.

Handel only has seven opus numbers, Op. 1 to Op. 7. Op. 1 to Op. 7 is all instrumental music – a combination of orchestral or chamber – and so I worked with Robina Young at Harmonia Mundi to do the complete Handel opus set. We already had the Op. 6 concerti grossi recorded and released under Andrew. With Richard we were able to fill in the chamber bits as well. The Handel Op. 1–7 is something I'm very proud of, and that also enabled us to re-engage with Harmonia Mundi. And actually, Richard's role allowed me to re-engage with David Rowe, our touring agent in America. A lot of the touring in the USA had been based on Andrew – because of the economic size of the baroque group. And so Richard's role enabled those two relationships to have a spark of life – Harmonia Mundi and the American touring.

Peter Ansell succeeded Lawrence in August 2007, with a wealth of experience organising tours with international symphony orchestras but – by his own admission – very little previous form in the world of early music. He'd never even visited Cambridge.

Maybe I had the impression that they were this old, fusty Cambridge-based outfit – and also, at that point, that it was all Christopher Hogwood. I'd never heard of Richard Egarr. I remember the move to Cambridge on the first day – moving into the office, and finding it was right next door to Christopher Hogwood's house, this four-floor Cambridge townhouse with creaky staircases, and no IT support, and I thought, 'Oh, my god. What have I done?' In a medium-sized company, you can just focus on what you're doing. But when you're in this very small environment and the printer suddenly stops working, it's a disaster that you've got to sort out yourself.

There was probably a season of work already in place, including an American tour planned with the Brandenburgs. Chris Lawrence had told me that an American tour always loses the money. In the end, actually, that tour made a decent profit because the exchange rate shifted, which meant that the fee income was more than we were anticipating. But I remember there were small projects planned too. I went to see Richard Egarr at the Handel House playing Corelli trio sonatas and I just couldn't see myself selling programmes like that. I felt that we'd got to do bigger things. And towards the end of my time there, we did. The last concert I attended as CEO was in Groningen in Holland where Richard played and directed Beethoven's Fourth Piano Concerto with Beethoven's Sixth in the second half. So we did get bigger.

I joined just at the start of the global financial crisis. One thing I didn't ask before accepting the job – a real schoolboy error – was the financial health of the company. It was OK. But once the financial crisis hit, I was looking down a double-barrel of trying to sell the AAM in the worst financial crisis in living memory, with a music director that no one had ever heard of – because I was talking to promoters in Germany and Austria, and for them the AAM equalled Christopher Hogwood. I asked Pavlo Beznosiuk,

'When was the last time the AAM did Vivaldi's *Four Seasons*?' I was thinking it was bound to have been a couple of years ago. He checked, and he said, 'Well, Hogwood did it fifteen to twenty years ago. We haven't done it since.' To cut a long story short, we came up with the idea of having a soprano singing arias related to each season in between the concertos.

It worked.

We presented at the Wigmore Hall – again, those Wigmore presentations always lost a lot of money. It's only 550 seats and, even if you filled it, the box office didn't really cover your costs. That was why the Development Board was formed by Christopher Purvis – it would raise money to support our London presence at the Wigmore Hall, and I would make money on top of that by touring. So we took the *Four Seasons* to the Sheldonian Theatre in Oxford and various other places, and it was quite a success. In fact later, when I was working at Intermusica, we schlepped the same project around Asia, and coined it in there as well.

Helpfully, Ansell found that he had an easy rapport with his music director.

Richard and I hit it off from day one. He was ambitious. He wanted to do big things. We had exactly the same sense of humour – we both love *Monty Python* and we had great fun on tours, really laugh-out-loud, belly-laughing fun. I loved working with him because he was so flexible as music director. Of course, there is a difference between music directors employed by an orchestra, and a founder-director. A music director employed by an ensemble can't put their foot down in quite the same way. The thing about Richard is that he's so inventive and he's such a can-do person that it was a joy working with him. We designed a project for 2009: Handel's greatest hits. And he would suggest a singer and I would say, 'Look, no one knows this random Dutch mezzo that you think is really, really good – we need someone else to sell this.' And he would take that on board and be very flexible about it.

When I first started, there was a bit of fuss regarding things called 'play days', where Richard was effectively re-auditioning the band. That caused a lot of consternation: in a small orchestra, where the string players had been in roughly the same position for quite some time, all of a sudden they were reapplying for their jobs. Again, that was part of my steep learning curve. There were a lot of panicked phone calls. The orchestra manager, Karen Foster, handled most of the player paranoia on the phones. But there were a few words in my ear on tour. Musicians, especially in a small ensemble, can be paranoid beings.

But there was a time in, I think it was about 2008–9-ish, when I really started to enjoy the job. Richard had been more firmly established in promoters' minds as the AAM, and so it became easier to sell. Staffing had changed; I brought in Andrew Moore to be orchestra manager – he's now the Head of Music at the Edinburgh Festival – and he freed up my time to concentrate on sales while he handled the personnel side of things.

Ansell stepped down in March 2010, succeeded in May that year by Michael Garvey – a former manager at the Orchestra of the Age of Enlightenment, who had also, crucially, worked for the Arts Council of England. By now – a quarter of a century after it had broken away from the AAM – the OAE was widely perceived as the Academy's principal rival. Garvey saw a need to differentiate between the two ensembles:

> I don't think I saw a huge distinction in the style or even the quality of the performance. I suspect some of the OAE's activity could be seen as quirkier, because it was player-led. Having come from the OAE, and knowing the period-instrument orchestras working in the UK, I decided that I wanted the AAM to have a USP, to be distinct. To not be like the other orchestras. I wanted the AAM to do what it should do, which was, in my opinion, baroque and early classical music.

The unofficial AAM cut-off point of 1827 had become softer and vaguer; now, in the interests of affirming the AAM's identity, Garvey drew a chronological line.

I remember there was a vaguely controversial programme that Richard Egarr did in my first couple of months, which had some Benjamin Britten in it. I didn't think we should be doing that. So I told him as much and we didn't do it afterwards. I was quite keen to ensure that we had a spot, in the panoply of what orchestras provide in the UK, that was ours and ours alone. I still maintain that orchestras have to have a home. That can be a geographic home, that can be a metaphorical home, or a spiritual home. But they need somewhere that they can relate to and a community that they can engage with. I wanted to focus far more on the UK than internationally, and that is what led to the relationship with the Barbican.

The AAM became Associate Ensemble at the Barbican Centre in London in 2013. Forty years after its foundation it now had a London home commensurate, in potential and stature, with its standing as a major international orchestra. The Barbican's two concert halls – the main 1,943-seat hall and its brand new 608-seat chamber venue, Milton Court, which opened in September 2013 – offered scope for a broad range of projects. Negotiations were protracted – Garvey describes a 'beauty parade'. 'We had to justify why it should be us rather than The English Concert, or the Sixteen, or John Eliot Gardiner,' he says. 'I suspect the fact that we were no longer a founder-led orchestra was a part of that. Unlike the Sixteen, and unlike John Eliot Gardiner's groups, we had transitioned to be something more than our founder. That gave us the potential for longevity.'

Christopher Purvis was at that point Chairman of the Barbican Centre Trust. 'Of course, I'm biased,' says Purvis. 'But it gave us greater scope to do things both in the small hall and in the large. Whereas anywhere beyond row E in St John's Smith Square, you can't see anything. And if you put more than twelve people on stage in the Wigmore, you're in danger of having them fall off. Which Richard Egarr did, by the way, on one occasion.'

The association with the Barbican was part of a wider process of consolidation. International touring was reasonably healthy. After departing to work at the agency Intermusica, Ansell had continued to find overseas opportunities for the Academy, without insisting on exclusivity. Spain, Australia, the Far East and the USA were still very much on the itinerary. But other fundamentals of the AAM's world were changing. The long-established office *chez* Hogwood at 10 Brookside had in 2008 been exchanged for less salubrious Cambridge digs on Newnham Road. It was, recalls Garvey, 'cold in the winter, too hot in the summer, far too small, and had the most miserable disgusting back yard which no one ever cleaned. I think it was owned by Clare College and we rented it for an extortionate rate.' The move to more pleasantly situated offices on King's Parade, in 2012, couldn't come soon enough.

Yet, even as the office space contracted, the AAM's staff count – and the range of its activities – were expanding. Garvey recalls,

> The staff structure grew slightly in my time, and this was criticised, but if there's any success that happened in my time, it's because of them. The staff initially included Simon Fairclough, who was Director of Fundraising; Andrew Moore, who was the orchestra manager; Toby Chadd, who did marketing; Elaine Hendrie, who went on for a long time after me and looked after finances remarkably well; and Samantha Martin, who was an office administrative assistant and went on to run concerts and education. And then Kate Caro, who was a concerts assistant. We were a strong team; we knew where one person started and the other person stopped, and we got on very well.

Three substantial new directions were developed by Garvey's team. Two were contingent on each other: for the first time, the AAM instituted a substantial, permanent education programme, and for the first time, from 2011, it was awarded core funding – or in the preferred jargon, National Portfolio Organisation status – by the Arts Council of England. As Garvey explains,

> Because I'd worked with the Arts Council before, on my first day I went to the local Arts Council office and said, 'Hello, I'm new on the job, why don't you fund us? What can we do to change that?' I did that in a nice and friendly way, and a relationship developed and grew as a result of the London–Cambridge axis. We were committed to being in Cambridge but by also performing in London, we brought an international quality back into

the region. The Cambridge Arts Council office liked that. But we recognised that in order to really tick Arts Council boxes, we needed to develop a line of educational activity.

That's quite difficult, in my opinion. Trying to tell a child what a cello is and how it's different from a double bass is hard enough, without then telling them about the difference between why this one is an eighteenth-century one and that one's a twentieth-century one. A = 440 or A = 442. All that historic and period-instrument stuff is not easy to communicate in standard music lessons. So we went for the upper end of the age range, and focused particularly on students at the Guildhall School of Music and Drama – that came out of the new relationship with the Barbican – and Cambridge University.

AAMplify – as the Education programme has become known – started in 2010 and is now a central part of the Academy's activities. In its first incarnation, it made £3 concert tickets available to students in London and Cambridge, organised 'side-by-side' orchestral masterclasses for aspiring young period instrumentalists, and offered arts-management traineeships for future administrators.

More visible to the traditional classical-music audience base was the AAM's decision – after nearly four decades as one of the best-selling recording orchestras of the digital era – to launch its own record label. Lawrence had resisted the idea, and prior to the late 1990s the idea that the AAM's foundational relationship with Decca could simply vanish would have seemed inconceivable. Now, though, with the AAM firmly re-established as an orchestra whose true home was the concert hall (and particularly the UK concert hall), Garvey felt that it was time to reaffirm its presence on disc.

When I first started, Harmonia Mundi were, in theory, exclusive with the orchestra. But they weren't funding recordings: we had to cover our own musician costs. They would pay for the recording, and sell the CD through their sales network. But this was the period when the cost of recording at the right quality was falling through the floor, because the equipment was cheap as chips. You no longer needed a studio and all the kit: you could hire that in yourself. And if we as the orchestra were funding the artistic costs anyway, we wondered, well, why don't we just make our own recordings?

The musicians were very keen to record, because they always are – always have been. Richard Egarr was particularly keen to make it happen too. I think we recognised quite early on that we weren't going to make any money from it, but that if we could not lose too much money, it would be a worthwhile investment. A CD sits on a shelf – or is in someone's CD player, or their car – far more regularly than we can physically perform. And of course it could go global.

We also realised that, if we were funding our own CDs, we could make them look the way we wanted them to look, in line with the rest of the orchestra's brand. My colleague Toby Chadd invested a huge amount of time and effort to make the discs themselves absolutely beautiful. They were collectors' items. And that was in line with our desire to make the AAM the absolute pinnacle of artistic standards.

The first release, catalogue number AAM001 of 2013, comprised an Egarr programme of early symphonies from Handel to Haydn. Egarr performances of J. S. Bach Orchestral Suites and the *St John* and *St Matthew Passions* both followed in 2014. An orchestra that had been created to serve the needs of the record industry was now making recordings to support the experience of live music.

Of Jubilees: Rubies and Diamonds

The Academy of Ancient Music celebrated its fortieth anniversary – its Ruby Jubilee – across its 2013–14 season. A year previously, though, the nation and Commonwealth had celebrated the Diamond Jubilee of the reign of Queen Elizabeth II. Here was history in the making: what could be more natural than that the Academy of Ancient Music, an ensemble that breathes and lives history, should play a central part in the festivities? Michael Garvey took the initiative.

They'd announced two years beforehand that to celebrate the Queen's Diamond Jubilee, there was going to be a river pageant on the Thames. I thought: 'Oh, that's funny: we do the *Water Music* all the time.' So I found out who was going to be curating the festival and I emailed him and said, 'Hello, I'm Michael Garvey, and I run an orchestra – you'll have heard of us – and I think that the perfect way to celebrate the Diamond Jubilee would be with the music that was written for a previous incumbent of the throne of England.' I got a nice email back saying, 'Thanks very much.' And that was that: not a yes, not a no. And then ten or twelve months later I got a phone call one morning to ask if we could talk about it. I couldn't believe it was actually coming true.

The Thames Diamond Jubilee Pageant took place on 3 June 2012. A flotilla of 670 vessels ranging from tugboats and historic warships to dragon boats, square-riggers, Dunkirk 'little ships' and royal barges paraded down the Thames from Battersea Bridge to Tower Bridge, with the Queen and Duke of Edinburgh on board the motor cruiser *Spirit of Chartwell*. Punctuating the 7.5-mile-long procession were what were called 'Musical Herald Barges', playing live music from groups as diverse as the Shree Muktajeevan Swamibapa Pipe Band, the Jubilant Commonwealth Choir and the Band of the Royal Marines. Bringing up the rear was the full London Philharmonic Orchestra; original music for the occasion had been commissioned from composers including Graham Fitkin, Jocelyn Pook and Howard Goodall. But first in line was Richard Egarr and the Academy of Ancient Music, playing Handel's original royal *Water Music* – a work that had been intimately associated with the group since Hogwood's pioneering 1978 Prom. Crowds of over 1 million spectators watched from the banks of the Thames; over 10 million watched the live BBC TV coverage.

Events of this nature don't simply fall into place. Garvey credits the AAM's orchestra manager Andrew Moore with the detailed planning of a performance that – even by the standards of the AAM – was distinctly out of the ordinary. 'He masterminded how to get twenty-five musicians on the top of a boat in the river when the instruments are delicate and ancient and precious. How do you put a harpsichord on a boat so it doesn't roll off? And what happens when it rains? And lo and behold, it did rain!'

In the traditional manner of the British high summer, it bucketed down all day. Temperatures were chilly, and while the eighty-six-year-old Queen and the ninety-year-old Duke of Edinburgh remained standing throughout the four-hour pageant, the experience of the AAM players varied (as is often the way in orchestras) depending on which instrument they played. Pavlo Beznosiuk remembers it as 'one of the most horrible days in my life. It was freezing. It was miserable. Nobody could hear us. We may as well have not been there.' The idea had been to broadcast the music to the crowds on shore via loudspeakers on the barge. In reality it was almost inaudible over the ambient noise. 'It was a complete wash-out. I remember getting off at Canary Wharf, which is just down the road from me, and walking home in the drizzle, then opening the gin and thinking why, why, why? That was a very long day.'

From the timpani, Benedict Hoffnung remembers it all rather more warmly:

It was good, because we stayed dry the whole day. We had a cooked breakfast on board the boat while everybody else – including my wife, who was standing on the riverbank – got absolutely soaked. It was actually very comfortable: we had a Perspex screen around us, which kept us dry and wind-free. It was a bit of a laugh.

Richard Egarr held it all together. 'We rehearsed the whole thing on the barge in late January or early February, and the weather was exactly the same as it was in June. So that was actually quite a good rehearsal! It was pretty wet.' Looking back, he is still glad to have been involved.

I mean, it wasn't a musical experience, and especially because we had amplification on the boat. The barge was pumping the sound out on both sides on these big plastic speakers, and of course, we were getting this horrible echo back from the banks. So, we were playing, and then getting two versions of it back at different times. You just had to try and keep time. But it was a wonderful thing to do. It was great fun to be part of it, and to see all those people was incredible.

In essence, it was all about profile: if any period-instrument orchestra was to be at the centre of national life, then that orchestra should be the AAM, the nation's flagship interpreters of Handel and his contemporaries. For Garvey, that was justification enough.

It worked – absolutely, it worked. It was a washout of a weekend and the BBC coverage was absolutely panned for being atrocious. But nevertheless there were tens of thousands of people lining the Thames that day, and we were centre stage. It was one of those moments when Christopher Purvis could wheel out his rich friends, and really milk those potential donors: because there was actually only one other orchestra in the entire country that was doing this, and that was the LPO, which couldn't be more different. So, look: isn't the AAM doing a really good thing at the moment?[7]

Damp as it was, the Jubilee Pageant served as a useful reminder of the Academy's stature as it entered its own anniversary season. On 8 December 2013 Lucie Skeaping presented a celebratory edition of the *Early Music Show* on BBC Radio 3: telling the story of the group's first four decades, but – with Egarr in the studio – placing the emphasis very much on the present and the future. 'There's always new ground to break and new things to learn. I think what's important is that we carry on the work that was done in those early days,' he told her.

We've started a record label, on which we've already released one record, *The Birth of the Symphony*, and a *St John Passion* is coming up. We're continuing a Bach cycle: it's strange that the Academy has never recorded the Bach Passions, so we've got the *John Passion* and the *Matthew Passion* . . . Music by [Dario] Castello that we're hoping to record complete. Also, we're exploring Monteverdi's operas in the next three years: we did *Orfeo* this year at the Barbican to start our season. Next year, we'll do *Poppea* and the following season we'll do *Ulisse*. And then in the three years after that, we're looking at exploring early nineteenth-century Italian opera – so perhaps Rossini, Donizetti. Who knows? There's plenty of work to do . . .

Not all profile-raising needs to be as spectacular (or as artistically unsatisfying) as the Jubilee Pageant. Garvey is particularly proud of the partnership that the Academy forged with the National Gallery as Resident Ensemble of the summer 2013 exhibition *Vermeer and Music:*

The Art of Love and Leisure. The exhibition, which ran from June to September, brought together for the first time three paintings in which Vermeer depicts music-making or musical instruments: *A Young Woman Standing at a Virginal*, *A Young Woman Seated at a Virginal* and *The Guitar Player*. The AAM's mission was to bring them to life. 'I was approached by Marjorie Wieseman of the National Gallery, and I could see that that would be a wonderful fundraising opportunity and it would elevate the orchestra's profile,' says Garvey. 'We agreed that the AAM would play 25 minutes of music in the exhibition, every hour on the hour, for five hours a day, four days a week.'

She changed her ticket prices accordingly so that when the musicians were there, it cost more to go to the exhibition. And as a result, those tickets absolutely flew out the door. The marketing was remarkable. We had Tube posters – the National Gallery's got a very large marketing pot – and they had a huge logo saying, 'Featuring live music performed by the Academy of Ancient Music'. We could never have hoped to make a marketing splash anywhere near that size.

We asked the musicians to find music that Vermeer himself might have heard – that was very easy for them to do – and we found space in the gallery for eight or maybe ten musicians at a time, including harpsichord or theorbo. The National Gallery had kittens, because all these musicians were surrounded by multi-million-pound works of art, and they expected to treat the gallery as if it was a backstage area. That was very funny. And our players became like rock stars because the galleries were absolutely rammed throughout the entire summer. People who go to art galleries don't usually hear live music; it was intended as background music and we expected the visitors to walk and talk. But they didn't: they stopped and listened. In fact, the Gallery took away the chairs to try to prevent people from sitting. It was a really good idea; really innovative.

Vermeer's paintings are flooded with a sense of almost transcendent tranquillity; a mind, and a painter's brush, moving on silence. And yet the images in the exhibition implied sound, emotion and vivid and intimate communication: in a word, music. Writing about the project in the *Guardian*, Richard Egarr explored the paradox. 'Period performance means using instruments as close as possible to the period when the music was written,' he explained, with the time-honoured patience of an AAM music director:

> With them we aim to create a sound as near as we can get to that which the composer would have heard, but what's more important is the sensibility of the time – the freedom. This music has to be passionate and free, and that is what we hope to convey as we play in the gallery alongside these Vermeers . . .
>
> We hope people will pay attention, but if they want to get up and leave, that's fine too. The idea of sitting down and listening in silence to a musical performance is only a twentieth-century one, after all. In Vermeer's time being involved in a musical performance was a live interactive experience. People weren't expected to be quiet. Throw things at us if you feel the urge. Well, maybe not while we're playing, but interact with us, or at the very least come and talk to us afterwards.[8]

The setting was intimate, rather than imposing. But in the year that it turned forty, the Academy of Ancient Music created a new and revelatory shared experience simply by remaining true to its founding principle: taking ancient music, and presenting it with intelligence, with imagination, and with an absolute devotion to both the spirit and the letter of its art.

11

THE TRIUMPH
OF TIME AND TRUTH

Michael Garvey stood down as Chief Executive of the Academy of Ancient Music in December 2013. 'It wasn't that I wanted to leave AAM at all,' he says. 'I really enjoyed it and loved the team and what we were doing.' But an opportunity to become Director of the BBC National Orchestra of Wales was too good to pass up. Christopher Purvis had stepped down from his epic and transformative tenure as Chair at the end of August that year, succeeded by Terence Sinclair, and Garvey's greatest regret about his departure is that it came at a time when continuity in the Academy's management would have helped ease the transition.

It's unlikely, however, that even Garvey would have been able to stave off the blow, in 2014, of the Arts Council of England's decision to drop the AAM from its National Portfolio: in other words, to axe the group's core funding. Since this funding had been granted to the AAM only in 2011, this was not the existential blow that it might have represented for a larger or more complacent orchestra. But it did require a certain amount of rethinking from Sinclair and the new Chief Executive, Jonathan Manners.

'My father had died just before Christmas 2013,' remembers Manners, who had built a strong reputation in the industry as Head of the Music Department at English National Opera.

I buried my father on the Friday, and I was in the AAM office first thing on a Monday morning. It was a baptism of fire. Whenever colleagues go through personal issues I genuinely believe that it's important that we all remind ourselves that it's just music. We do things as well as we can, all of the time – that's our job. But at the sacrifice of personal health? No, it isn't worth it. And, funnily enough, when I had the call from the Arts Council to say that we had lost the funding, I knew exactly what was required for the Academy to go on from there, and what I had to do for the organisation. And I concluded that I had to walk away.

I remember hearing the Academy performing the *St Matthew Passion* at King's College on Good Friday, and thinking quite how special the AAM is. It's such a remarkable group of people. But I just didn't have the fight in me, at that time, to take the organisation forward.

Manners left the AAM in August 2014, after eight months. In 2016, he took up a new post as Chief Producer and Artistic Director of the BBC Singers, though he is still touched by the sympathy shown by the AAM musicians when they learned of his decision.

Garvey's and Manners's departures coincided with the loss of several long-serving office staff, as well as the cancellation of the ACE grant: Ed Hossack, Manners's successor, was invited in July 2014 to serve as Acting CEO; as he puts it, 'to steady the ship'. He was offered the post on a permanent basis later in the autumn, but found his immediate options limited:

I always think of the history of an organisation as a sort of cycle. There should have been a cycle of renewal, with a new chairman, a new chief executive, the renewal of NPO funding: that was the moment when the AAM would really fly. For obvious reasons, that didn't happen. So my approach was very much 'heads down, let's just survive'. There was certainly work in the diary: Michael and Andrew [Moore] had done amazing work to find the tools and the opportunities. But the staff were unsettled because of the turnover of senior staff, and a little bit burned out by the real achievement of the fortieth-anniversary gala.

The fortieth-anniversary season had concluded in heroic style at the Barbican on 21 July 2014 – with Egarr conducting the AAM and its

Choir, augmented by AAMplify performers from London, Cambridge and Manchester, in a programme of Haydn's 104th, Mozart's 41st and Beethoven's Ninth Symphonies. A few weeks previously, in June, the AAM had hosted its first ever fundraising gala: a black-tie event for 250 guests, held at Hatfield House, and featuring a three-course champagne dinner and a private recital by Egarr and the mezzo Joyce DiDonato. It was a success, raising £60,000. But organising one-off prestige events of this sort places immense pressure on a small organisation. The public sees the serenely gliding swan, but not its feet, paddling frantically beneath the water.

'So yes, I think there was a sense of pause,' remembers Hossack. 'And there really wasn't the money in the bank to do anything other than pause. At that point, Chris Hogwood was still alive.' The personal and artistic tragedy of Hogwood's early death that September would – exactly as he had hoped – inject new financial strength into the orchestra to which he had dedicated his life. It became known during 2015 that Hogwood had left just over £1m[1] to the AAM, which the Board (in keeping with the wishes that he expressed during his final months) designated to support 'out-of-the-ordinary projects that would otherwise not be affordable'.[2] For Hossack, it was a liberation:

> When the Hogwood legacy became clear, the extent of that legacy
> – and the fact that it was really restricted – gave the organisation
> the opportunity to develop more of an outgoing, entrepreneurial,
> adventurous culture. But you can't turn an orchestra around on a
> dime. It takes time to secure the work, to get concerts in the diary.

One decision was pragmatic, but positive: renegotiation of the ongoing and artistically successful Barbican partnership, despite the disappearance of the Arts Council funds that had originally underwritten the AAM's financial risk on these high-profile (but costly) concerts.

> It's a golden ticket for an orchestra to be resident at a venue. And
> the fact that the Orchestra of the Age of Enlightenment is only
> 'resident' at the Southbank, while the AAM is Associate Ensemble
> at the Barbican is a real coup. Overall, I think it was a really very
> sound move – a key part of the orchestra's strategy.

Other decisions were equally pragmatic, but more painful: a plan to resume the Hogwood–Levin Mozart cycle was no longer financially viable in the absence of Hogwood. It was quietly shelved. But as the situation stabilised, and with the reassuring presence of the Hogwood legacy on the balance sheet, other projects became possible. Even now, the AAM still had new territories to explore. On 3 May 2016 the Academy became the first European orchestra to play in the new Prince Mahidol Hall in Bangkok, Thailand. (Egarr conducted the soprano Vivica Genaux in arias by Vivaldi as well as the inevitable Handel *Water Music*, before proceeding to Beijing and Shanghai.) 'Great fun,' remembers Hossack, 'particularly for the orchestra manager, who was incredibly allergic to peanuts.'

But the real quiet revolution was happening closer to home. In 2017, when the countertenor Michael Chance – an old collaborator of the Academy – launched a new summer opera festival at the Grange in Hampshire, Hossack persuaded him to appoint the AAM as one of the festival's two orchestras in residence – playing for baroque and classical operas, while the Bournemouth Symphony Orchestra handled the later repertoire. 'The Board had been looking to me for some time to get a residency with one of the summer opera festivals,' recalls Hossack – the Orchestra of the Age of Enlightenment's annual block of well-paid work at Glyndebourne was a long-standing source of envy.

'Opera was something that AAM had increasingly looked to over the last few years, with Richard directing the semi-staged Monteverdi operas at the Barbican at the beginning of each year. But that relationship with Grange Festival was beneficial for the profile of the orchestra: a really interesting artistic partnership with Michael Chance and his new company, and work for our musicians across the summer,' says Hossack. Jean-Luc Tingaud conducted the AAM in the Grange's inaugural staging of *Il ritorno d'Ulisse* in June 2017; subsequent seasons included Handel's *Agrippina* with Robert Howarth, and (in 2019) *Le nozze di Figaro* with Egarr.

The grassroots needed watering too. 'There hadn't been a dedicated, full-time education and outreach staff member,' says Hossack.

So I made that happen. We did workshops with Cambridge primary schools for the first time. It took time to set up education and outreach work with an organisation that wasn't really financially sustainable. It wasn't a priority; then it became a priority and

I'm very proud to have achieved that. The aim was to stop and consider where we were in Cambridge and the East of England – an area that is not well served by music education. It was an opportunity to get close to the local Arts Council as well; to make sure that relationship was kept alive. But it was also about trying to create more of a coherent link between the identity of the group and its function.

The AAM is placed differently to other orchestras, purely because of its name: the Academy of Ancient Music. I really wanted to establish that 'non-musical musical' aspect of the AAM's whole ethos; the link with academia. There were existing links with various universities and music colleges around the country, particularly with the Guildhall. There was primary-school work in the community. This was all great. But it simply wasn't enough. For me, it was more than just working with schools or just working with music-college students. It was about collaborating with the Fitzwilliam Museum or working with Addenbrooke's Hospital on their collection of musical artefacts. One of the biggest achievements of my time was the concept and creation of the Hogwood Fellow.

The idea of appointing a specialist scholar or artist to work on major projects with the Academy came to Hossack immediately after Hogwood's memorial service.

There was an informal gathering that Chris Lawrence and I attended together at Pembroke College. The fundraisers from the two Cambridge colleges which he had remembered in his will, as well as the two London colleges – the Royal College and the Royal Academy – were all there, and I said, 'You will all be appointing Hogwood scholars, won't you?' They all said, 'Yes.' And I just thought: well, the AAM should do the same. We should have our own Hogwood scholar. Robert Levin was the ideal first candidate: someone who would perform with the orchestra, who was very close to the musicians, incredibly creative, incredibly scholarly, and who could also write. And that, for me, went beyond business as usual for an orchestra.

Levin was appointed inaugural Hogwood Fellow in 2017; he was followed by the bassist, composer and educator Sandy Burnett, the visual artist Emma Safe and the present author.

A renewed commitment to scholarship had practical and artistic benefits. Oboist and orchestral fixer Lars Henriksson assisted Hossack in devising saleable, practical touring programmes that could be marketed to concert promoters. 'It's not just, "What do I want to play?" It's also, "What will this orchestra benefit from?"' says Henriksson.

> The Board had a very strong idea of what they wanted for the orchestra – they wanted the past glory to return. The Artistic Director wanted to do stuff that he enjoyed, and the CEO had, of course, to sell concerts. I produced a number of programmes – there's one with the Brandenburg Concertos 4 and 5, and Telemann's *Don Quichotte*, that I still see being recycled to this day.

The AAM's fledgling label pivoted, quietly, to focus once more on music that deserved rediscovery, and that sparked the passion of its Music Director. In January 2016, at St George's Church, Chesterton, Egarr and a chamber-sized AAM recorded the first book of *Sonate concertate in stil moderno* of 1621 by Dario Castello (1602–1631). It was another luxury product in the spirit of Florilegium, with carefully chosen artwork, sleeve notes by the Academy's theorbo player William Carter and a spirited publicity campaign from Egarr himself, whose enthusiasm matched – in spirit, if not his exact choice of words – the missionary zeal of the young Hogwood:

> Twelve incredible, ball-busting sonatas by this wacky early-seventeenth-century virtuoso guy called Dario Castello, who probably was a bit like Eric Clapton and Jimi Hendrix. The album, from the Academy of Ancient Music, features incredible solos by our two lead violinists, Pavlo Beznosiuk and Bojan Čičić; Josué Meléndez on cornetto, which is a kind of kinky leather-covered banana; Benny Aghassi on a bassoon bazooka; Sue Addison on a raspy trombone; and myself and Bill Carter on continuo and organ and theorbo, and finally Joseph Crouch on a very strange violin–cello hybrid. Buy it, put it on really really loudly in your living room and you'll have a great time.[3]

Critics seemed to agree. 'So eventful are these 12 trio- and quartet-sonatas that you can indeed find yourself gorging greedily,' wrote Lindsay Kemp in *Gramophone*.

> The difficulty of these sonatas was acknowledged by Castello but the AAM's expert players are gleefully equal to the job, and, in music which must sometimes feel rather like a bucking bronco, know when to rein it in and when to give it its head. A joy for ear and spirit.[4]

The disc also placed – front and centre – the playing of violinists Pavlo Beznosiuk and Bojan Čičić. It was a signifier, though no one then knew it, of things to come. After a decade as leader, and having played regularly with the AAM since 1985, Beznosiuk stood down in August 2017. Čičić became leader on an official basis from April 2018, though, like Beznosiuk, he had a long history with the group. Born in Croatia, he belongs to a generation of baroque violinists who have lived their entire lives in an early-music world shaped by the Academy of Ancient Music. He can't recall, exactly, the date of his first concert with the AAM (it was a *Messiah* at the Sheldonian Theatre, Oxford, somewhere around 2010). But he struggles to remember a time when the Academy was not a presence on his musical horizon.

> The first time I heard them was maybe in 2001 or 2002. They came to Vienna, and I was still living in Zagreb. I took a train to see the concert, and I remember that Anthony Pay was playing the Mozart Clarinet Concerto. And afterwards, to save money, I stayed with a friend, [AAM cellist] Joe Crouch, and took a train back home the next morning – back to Zagreb. So that was the first time I heard them live, all those years ago.

But even before he'd heard the Academy play, Čičić had been drawn into its orbit. As a violin student in Zagreb, a masterclass with Catherine Mackintosh had inspired him to make the transition into baroque playing.

> I played Bach's A Minor Fugue for her. And by that point, I was already interested in listening to recordings – I had some

Jordi Savall CDs, I had some Reinhard Goebel recordings, and *Romanesca* with Andrew Manze. I loved that sound world, so I went, of course, to this masterclass. It was a complete revelation to see musicians approaching music almost like a hobby, or a passion – where it's not only about the music, but also the society in which composers lived, the formation of orchestras, how would it sound, what the music might mean. These musicians just had a much wider breadth of knowledge than the ones that I was used to. It appealed to the curious side of my nature. And at the same time, it kept a sort of modesty: well, this might not be the truth, but it's a version of it that we believe in.

Mackintosh invited him to Aestas Musica, her baroque summer course in Croatia.

'Other teachers there included Jennifer Ward Clark, Nicolette Moonen and Laurence Cummings, so that's where my connection with AAM began,' he recalls.

I was in love with period performance and knew that I had to try and do this with my life, but it was a totally different world. At the time it wasn't available to me unless I went abroad. After graduating, I joined the Zagreb Soloists, but after a year working there, in 2003 I decided to do something about my love of early music and moved to France to study at the Paris Conservatoire. During my studies there, I was mainly playing French music, or German music in a French way, but not much Italian music. I learnt more about German and Italian repertoire from Rachel Podger when I went to study at London's Guildhall School of Music and Drama, where I finished my MA in Performing Arts in 2007.

I remember Lars Ulrik Mortensen in a masterclass saying that early-music students should start by playing only French baroque in the first year, move on to Italian style for the second and then go into German style for the third. I was very lucky to have had that in my own education, so I would tend to agree with this statement.[5]

The Castello disc had been a passion project of Egarr's. But with a more ambitious overview, it was possible to align the multiple poles of fundraising, profile-raising, live performance and recording in a way that made much larger projects feasible. The days when the music director had an idea and Decca simply wrote a cheque and booked a studio – followed by a multi-date promotional tour – are a distant memory in the twenty-first century. A major recording project now has to be part of a much more comprehensive (some would say healthier) artistic and organisational outlook. If the music director believes in a work, the whole organisation needs to align behind them.

Egarr felt that way about Handel's mighty, neglected *Brockes Passion* – a setting of the Passion story as retold by the Hamburg poet Barthold Heinrich Brockes (1680–1747), and first performed in Handel's former home of Hamburg at Easter 1719. 'It's something I was talking about for many years, and we just managed to get it together,' says Egarr.

> There are three great Passion-related pieces by Handel. You have the early Italian Catholic one, *La Resurrezione*. And you have the one for England: *Messiah*. And then we have this one for Germany. Because of the content, and the fact that it is so obscenely gory and graphic, it didn't appeal to English taste at all. There are a couple of German recordings, and Nic McGegan did it in Hungary. But it's a real masterpiece: of the three, I think it's right up there.

But an unfamiliar evening-long choral epic, with twelve soloists (including three drawn from within the AAM Choir itself) is no longer something that can be thrown together for a commercial recording at a few months' notice. A new edition had to be prepared (edited by Leo Duarte), plans needed to be co-ordinated with partner organisations such as the Barbican, and of course money had to be raised. Over a hundred individual friends and supporters of the AAM contributed to the project, and for the subsequent release of the recording individuals could sponsor specific roles and sections in the Passion – including Jesus, the Evangelist, Judas and Pilate. Hogwood Fellow Sandy Burnett helped co-ordinate the various strands of the project, while the AAM's new Chief Executive Alexander Van Ingen had overall responsibility. Hossack had stepped down in early 2017 – his daily four-and-a-half-hour commute to Cambridge from south-west London had become unsustainable – and was succeeded by Van Ingen, who joined the AAM in April 2017 from (a playful but largely coincidental quirk of fate) Decca.

'I think it's fair to say that the AAM record label is never likely to be commercially successful,' says Van Ingen.

It will cover the cost of initiating a project from the ground up. But there are other ways that the label contributes to the organisation. You might not earn money from a recording like the *Brockes Passion*, but it does enable you to raise money because you can create an interesting product or project. It allows a significant expansion of brand awareness, which, again, can be a catalyst towards being able to raise money for the organisation centrally. We realised early on that AAM has a huge number of listeners online – and in three years we turned it into the most listened-to period-instrument ensemble in the world.

That doesn't bring you much money, because most of the AAM's recordings are owned by Universal. But it is a significant thing when it comes to raising money; it's about attracting new donors and telling donors the story of the organisation, and what it is that they're supporting. Everybody wants to support a successful organisation. And when it comes to the CD, you want to really be able to see it, to feel it, to understand it, to smell it. So that's why we did *Brockes Passion* with a big 220-page booklet, full-colour artwork and all the extra recordings of the Jennens translations – just to make it the most complete it could be. We found that people who bought it at concerts were typically buying copies in pairs, because they wanted to give one as a gift to someone else. They could see that this was a special product. The Dussek Mass and Eccles's *Semele* were released in a similar format.

Meanwhile, after two years of preparatory work, Egarr conducted the *Brockes Passion* at the Barbican on Good Friday 2019 – the 300th anniversary of the work's first performance in Hamburg. The recording, taken from the rehearsals and performance, and adorned with cover art by Hogwood Fellow Emma Safe, was released in October 2019. Once more, the Academy of Ancient Music was redefining the public perception of a major choral work by Handel, and on no one's terms but its own.

'We had plenty of donors who, having said they were going to leave, not only came back into the fold, but started giving us more money because they really, suddenly, felt that they were part of an organisation that was going somewhere, and was dynamic,' says Van Ingen.

'The AAM supported it massively,' says Egarr.

> I mean, it was a huge project, with the new edition and the new translations. It was quite something. So it was really a spectacular vote of confidence by the AAM, not just in me, but in that kind of project and that kind of research and scholarship. Because there are still pieces which deserve that kind of attention – which have been forgotten, if you like.

One such buried masterwork was Jan Ladislav's Dussek's *Messe Solemnelle* (1811) – the focus of Egarr's next major act of musical archaeology. 'I've been keen on Dussek for a good decade: a totally neglected and really important composer. I'd read in a dissertation that one of his last pieces was this Solemn Mass, and I knew that the manuscript was in the conservatory library in Florence.' First attempts to obtain the score fell on the stony ground of Italian bureaucracy, but in July 2015, Egarr took matters into his own hands. 'I was on holiday in Florence with my new wife. We were just sort-of wandering around and I thought, "Let's just go to the conservatory library and see if anybody's there." It was a Sunday. It was a stupid idea. We rang the bell. A lady opened the doors, and within forty-eight hours, I had a beautiful digital copy of the manuscript.'

Egarr's recording of Dussek's *Messe Solemnelle* would be recorded along the same deluxe lines in October 2019. John Eccles's 1707 opera *Semele* (a collaboration with Cambridge Handel Opera Company, conducted by Julian Perkins) followed shortly afterwards, complete with booklet essay by Stephen Fry. Both were nominated for *Gramophone* awards in 2021; the Dussek was victorious in its class. And both were released into a musical world that had – once again, and this time without warning – changed beyond recognition.

Transformation in a Time of Covid

Some changes can be anticipated. In August 2018, Richard Egarr announced his intention to stand down as the AAM's Music Director at the end of the 2020–21 season. Like his predecessor, and like his old friend Andrew Manze, Egarr has always had catholic tastes, with an appetite for repertoire far beyond the Academy of Ancient Music's core territory. What do they know of ancient music, who only ancient music know? Unlike some of the more doctrinaire Continental practitioners, British early-music performers have thrived on open-mindedness and pragmatism. Hogwood had his Martinů; in 2016 Egarr recorded a sparkling *HMS Pinafore* with Scottish Opera. 'The idea came to us one night at a post-recording-session dinner and lots of wine, after we'd recorded the *St John Passion*: I looked round the table and said, "Wouldn't this be a great cast for a Gilbert and Sullivan production?!"' he told *Presto Music*.[6]

For the Academy of Ancient Music, however, the chronological parameters remained fixed, with the 1820s as Ultima Thule: thus far, and no further. 'I think that the Board felt that was the AAM brand,' says Egarr.

> I can understand that, but for me that was necessarily a little bit of a disappointment. I would've loved to have done some Mendelssohn, and I know the players would, as well. I would have loved to have done more Beethoven – I only ever did three of the symphonies. But I mustn't grumble too much, because I was able to do some really wonderful things – especially the *Brockes Passion* and the Dussek Mass – that the AAM has been 150 per cent behind. That's absolutely what the AAM is about. It's about breaking ground within the parameters that they've set, and it's been nice to be able to find repertoire that still needs that approach.

A new post as Music Director of San Francisco's Philharmonia Baroque Orchestra offered an opportunity to explore areas closed to the AAM. Egarr planned to conclude his opening season in San Francisco with a period-instrument performance of Tchaikovsky's Fourth Symphony.

> That was something that was very important to me – to be able to spread my musical wings in the early-music world, and also branch forward into a later repertoire as well. I realised that was not going to happen with the AAM, so it was a natural progression.
>
> I'm not going to do an Andrew and just say no to directing from the harpsichord – but I've always had a very broad taste in

music. I've done Bruckner symphonies and new music as well. I'm taking over the Philharmonia Baroque Orchestra at the same point that I took over the AAM. Nic [McGegan] steered that orchestra brilliantly for the last thirty-five years, and now I'm trying to take it in a slightly different direction.

Of course, for the music director of a conventional symphony orchestra, a fifteen-year tenure would be a marathon. The transition to a more conventional model of artistic leadership is further evidence that the early-music scene has come of age; in that regard, as in so many others, the AAM has led the field. Egarr was also acutely aware that throughout the second decade of the twenty-first century, the AAM was navigating choppy financial and administrative waters. However unavoidable the reasons, it's rarely conducive to consistent artistic planning when an organisation gets through five chief executives in ten years. 'I've genuinely enjoyed working with every one of them,' says Egarr. 'Unfortunately, that kind of instability is not good for an orchestra.' The formation of a players' committee (for the first time in the AAM's history) in the summer of 2019 suggests that uncertainties were starting to filter through to the musicians themselves. Amid the growing economic instability of the late 2010s, it's easy enough to understand why a musician as ambitious as Egarr might seek calmer seas in which to steer his creative course.

Van Ingen initiated the process of seeking a successor. Meanwhile, there was the day-to-day business of running an orchestra – planning tours, concert series and recordings. 'We got back into the States,' he says. 'We were lining up a nice Australia tour, again, having not been there for some years.'

In the 2019–20 season – as it would transpire, Egarr's last relatively normal season as Music Director – the AAM played 26 concerts: in London, Cambridge, Bury St Edmunds, Oxford, Malvern and Bath, as well as in Germany, the Netherlands, Turkey and the USA (Los Angeles and San Francisco). There were recorded collaborations with the chamber choir VOCES8 and the soprano Chen Reiss. With the success of the recent recordings, and the approach of the Academy's fiftieth anniversary, plans began to take shape for a major recording project with a special significance: a piece of unfinished business. Van Ingen began to draw plans to resume the long-abandoned Mozart piano concerto cycle with

Robert Levin. On 11 March 2020, he announced his departure for a new role at the head of the Philharmonia Orchestra, effective from September that year.

'I was very torn,' he says.

> It was something that was going really well. I felt I was leaving too early, because the fruits of our labours had only just started to bloom, but I was given a lot of sweet-talking by the Philharmonia and I thought, 'Well, something like that only comes up once.' I thought I'd give it a crack. How that turned out is a completely different story, and one for a different book.

Twelve days later, on 23 March 2020, in response to the global Covid-19 pandemic, the government of the United Kingdom announced a nationwide lockdown. At a stroke, every concert venue was closed and every public concert cancelled for what (it was initially assumed) would be a period of several weeks. In the event, it would effectively end public music-making under normal circumstances for most of the next two concert seasons: a disruption in national (and international) concert life without precedent in peacetime. On 14 March 2020 the AAM had played a programme of baroque lollipops at Leeds Town Hall. The final item – Bach's Cantata No. 51, 'Jauchzet Gott in allen Landen' – would be the last music that the Academy would play in public for the foreseeable future. Performances of Bach's *St John Passion*, in Cambridge and London, Handel and Herschel at King's Lynn, and Monteverdi's *Ulisse* at Longborough Festival Opera were among the projects cancelled or indefinitely postponed.

In these circumstances – with a departing music director and no confirmed successor, with all live public performance on ice, plus staff operating in isolation and halfway through a relocation to new offices on St Matthew's Street, Cambridge – Van Ingen's successor John McMunn took up his post on 1 September 2020. In accordance with general practice during the Covid pandemic he was interviewed via the digital platform Zoom, but he knew what he was stepping into. As a former choral scholar at King's College, Cambridge, McMunn had grown up, musically, alongside the AAM, in the same artistic and academic milieu (a generation or two removed) that had nurtured Hogwood, Munrow, Manze and Egarr.

He sang with the Academy on numerous occasions during the triumvirate era, appearing briefly as a soloist on Stephen Cleobury's 2006 AAM recording of Purcell's *Music for Queen Mary*. 'I remember feeling very privileged to work alongside the members of the band,' he recalls. Having decided to move into management, in 2014 and 2015 he'd worked in the AAM's marketing and fundraising teams under Jonathan Manners and Ed Hossack, before going on to serve as General Manager of Paul McCreesh's Gabrieli Consort and Players. His first priority – even before he accepted the post – was to appoint Egarr's successor.

> The selection process began a long time before I was on the team. But I had a conversation with Philip Jones, who was then Chair of the Board, when I was thinking about applying and I asked, 'Has this appointment been made?' If the answer had been 'yes', then I wouldn't have been as interested overall as if the answer was 'no'. It's a key relationship. There was a real, amazing, opportunity to join with someone else who was new and to put forth an entirely new vision.

The man who would shape that vision was the harpsichordist, organist and conductor Laurence Cummings. On 18 November 2020, it was announced that effective from the start of the 2021–2 season he would be the next Music Director of the Academy of Ancient Music – only the third in its forty-eight-year history. In a radical departure for the Academy, his musical roots lay not in Cambridge, but at Christ Church College, Oxford – though as a trustee of the Handel House Museum and Artistic Director (since 2011) of the Göttingen International Handel Festival, his musical imagination was very much at home in the ancestral heartlands of the Academy's repertoire.

'It was the AAM's recordings with Christ Church Choir that actually inspired me as a teenager,' says Cummings. 'So in a funny kind of way, I feel like the orchestra was part of my musical education – particularly when I was at Oxford. It was the late 1980s so it was the zenith of the period-instrument movement. All the lectures were centred around that – and obviously, although Chris Hogwood was based in Cambridge, we were very much aware of what he was doing.' As Head of Historical Performance at the Royal Academy of Music from 1997 to 2012,

Cummings would have regular dealings with Hogwood. 'He was the visiting international professor, so I had a lot of interaction with him. The students and I went to his house in Cambridge, and played his instruments and saw his library – he was incredibly generous with all that. So, yes, I feel like I knew him well.' Still, the call from the AAM came as a surprise.

> I had never worked with them before, so it was rather nice to come in with a clean slate. Actually, I had done one concert of a three-concert tour earlier that year. But then the tour got cut short because of Covid and the management felt that the orchestra should have the chance to work more with the person who would be their musical director. I had to audition. They said, 'We're interested in you, we've got this position, would you mind auditioning?' It was the August of the pandemic year, 2020, and I was delighted to do that after eight months of not having done anything at all. We had a baroque day and a classical day. For the baroque day I did a Handel flute concerto with Rachel Brown, a Handel concerto grosso, and a big Rameau suite from *Dardanus*. And then, for the classical day, we did Mozart's *Idomeneo* overture and ballet music, and a Haydn symphony – No. 49, *La Passione*. It was wonderful coming together and I was delighted that I got the job.
>
> It had been a tricky time. The first concert I did was when I'd been appointed but before I was in post. And it was a chamber concert up in West Road to no audience – freezing cold because the University insisted on having ventilation from outside, and it was February.

This was spring 2021, when – due to prevailing advice about transmission of the Covid virus – such concerts that did take place did so with no audience and masked musicians seated at least six feet apart, with doors propped wide open to maintain a healthy draught.

> The weirdest thing was travelling back to London with no one else on the train. Arriving at King's Cross at 10.30 p.m. on a Friday night, I was the only person on the platform. It was dystopian, really. Of course everyone was just very grateful to be playing,

because for such a long time we'd been unable to do anything at all.

For McMunn, too, the pandemic dominated the first days of what should have been a thrilling new role: working alone amid yet-to-be-unpacked boxes in the empty office, with all music-making and AAMplify work cancelled and staff working remotely. Like orchestral managers across the world, McMunn and his Head of Planning & Operations Fiona McDonnell (who had joined the AAM just a few months before him) found themselves forced to make and remake artistic plans within the restraints of changing, restrictive (and often contradictory) public health regulations. 'I was appointed in early June 2020, with an official start date of 1 September, but I more or less started immediately. What planning there was, was cancelled pretty quickly,' he remembers. The bare facts stated in the AAM's August 2020 annual report paint the overall picture as concisely and comprehensively as any such document allows. 'The 2019–20 season was a tale of two halves,' it begins.

Between the first lockdown and 31 August 2020, the orchestra was forced to cancel 19 concerts in the UK and internationally, and countless other projects were paused or postponed indefinitely . . .

There were nevertheless creative opportunities amidst the disruption. Closure of concert halls and recording studios forced our activities online, and between March and June 2020 we released 12 full-length concerts on YouTube, an initiative branded 'Streaming Sundays'. To date, these performances have received nearly 1.5 million views. From June, we began curating weekly playlists on Spotify highlighting AAM's rich and varied catalogue of recordings. #SpotifySundays featured tracks selected by a series of guests (past and present music directors, principal players, trustees and staff) and were released with detailed notes and personal reflections on the works included. Through these efforts we increased our Facebook followership by more than 13 per cent to 44,437; grew YouTube subscriptions by 161 per cent to 16,200; and maintained an average of more than 1 million monthly listeners on Spotify, 50 per cent of whom are under the age of thirty-five.

These achievements are cold comfort of course to our talented freelance musicians, who saw their livelihoods decimated in the second half of the year. From the very beginning of the pandemic, AAM has been determined to help musicians and save our world-beating industry from collapse. Efforts to this end have included the launch of a players' fund, which has paid more than £36,000 directly to players to date, drawing down reserves to pay fees for all concerts cancelled in the first months of the pandemic, and a series of closed-door projects ranging from in-house 'player days' to an online performance as part of the 'Live from London' series promoted by our partners VOCES8. At the time of writing, it appears as if an end to the past year's disruption may be in sight . . .[7]

The optimism of August 2020 was premature; a tentative return to concert life that autumn was disrupted by a further lockdown, extending (with a brief Christmas respite) from early November 2020 to May 2021. Grants from the Arts Council's Cultural Recovery Fund were supplemented by one particular AAM-specific financial resource: the Hogwood legacy. Although the legacy had been officially designated for special artistic projects, £45,000 was released in order to support AAM musicians who had lost work during the Covid period. Hogwood never foresaw a pandemic (no one did), but it's impossible to doubt, even for a minute, that this was exactly what he would have wanted. Once more, every opportunity was taken to return to live performance as soon as, and in whatever form, possible.

In addition to own-promoted live-streamed programming, the organisation continued to work closely with partners at the Barbican Centre, presenting a seasonal performance of Handel's *Messiah* in December 2020 and Vivaldi's *The Four Seasons* in June 2021 on the Barbican's own 'Live from the Barbican' platform. These performances reached digital audiences of 3,000 and 500 respectively; in-person audiences were allowed back in the Hall for the Vivaldi, which sold out at the government-mandated maximum capacity of 50 per cent (or *c.* 1,000 audience members). The orchestra also returned to VOCES8's 'Live from London' digital festival in March 2021 with a performance of J. S. Bach's *Mass in B minor*, released on Easter Sunday, 2021. Surpassing viewership for AAM's previous festival appearance, this 'as live' on-demand performance reached nearly 5,000 people across individual and season-ticket sales, and excerpts from the concert have now been viewed nearly 100,000 times on YouTube.[8]

By the early summer of 2021, with mass-vaccination programmes being rolled out across the UK population, it appeared that the storm had been weathered. On Sunday, 27 June 2021, at the Barbican, and in front of a live audience, Richard Egarr directed his final concert as Music Director of the Academy of Ancient Music – two Corelli concerti grossi, and Vivaldi's *Four Seasons*, with Rachel Podger as soloist, plus (a classic Egarr touch) one last rediscovery: a neglected sinfonia by Maria Margherita Grimani (1680–c. 1720). In the same hall, on Sunday, 28 September 2021, Laurence Cummings conducted his first. It was an expansive and joyous statement of intent: a blaze of renewal and light. The AAM and its chorus – plus soloists Mary Bevan, Rachel Redmond, Stuart Jackson, Ashley Riches and Matthew Brook – performed Haydn's *The Creation*, with specially commissioned 3D-mapped projections by the visual artist Nina Dunn. 'Sheer, exhilarated, heaven-storming joy,' declared the critic Boyd Tonkin of *The Arts Desk*.

> The AAM's incoming Music Director Laurence Cummings commanded his substantial orchestra, a 26-strong chorus, five soloists and even Alastair Ross's striking, historically informed continuo – an 1801 Broadwood fortepiano. They endowed Haydn's Enlightenment-era vision of a sin-free universe with proper grandeur as well as all the tenderness, humour and warmth written into this glorious score . . . Just now, though, we have earned a little unshadowed bliss. Cummings delivered it gift-wrapped.[9]

'A piece like *The Creation* is theatre of the mind,' says Cummings.

> I love collaborations because it makes you examine what you want to achieve from whatever performance you're putting on. That was certainly the case with *The Creation*: to do a work that's

not normally staged in a sort of semi-staged version, where the singers are all off-copy and singing from their hearts – to me, it brings the whole piece alive. If, in a building like the Barbican, you can make changes to the architecture so that it becomes a different experience, you really are taking people on a journey. That is something that excites me.

I was pleased with the choice of *The Creation*. It seemed like the right piece, and when we got there it was very zeitgeist-y. It was incredible to have that 'Light' chord so early on into the piece. It made the Barbican explode. It felt like we were all coming alive again.

12

POSTLUDE: THE PAST, LOOKING FORWARD

Any powerful artistic personality imparts something of themself to the organisation that they lead. But a truly great artistic leader is unselfish. The imprint of Christopher Hogwood's personality seemed, for many years, to be part of the very being of the Academy of Ancient Music – though Hogwood never willed it, and went to endless, self-denying lengths to ensure not only that his personal celebrity could be turned to the benefit of the group (and the art) as a whole, but that the Academy would remain receptive to artistic visions very different from his own.

Laurence Cummings will have been in post for only two full seasons when the Academy of Ancient Music reaches the fiftieth anniversary of that autumn morning in 1973 when Christopher Hogwood and Peter Wadland assembled a group of players in a church in Petersham to see if it was practical – or even possible – to assemble a first-class professional orchestra using period instruments. It's evident, however, that he has already made a positive impression.

'He's clear,' says Benedict Hoffnung. 'He doesn't beat around the bush. He's very good at directing from the keyboard. He's musically mature, and he can do everything you need. It's a good appointment.' 'I'm thrilled that he's the new director,' says Rachel Brown. For Bojan Čičić, playing under Cummings 'is like coming home':

He was the harpsichord teacher on the first summer course I attended in Croatia, so he goes back to the very beginnings of my serious involvement with early music. He still has that pioneering generational spirit where people are curious and trust each other – and know that other people are also curious. It's a broader way of thinking about and making music: the players trust and support Laurence. There's a mutual communication going both ways, and there's more freedom to play the way we would like to play, rather than the way, maybe, that Richard wanted us to play. To me, it feels that we are getting back our house style.

'The thing I feel strongly is that the orchestra should play to its strengths,' says Cummings,

which is pretty much everything from the seventeenth and eighteenth centuries. So we should be doing very small-scale things and very large-scale things. Obviously, we are in a good position to be doing that: we have some of the best players in the world, and we get to work with the finest singers as well. Unusual combinations of performers is good, for me – and unusual repertoire, of course, is part of the organisation's heritage. We should be doing that: championing the works that no one else does. We've just done the Zipoli *Vespers*, which is very rarely heard. And I'm trying to approach these works so that they don't feel like we're doing something dusty from a library.

Obviously we're looking to the fiftieth anniversary. We're doing a Haydn oratorio project with the Barbican: *The Creation* in 2021, *The Seasons* in 2022. For now, it's valid to say we're carrying on as we're carrying on. But actually that's our strength – I don't feel the organisation needs to change direction. What it needs to do is build on what we have, to carry on being excellent, and to be as clearly led as possible. I'm very inspired by Peter Holman's book *Before the Baton*. Holman points out that the conductor is the anachronistic person in the room because, in fact, conducting hadn't been invented yet! That's why I almost always direct from the keyboard – to give the players a sense of empowerment.

For Cummings, however, scholarly principles serve to enable artistry. 'We're moving into Beethoven,' he says.

So I suspect that's going to need a little bit of arm-waving! But we just did the Mozart 'Jupiter' Symphony at the Barbican, and I lifted my hands off the keyboard only twice. I was pleased that it worked, because it makes such a different energy with orchestra. But the exciting thing about us doing Beethoven and possibly Mendelssohn is that as we go into this new repertoire, it'll be as if we're playing modern music. Some of the other period-instrument orchestras have done quite a lot more of that, and I think it becomes a little bit . . . well, it's part of their repertoire. Whereas this is *not* our repertoire. I want to go into it with a ground-breaking mentality.

Early Beethoven would be a good extreme for us to be aiming for. I don't think we should be moving to compete with some of the other, bigger orchestras – the seventeenth and eighteenth centuries should be our heartland. I think the most important thing for me is that we adopt the same *modus operandi*, which is to go back to the sources all the time, to use the instruments, and to use the players who are specialists in this repertoire – whichever repertoire it happens to be. And we do it to bring the music to life for a contemporary audience. It's never enough just to get it right. You have to find a way to engage the listener.

So, for instance, with the Zipoli we re-enacted an imaginary church service in eighteenth-century South America, complete with processions and the indigenous music that could have been found when the missionaries arrived. Yes, you could say that it's all speculative. But so much of what we do is speculative. We'll never know everything. If you can make the music come alive and make people feel they've experienced it through a historical lens, then I feel we've done our job. And they go away feeling changed, if that doesn't sound too pretentious. But feeling that they've experienced something, and it was worthwhile.

That's really the most important take-home for me, from any treatise that you read. Obviously, we want to get all the details as close to accurate as we can, but there will always be a final chapter saying that the duty of the musician is to move the soul of the listener.

Meanwhile, McMunn and his management team work behind the scenes creating the conditions that enable Cummings and his musicians to bring the music to life. The AAM that is celebrating its half-century is both an orchestra and a choir. (Cummings has dropped the distinction between chorus and orchestra: they are all, now, simply the Academy of Ancient Music.) It is also a record label and an online force – a former recording orchestra that has completely redefined itself as a live ensemble, and in doing so has found itself uniquely well placed to take advantage of the internet age. It is a vital (and expanding) provider of music education: AAMplify, now under the energetic leadership of oboist, scholar and animateur Leo Duarte, is a central and integral part of its working schedule. McMunn's role is to sustain and build on the results of fifty years of achievement, so that the Academy of Ancient Music can flourish in a musical world unlike anything its founders could have foreseen. What course does he propose to set?

'To be honest, it's a really difficult question to answer,' he says,

both because we're a mature organisation at this stage, and because the historically informed-performance movement has been hugely successful. It's succeeded in changing how the industry overall thinks about playing music, especially seventeenth- and eighteenth-century repertoire. The entire approach that symphony orchestras take now, especially to our core repertoire, has changed utterly in the past fifty years. And that presents a real challenge both to AAM and other HIP orchestras – when the Scottish Chamber Orchestra is playing on valveless trumpets and natural horns, what's the point of AAM? But I think the answer to the question is implicit in this difficulty because while the movement overall has been hugely successful, it's not as if it's all 'done'.

I used to work with Paul McCreesh and he instilled a belief in me that historical performance is a methodology, and not a repertoire – and a methodology isn't 'done'. It's something that you continue to apply. So I think the future of AAM is continuing to apply all of the same approaches to the work that we have done previously – continuing to challenge assumptions and to innovate. And there's still loads of work to be done, frankly. There's loads of research that's ongoing around pitch, around instrument technology. There's endless work being done on improving our ability to play the instruments to the highest level, and how best to ornament the works that we play. But also, there are loads of frontiers in repertoire, not just for AAM – pushing a little bit earlier into the seventeenth century, and (dare I say?) later, just getting a bit more comfortable living in the nineteenth century than we have been previously – but for all classical music organisations, exploring music by women and ethnically diverse composers. There's a remarkably pernicious idea that somehow women and composers of colour didn't exist in the eighteenth century, but they very much did. We should be championing and advocating for the performance of their works.

And then there's the question of how we present our work to audiences. So much of what Laurence and I have done already in the past two seasons has been around what I used to think of as 'exploding the concert hall'. There's nothing less historical than performing in the Barbican because, of course, there were no modern concert halls in the eighteenth and seventeenth centuries. So it's a little bit anachronistic. Our residences in London and Cambridge are hugely important, but we shouldn't let ourselves get too comfortable in the standard annual planning cycles of modern orchestras.

This means we need to continue to experiment like we did with *The Creation*, which riffed on the eighteenth-century concept of Theatre of the Mind, using 3D-mapped immersive projections. And there are other kinds of interdisciplinary experiments that we need to continue to explore – with actors, with onstage presentation, with dancers. And then there's the question of reach, which I think we're all really mindful of today, ensuring that not only is the work that we do in London and Cambridge accessible, but that we're accessible to audiences that don't live in London and Cambridge, or indeed even in the UK.

To this end, we're looking at ways in which we can reinvigorate the regional touring programme that we used to have pre-pandemic in the UK as well as our international touring, but also ways in which we can reach people through new means, through digital-content creation, through social media. So much of AAM's prestige and brand is built on its unrivalled recording catalogue. The recording catalogue of the future isn't just audio; it includes video, and other digital bits. And it's shareable: not just through the dissemination of a physical recording or even through an audio streaming service, but on TikTok and YouTube and WhatsApp. AAM is already a leader in leveraging these digital channels, but we can always – and we must! – do more.

And then the final bit – and I'm biased because one of the first things that I did as Chief Executive was to help facilitate the process that appointed Laurence Cummings – the future of the AAM, whatever it is, is going to be built around Laurence. If you look at the real success of the orchestra historically, it was anchored by really strong associations with individuals – Christopher Hogwood or Andrew Manze or Richard Egarr. Like all performing ensembles, we need to have a 'dominant artistic personality'. It's a strange way to describe Laurence, because he is not particularly a dominant personality. He's a very collaborative musician – but he still needs to sit at the heart of our work. That's going to create – in a really exciting way – a more collegial and collaborative AAM, but it will nevertheless be Laurence's AAM.

So what do the next fifty years of AAM look like? Hard to say, but I think it will be collaborative with our acclaimed musicians playing alongside Laurence and not *for* Laurence. I think it can't help but be innovative, with our core repertoire – the *Messiah* and the *Four Seasons* – sitting alongside new discoveries and unjustly forgotten works. It will be accessible, with performances that feel modern, that aren't just standard white-light concert-hall symphony-style presentations. And hopefully it will be global, not just through our touring programme, but through the production of a whole new catalogue of shareable content that will take historical performance out to the masses in the same way the compact disc did in the 1980s and 1990s.

Ultimately, if there's anything I've learned in my time managing orchestras, it's that you can make plans – what's the phrase? The gods laugh when men plan? Something like that – but exactly what the future holds, who can say? You'll have to read the second volume of this book in fifty years' time. Some of it will look like what I've laid out. A lot of it won't. But that's the beauty of live performance and I, for one, can't wait to see what happens and what surprises may yet be in store for us all.

One prospect, however, looks certain. No one was more surprised than Robert Levin to learn that the AAM Mozart piano concerto cycle – left suspended in 2003 and apparently doomed to remain unfinished after Hogwood's death – would finally be completed. 'Twenty-one years went by, and Chris left us for a better world, and – to my absolute amazement – the Academy has decided to bring this project, which is certainly a legacy item, to its fruition,' says Levin. 'We planned to start in 2020, and then of course Covid came into play and that caused everything to be delayed a bit. But then, starting in August of 2021, we went into the studio and began to record the remaining five discs.'

The AAM's Head of Development Liz Brinsdon spearheaded the necessary fundraising, while McMunn and McDonnell put the project together. McMunn recalls that:

After I was appointed, very soon it became clear that we weren't going to be able to have anything like a normal season in 2020–21. So we struck on the idea of finally completing the piano concerto cycle. But of course, it's wheels within wheels. For the past twenty years, it had been an ambition, not just of Bob's but of the AAM's. I think the pandemic just gave us the opportunity at long last to say, 'OK, this is the time. We have to do something to help our musicians. This is work we can deliver behind closed doors. We need to do this.' And everyone, on the Board and on every other side of the organisation said, 'Yes, absolutely.'

'Of course, over the years, there have been personnel changes in the band, but there is a remarkable number of members of the orchestra who have long played with the AAM and whose work I know very well,' says Levin.

They were on board at the beginning of the project, and they're still there. Actually, one of the violas came up to me and said, 'You've never sounded better,' and it made me so happy to hear

that, because entropy being what it is I'm no longer the whipper-
snapper that I was when we began the series, and I have to work a
little bit harder at certain things. But my general approach is based
on notions of Mozart's vernacular and, fortunately, by the time I
embarked on the project with Chris in 1993, I had been working
for close to thirty years on my studies of Mozart's lingo. I'm not
sure that people listening to these latest discs that complete the
cycle are going to be able to divine that there's a twenty-one-year
hiatus between the first eight and the last five.

Inevitably – like all the best-laid plans during the Covid pandemic –
the recording process took longer than anticipated. But that, too, has had
an unexpectedly happy outcome. The delay allowed recording sessions to
be conducted by both Richard Egarr and Laurence Cummings, united
in a decade-spanning shared project with one of most beloved of the
Academy's many musical friends. 'It was very emotional when we came
to the end of it,' says Cummings.

And I could tell that Robert was . . . well, obviously he was the
way you feel at the end of a recording, which is tired. But he was
also elated that it had actually come to an end. And, of course,
we've done such wonderfully interesting things – not limited to
playing them on Mozart Stein copies. Robert actually recorded
K.175 on the organ in Dulwich, and we had the Tangentenflügel
and the Stein harpsichord for the Triple Concerto, which really
delineated the three different parts in a way that's quite hard to
achieve otherwise. I love the fact that it's been adventurous as well
as scholarly.

Adventurous as well as scholarly: in other words, absolutely in the
tradition of historically informed performance that Hogwood established,
and which the Academy of Ancient Music continues to affirm. When
the remaining Mozart discs are released by the AAM's own label, it will
represent more than just the most comprehensive Mozart concerto cycle
ever recorded on period instruments – a project that Levin describes
as 'central to my identity as an artist'. It will be a document spanning
three decades of the Academy of Ancient Music's history, embracing all

three of the group's music directors. It'll be a homage to the memory and achievement of Christopher Hogwood, and a statement of faith in the future: in the AAM's artistic renewal, and in the enduring value of studying, playing and recording ancient music in a way that makes it sound forever new.

Christopher Hogwood liked to sign off his letters with the word *sempre* – 'always'. But three centuries earlier, as the first incarnation of the Academy of Ancient Music approached its half-century, its chronicler Sir John Hawkins signed off, in the manner of the eighteenth century, with an altogether more rococo flourish. The members of the Academy, he wrote:

> flatter themselves that the studies of such men as Palestrina, Tallis, Byrd, Carissimi, Colonna, Stradella, Purcell, Bassani, Gasparini, Lotti, Steffani, Marcello, Buononcini, Pergolesi, Handel, Perez, and many others, abounding in evidences of the deepest skill and finest invention, when duly attended to, will be thought worthy the admiration of every musical ear.[1]

Hawkins was hardly in a position to add Mozart, Haydn, Beethoven or Sir John Tavener to that list; he might not even have been aware of Zipoli or Dario Castello. But from a distant century and a different world, his argument holds true:

> A society founded on principles like these can hardly fail of proving an inexhaustible fund of benefit and entertainment. Here the student in the musical faculty will find the means of forming his style after the most perfect models. Here the timid and modest performer may acquire that degree of firmness and confidence which is necessary for displaying his excellencies in public. Here the ingenuous youth, who prefers the innocent pleasures of music to riot and intemperance, may taste of that mirth which draws no repentance after it; and hither may those repair to whom the studies or labours of a day must necessarily endear the elegant delights of a musical evening.

Padre Paolo Sarpi resigned his breath with a prayer for the Republic of Venice, which it is to be hoped every friend of the

Muses, applying it to the Academy of Ancient Music, will adopt; and in the words of that excellent man cry out,

ESTO PERPETUA!

REFERENCES

Unless otherwise indicated, direct quotations in the text are taken from interviews with the author. For a list of interviewees and the dates of interviews or written communications, see page 232.

Chapter 1: Ancient Music
1. Timothy Eggington, *The Advancement of Music in Enlightenment England*.
2. Ibid.
3. John Hawkins, *An Account of the Institution and Progress of the Academy of Ancient Music*, edited by Christopher Hogwood.
4. Christopher Hogwood on the AAM website, http://web.archive.org/web/19970402210003/http:/www.aam.co.uk/edu/9611edu.html; accessed June 2023.
5. Eggington, *The Advancement of Music*.
6. Hawkins, *An Account of the Institution*.
7. Ibid.
8. Ibid.
9. Ibid.

Chapter 2: The Piper and the Lyrebird
1. Nick Wilson, *The Art of Re-enchantment*.
2. Ibid.
3. Ibid.
4. James Bowman, 'Christopher Hogwood', Dictionary of National Biography.
5. Elizabeth Roche, '"Coming events cast their shadows before": Christopher in Cambridge, 1960–67', *Early Music*, vol. 44 no. 1 (February 2016), pp. 11–20.
6. Ibid.
7. Bowman, 'Christopher Hogwood'.
8. Paul Thwaites, http://www.semibrevity.com/2011/09/how-famous-is-scholar-conductor-and-harpsichordist-thurston-dart-40-years-on-part-2/; accessed June 2023.
9. Paul Thwaites, http://www.semibrevity.com/2012/02/the-forgotten-harpsichord-teacher-of-christopher-hogwood-colin-tilney/; accessed June 2023.
10. Roche, '"Coming events"'.
11. Zuzana Růžičková and Wendy Holden, *One Hundred Miracles: A Memoir of Music and Survival*.
12. Roche, '"Coming events"'.

13. Nicholas Kenyon (ed.), *Authenticity and Early Music*.
14. 'Tributes to David Munrow', *Early Music*, vol. 4 no. 3 (July 1976), pp. 376–80.
15. Richard Bratby, *Forward: 100 Years of the City of Birmingham Symphony Orchestra*.
16. 'Tributes to David Munrow'.
17. 'Happy Birthday, Christopher Hogwood!', *Gramophone* podcast produced by Anthony Fabian, 9 September 2011.
18. Thwaites, http://www.semibrevity.com/2012/02/the-forgotten-harpsichord-teacher-of-christopher-hogwood-colin-tilney/; accessed January 2022.
19. Kenyon (ed.), *Authenticity and Early Music*.
20. Harry Haskell, *The Early Music Revival: A History*.
21. Ibid.
22. 'Tributes to David Munrow'.
23. 'Happy Birthday, Christopher Hogwood!'
24. Ibid.
25. Quoted in Kenyon (ed.), *Authenticity and Early Music*.
26. Interview with Gerhard Persché, translated by John Pehoe, *Opernwelt*, 1984.
27. Ibid.
28. Ibid.
29. 'Happy Birthday, Christopher Hogwood!'
30. Interview with Nicholas Kenyon, 1983.
31. Ibid.
32. Wilson, *The Art of Re-enchantment*.
33. Interview with Nicholas Kenyon, 1983.
34. *The Early Music Show*, BBC Radio 3, 8 December 2013.

Chapter 3: Creating a Sound

1. 'Happy Birthday, Christopher Hogwood!'
2. Interview with Lucie Skeaping, *The Early Music Show*, BBC Radio 3, 8 December 2013.
3. Wilson, *The Art of Re-enchantment*.
4. J. M. Thomson (ed.), *The Future of Early Music in Britain*.
5. Ibid.
6. James Jolly, obituary of Peter Wadland, *Independent*, 1 July 1992.
7. 'Envisaging Soundscapes', *Eye* magazine, issue 39 (spring 2001).
8. *The Times*, 23 November 1974.

Chapter 4: Making a Name

1. *Herne Bay Press*, 24 May 1974.
2. *Lynn Advertiser*, 5 August 1975.
3. Ibid., 27 July 1976.
4. Ibid.
5. *Hindustan Standard*, 18 November 1976.
6. Ibid.
7. Unidentified Hong Kong newspaper in C. Hogwood Archive.
8. Ibid.
9. *Hong Kong Tiger Standard*, 5 December 1976.

10. *Guardian*, 2 August 1978.
11. Thomson (ed.), *The Future of Early Music in Britain*.
12. *Guardian*, 2 August 1978.
13. Ibid.
14. *The Times*, 2 August 1978.
15. *Daily Telegraph*, 2 August 1978.
16. 'Tributes to David Munrow'.
17. *Gramophone*, October 1986.
18. Interview with Bruce Duffie on WNIB, 1 May 1990, www.bruceduffie.com/preston.html; accessed June 2023.
19. *Gramophone*, December 1979.
20. Paul Griffiths, *The Times*, 28 December 1979.

Chapter 5: Mozart and *Messiah*

1. *Come Back Mozart*, BBC Two, 15 February 1980; script by Christopher Hogwood in CH archive.
2. Ibid.
3. Thomson (ed.), *The Future of Early Music in Britain*.
4. *The Early Music Show*, 8 December 2013.
5. Ibid.
6. Obituary in *The Strad*, 6 January 2020; www.thestrad.com/featured-stories/dutch-violinist-and-musicologist-jaap-schröder-dies-aged-94/9970.article; accessed June 2023.
7. *The Early Music Show*, 8 December 2013.
8. Nigel Simeone, *Classical Music*, March 1979.
9. Alan Rich, *New York* magazine, 15 September 1980.
10. *Gramophone*, May 1983.
11. Wilson, *The Art of Re-enchantment*.
12. Alan Rich, *New York* magazine, 15 September 1980.
13. *Port Talbot Guardian*, 23 December 1976.
14. Quoted by David Vickers, *Gramophone*, November 2006
15. Ibid.
16. Ibid.
17. Ibid.
18. *Stereo Review*, March 1981.
19. *New York Times*, 19 October 1980.
20. *Gramophone*, April 2015.
21. 'Happy Birthday, Christopher Hogwood!'
22. Bratby, *Forward*.
23. *Guardian*, 5 November 1979.
24. Ibid.
25. *Spectator*, 3 November 1979.
26. Ibid., 10 November 1979.
27. Ibid., 24 November 1979.

Chapter 6: Revolution and Counterrevolution

1. Quoted in Wilson, *The Art of Re-enchantment*.
2. https://youtu.be/XXVpFbIucgo; accessed June 2023.
3. Kenyon (ed.), *Authenticity and Early Music*.
4. *She* magazine, May 1981.
5. https://www.youtube.com/watch?v=jxsleLrDIiQ; accessed June 2023.
6. https://www.officialcharts.com/charts/albums-chart/19850310/7502/; accessed June 2023.
7. Quoted in Colin Lawson, '"Attractively Packaged but Unripe Fruit"; the UK's Commercialization of Musical History in the 1980s', *Performance Practice Review*, vol. 13 (2008) no. 1. DOI: 10.5642/perfpr.200813.01.04; accessed June 2023.
8. *Early Music*, vol. 12 no. 1 (February 1984), pp. 3–12.
9. Ibid.
10. *The New York Times*, 11 January 1998.
11. Richard Taruskin, *Text and Act: Essays on Music and Performance*.
12. Ibid.
13. Richard Taruskin, *Text and Act: Essays on Music and Performance*, p. 149.
14. *The New York Times*, 25 December 1988.
15. John Butt, *Playing with History*.
16. Helen Wallace, *Spirit of the Orchestra*.

Chapter 7: A New-Created World

1. *Canberra Times*, 10 June 1988.
2. *Melbourne Morning Daily*, 17 June 1988.
3. Letter from Paul Myers to Jasper Parrott, 11 March 1988.
4. *Gramophone*, March 1991.
5. Classics Today, 2012, https://www.classicstoday.com/review/reference-recording-creation-hogwoods-finest-performance/
6. Letter from Barry Guy to Paul Hughes, 17 April 1987.
7. *Guardian*, 11 February 1986.
8. Ibid., 22 February 1986.
9. Taruskin, *Text and Act*.
10. *Independent*, 6 October 1992.
11. *Early Music Quarterly*, summer 1999.
12. Quoted in Wilson, *The Art of Re-enchantment*.

Chapter 8: Building to Last

1. *Gramophone*, April 1992.
2. *Early Music Quarterly*, summer 1999.
3. *Gramophone*, April 1997.
4. *Early Music Today*, April–May 1997.
5. *Early Music Quarterly*, summer 1999.
6. *The Times*, 25 October 2004.

Chapter 9: Triumvirate and Succession

1. *Gramophone*, January 2001.
2. *Independent*, 17 November 1999.
3. *BBC Music Magazine*, 20 January 2012.
4. *The New York Times*, 14 June 1998.
5. *Gramophone*, December 1997.
6. Programme note by composer, https://www.wisemusicclassical.com/work/8509/Eternitys-Sunrise--John-Tavener/; accessed June 2023.
7. John Tavener, *Total Eclipse*, preface to the published score.
8. *Observer*, 25 March 2001.
9. *Guardian*, 14 March 2003.
10. Ibid., 15 December 2006.

Chapter 10: Renaissance

1. *Herald*, 27 April 2016.
2. *China Daily*, 15 October 2008.
3. *Daily Telegraph*, 17 March 2009.
4. *Opera*, January 2010.
5. *Boston Globe*, 25 February 2008.
6. Andrew Druckenbrod, *Pittsburgh Post-Gazette*, 30 April 2007.
7. *The Early Music Show*, 8 December 2013.
8. *Guardian*, 26 June 2013.

Chapter 11: The Triumph of Time and Truth

1. The precise sum was £1,064,552.00.
2. AAM Report and Accounts, 31 August 2015.
3. https://www.youtube.com/watch?v=f81NFG5jugI; accessed June 2023.
4. *Gramophone*, December 2016.
5. Interview for AAM website, https://aam.co.uk/what-makes-music-authentic-is-emotion-an-interview-with-aam-leader-bojan-cicic/; accessed June 2023.
6. https://www.prestomusic.com/classical/articles/1510--interview-richard-egarr-on-hms-pinafore; accessed June 2023.
7. AAM Financial Statements, 31 August 2020, Companies House.
8. AAM Financial Statements, 31 August 2021, Companies House.
9. http://content.theartsdesk.com/classical-music/creation-academy-ancient-music-cummings-barbican-review-back-choral-paradise; accessed June 2023.

Chapter 12: Postlude: The Past, Looking Forward

1. Hawkins, *An Account of the Institution*.

Interviewees

Interviews were carried out via Zoom, telephone and email between January 2021 and September 2022.

Peter Ansell, 24 January 2021

Pavlo Beznosiuk, 25 February 2021

David Blackadder, 22 February 2021

James Bowman, 28 January 2021

Rachel Brown, 6 April 2022

Bojan Čičić, 7 April 2022

Lydia Connolly, 15 July 2022

Laurence Cummings, 22 August 2022

Leo Duarte, 10 August 2022

John Dunkerley, 25 November 2021

Richard Egarr, 29 January 2021

Anthony Fabian, 17 November 2021

Simon Fairclough, 2 February 2021

Michael Garvey, 18 May 2021

Paul Goodwin, 12 February 2021

Barry Guy, 25 March 2021

Michael Haas, 26 April 2022 (correspondence)

Judith Hendershott, 13 December 2021

Lars Henriksson, 2 September 2022

Benedict Hoffnung, 15 March 2021

Maya Homburger, 25 March 2021

Ed Hossack, 4 March 2022

Paul Hughes, 25 January 2021

Heather Jarman, 22 January 2021

James Jolly, 4 March 2022

Sir Nicholas Kenyon, 25 May 2021

Dame Emma Kirkby, 4 February 2022

Colin Kitching, 23 February 2022

Christopher Lawrence, 15 January 2021

Robert Levin, 7 February 2022

Catherine Mackintosh, 6 December 2021

John McMunn, 20 June 2022; 5 September 2022 (correspondence)

Jonathan Manners, 23 May 2022

Andrew Manze, 29 January 2021

Marshall Marcus, 6 February 2021

Sir Roger Norrington, 31 January 2022

Jasper Parrott, 5 February 2021

Anthony Pleeth, 8 December 2021

Christopher Purvis, 9 February 2021; 6 December 2022 (email)

Sir Konrad Schiemann, 17 November 2021

Simon Standage, 23 February 2021

David Thomas, 8 February 2021

Alexander Van Ingen, 7 July 2022

BIBLIOGRAPHY

Bowman, James, 'Christopher Hogwood', *Oxford Dictionary of National Biography* https://doi.org/10.1093/odnb/9780198614128.013.108585 (Oxford University Press, published online 15 February 2018)

Bratby, Richard, *Forward: 100 Years of the City of Birmingham Symphony Orchestra* (Elliott & Thompson, 2019)

Butt, John, *Playing with History* (Cambridge University Press, 2002)

Eggington, Timothy, *The Advancement of Music in Enlightenment Britain* (The Boydell Press, 2014)

Haigh, Caroline, John Dunkerley and Mark Rogers, *Classical Recording: A Practical Guide in the Decca Tradition* (Routledge, 2021)

'Happy Birthday, Christopher Hogwood!', *Gramophone* podcast produced by Anthony Fabian, 9 September 2011

Haskell, Harry, *The Early Music Revival: A History* (Thames and Hudson, 1988)

Hawkins, John, *An Account of the Institution and Progress of the Academy of Ancient Music* [1770], edited by Christopher Hogwood (Cambridge University Press, 1998)

Haynes, Bruce, *The End of Early Music* (Oxford University Press, 2007)

Henley, Darren, and Daryl Easlea (eds), *Decca: The Supreme Record Company – The Story of Decca Records 1929–2019* (Elliott & Thompson, 2019)

Hogwood, Christopher, *The Trio Sonata* (BBC, 1979)

—, *Handel* (Thames and Hudson, 2007)

Kelly, Thomas, *Early Music: A Very Short Introduction* (Oxford University Press, 2011)

Kenyon, Nicholas (ed.), *Authenticity and Early Music* (Oxford University Press, 1988)

Lebrecht, Norman, *The Maestro Myth* (Citadel Press, 1991)

Mohr-Pietsch, Sara, *A New Heaven: Harry Christophers and the Sixteen* (Faber & Faber, 2019)

Růžičková, Zuzana, and Wendy Holden, *One Hundred Miracles: A Memoir of Music and Survival* (Bloomsbury, 2019)

Taruskin, Richard, *Text and Act: Essays on Music and Performance* (Oxford University Press, 1995)

Thomson, J. M. (ed.), *The Future of Early Music in Britain* (Oxford University Press, 1978)

Wallace, Helen, *Spirit of the Orchestra* (Orchestra of the Age of Enlightenment, 2006)

Wilson, Nick, *The Art of Re-enchantment* (Oxford University Press, 2014)

Zaslaw, Neal, *Mozart's Symphonies* (Oxford University Press, 1989)

INDEX

NB. AAM is used throughout the index to refer to
the Academy of Ancient Music (established 1973).